AD[illegible]

SPY SITES OF PHILADELPHIA

"Growing up in the Philadelphia area, I heard a lot about the region being the birthplace of American democracy but very little about its connection to espionage. Now, preeminent intelligence historians Keith Melton and Bob Wallace have filled that gap in my knowledge with their terrific book *Spy Sites of Philadelphia*."

—**BILL HARLOW,** former CIA Director of Public Affairs (1997–2004) and coauthor with George Tenet of *At the Center of the Storm: My Years at the CIA*

"The Melton and Wallace team does not disappoint. There are well over 100 short profiles of operatives in the world of espionage, each one worth their own book. As an ex-agent, I am amazed to discover how many 'colleagues' I have."

—**JACK BARSKY,** ex–KGB illegal and author of *Deep Undercover: My Secret Life and Tangled Allegiances as a KGB Spy in America*

"In the third book of their Spy Sites series, the authors once again provide a lively and entertaining perspective, this time taking us to Philadelphia where the 'second oldest' profession has been practiced for almost 250 years. This is a highly recommended book for anyone interested in espionage, or simply seeing the historic sites of Philadelphia. To the general public, most of the historic details will be new and fascinating."

—**KENNETH A. DAIGLER,** author of *Spies, Patriots, and Traitors: American Intelligence in the Revolutionary War*

SPY SITES

OF PHILADELPHIA

OTHER TITLES OF INTEREST FROM

GEORGETOWN UNIVERSITY PRESS

American Spies: Espionage against the United States from the Cold War to the Present

by Michael J. Sulick

Spies, Patriots, and Traitors: American Intelligence in the Revolutionary War

by Kenneth A. Daigler

Spy Sites of New York City: A Guide to the Region's Secret History

by H. Keith Melton and Robert Wallace with Henry R. Schlesinger

Spy Sites of Washington, DC: A Guide to the Capital Region's Secret History

by Robert Wallace and H. Keith Melton with Henry R. Schlesinger

To Catch a Spy: The Art of Counterintelligence

by James M. Olson

SPY SITES OF PHILADELPHIA

A GUIDE TO THE REGION'S SECRET HISTORY

H. KEITH MELTON AND ROBERT WALLACE

WITH HENRY R. SCHLESINGER

GEORGETOWN UNIVERSITY PRESS
WASHINGTON, DC

All statements of fact, opinion, or analysis expressed are those of the authors and do not reflect the official positions or views of the CIA or any other U.S. Government agency. Nothing in the contents should be construed as asserting or implying U.S. Government authentication of information or Agency endorsement of the authors' views. This material has been reviewed by the CIA to prevent the disclosure of classified information.

Library of Congress Cataloging-in-Publication Data

Names: Melton, H. Keith (Harold Keith), 1944- author. | Wallace, Robert (Retired intelligence officer), author. | Schlesinger, Henry R., contributor.
Title: Spy Sites of Philadelphia : A Guide to the Region's Secret History / by H. Keith Melton and Robert Wallace ; with Henry R. Schlesinger.
Description: Washington, D.C. : Georgetown University Press, [2021] | Includes bibliographical references and index.
Identifiers: LCCN 2020010258 (print) | LCCN 2020010259 (ebook) | ISBN 9781647120177 (paperback) | ISBN 9781647120184 (ebook)
Subjects: LCSH: Espionage--Pennsylvania--Philadelphia--History. | Espionage--United States--History. | Spies--Pennsylvania--Philadelphia--History. | Philadelphia (Pa.)--Guidebooks.
Classification: LCC UB271.U5 M445 2021 (print) | LCC UB271.U5 (ebook) | DDC 327.1209748/11--dc23
LC record available at https://lccn.loc.gov/2020010258
LC ebook record available at https://lccn.loc.gov/2020010259

♾ This book is printed on acid-free paper meeting the requirements of the American National Standard for Permanence in Paper for Printed Library Materials.

22 21 9 8 7 6 5 4 3 2 First printing

Printed in the United States of America.
Cover designer, Tim Green, Faceout Studio.
Cover images courtesy of Getty Images (tri-corner hat) and Shutterstock.
Text designer, Paul Nielsen, Faceout Studio.
Cartographer, Chris Robinson.
Acquisitions assistant, Maja James.
Production assistant, Rachel McCarthy.

CONTENTS

PREFACE

We invite you to retrace the steps of the country's Founding Fathers and citizens of Philadelphia and the Delaware Valley, not as statesmen or soldiers but as spies. Possibly you may be surprised to encounter men and women who put their lives and fortunes at risk to infiltrate enemy camps, collect sensitive information, and undertake deadly missions of disruption and sabotage. These stories from Philadelphia are part of America's silent and secret espionage history.

In *Spy Sites of Philadelphia*, you will visit more than 150 sites where spies lived and conducted their clandestine operations. Walking the same streets as they once did links us to an often-unrecognized piece of American history. Even today the strangers you encounter on Market Street could be there for a far different purpose than what their tourist attire suggests.

Based on our collaborative work on intelligence history during the past two decades, we developed an extensive database of espionage-related locations in the United States. Some locations are scattered throughout intelligence literature, official documents, government reports, affidavits, and indictments. Resources of the Library of Congress and the National Archives and Records Administration were accessible and invaluable. Newspaper accounts of spies' arrests and trials describe the circumstances of their espionage and locations of arrests; their residences provide an immediacy that brings these people and events to life. Of particular value was the private assistance from family members of now-deceased relatives who were central to the cases. A selected bibliography is included for readers whose interests extend to greater detail on the stories behind the sites presented here.

Certain cities, such as Philadelphia, New York, and Washington, DC, are especially rich in spy sites. Philadelphia can rightly claim the title of both the "Birthplace of American Democracy" and "Birthplace of American Espionage." Before the ratification of the Declaration of Independence, the Continental Congress created the Committee of Secret Correspondence and launched covert operations to supply George Washington's army. The Founding Fathers did not shy away from spying; rather, they saw it as essential to winning independence. As a result, Philadelphia offers some of the earliest spy sites in American history. From early actions taken in the city, patriot espionage spread across the colonies and into Europe.

In compiling the book, we found 18th-century addresses have changed over the decades, and buildings have been demolished, remodeled, or adapted to other uses. Private homes where spies once lived were purchased by new owners who may have been unaware their residences occupy a place in America's clandestine history. We have attempted to make any changes clear and request, as you visit any nonpublic place we identify, that you please respect the property rights and personal privacy of present-day owners.

We recognize that a book of spy sites is, by definition, incomplete. Many operations remain unknown except to the participants or to those authorized to read secret files. Some well-known spies who operated in Philadelphia and the Delaware Valley used multiple operational sites for their espionage and revealed few. For each primary site discovered and identified, we offer a condensed story of the associated spy's activities. The narrative proceeds chronologically and includes surprising, glorious, and notorious episodes. We have written each entry with sufficient fullness to convey a stand-alone story about the site, individual, or operation. To do so, in a few instances, we repeat certain details that appear elsewhere in the book, but we have attempted to keep this to a minimum. We appreciate the reader's patience with this necessary redundancy.

Finally, if you know of a spy story and a site not included in this book, we would love to hear about it and welcome your joining us in these espionage adventures. We hope *Spy Sites of Philadelphia* will whet your appetite for America's secret history, beginning with where it all began and where you can expect the unexpected.

ACKNOWLEDGMENTS

Spy Sites of Philadelphia represents the third in a series of works that capture the history of espionage in the United States as practiced in the three major cities of the nation's development. In 1775 Philadelphia was the largest city of the colonies and the unofficial capital, while New York, a locus of trade with its commercial harbors, became the British center of occupation. Operational sites for spies on both sides of the Revolution were numerous in both cities. Once Washington became the new nation's capital in 1790, espionage grew there along with the city.

Discovering spy sites in each city, the history surrounding them, and the people whose secret activities made each significant required the generous help of many others. We particularly acknowledge the assistance of John Pollack of the Kislak Center for Special Collections, Rare Books and Manuscripts, at the University of Pennsylvania and Tiffany Miller, the reference assistant with the Special Collections Research Center of Syracuse University Libraries. Supersleuth Rayna Polsky tracked down spy properties in Bucks County, Pennsylvania. Allison Olsen of the Architectural Archives at University of Pennsylvania; Danielle McAdams of the Pennsylvania Academy of Fine Arts in Philadelphia; Brenda Galloway-Wright, the associate archivist at the Charles Library of Temple University; and Lisa Minardi at the Lutheran Synod Archives—all were instrumental in obtaining images and permissions from their respective organizations.

We received exceptional assistance from staff and volunteers at the Athenaeum of Philadelphia, the Laurel Hill Cemetery, the site PhillyHistory.org, the University of Michigan's William L. Clements Library, the Fireman's Hall Museum, the University of Pennsylvania's Museum of Archaeology and Anthropology, the Historical Society of Pennsylvania, the Theatre Historical Society of America, the Royal Heritage Society of the Delaware Valley, the Yale University Art Gallery, the White House Historical Association, and the White House's curatorial staff.

The list of those contributing information as well as images is extensive. We gratefully acknowledge assistance from the University of Pennsylvania Archives; Historical Society of Bensalem Township; Office of Strategic Communication, US Army John F. Kennedy Special Warfare Center and School, Fort Bragg, North Carolina; Department of History, US Naval Academy; Philadelphia's Underground Railroad Museum at Belmont Mansion; Free Library of Philadelphia; Chester Rural Cemetery; Mikveh Israel Cemetery Trust; Arch Street Friends Meeting House; Valley Forge National Historical Park; Forest Hills Memorial Park; Philadelphia City Archives; and the Union League of Philadelphia. We particularly acknowledge Nancy J Perkins and David Mink for graciously sharing historical information from their respective families.

Special appreciation is extended to intelligence historian Hayden Peake for invaluable guidance and suggestions throughout the creation of the book and for fact-checking the manuscript. David Robarge of the Central Intelligence Agency's history staff added context to many lesser-known 20th-century espionage cases. FBI historian Dr. John Fox, Bill Kline, and Keith Clark shared their considerable knowledge of spy craft. Particularly helpful to our research were John A. Nagy's books *Spies in the Continental Capital: Espionage across Pennsylvania during the American Revolution* and *Invisible Ink: Spycraft of the American Revolution*.

From the earliest discussion in 2014 of this spy sites trilogy, Donald Jacobs, our editor at Georgetown University Press, has been a steady hand in overseeing the structure and publication of each volume. We are indebted to Glenn Saltzman and her staff for exceptional book design and quality printing. Our special appreciation is extended to Vicki Chamlee for her copyediting work. Over nearly two decades, we have benefited from the sound counsel of our literary agent, Daniel Mandel, whose expertise on business and legal matters enables us to concentrate our attention on research and writing.

For able day-to-day editorial and photographic support, as well as needed encouragement, we thank Manny Simantiras, Corinna P. Sicoutris, Karen Melton, Mary Margaret Wallace, Melissa Schlesinger, and Brian Wainger. We hope all who contributed are proud to have been a part of this effort.

ABBREVIATIONS

APL	American Protective League
BOI	US Bureau of Investigation
BSC	British Security Coordination
CIA	Central Intelligence Agency
COI	Office of the Coordinator of Information
CPI	Committee on Public Information
CPUSA	Communist Party of the United States of America
CSO	consular security officer
DCI	director of Central Intelligence
DRG	Sabotage and Intelligence Group (component of Soviet intelligence)
FBI	Federal Bureau of Investigation
FDR	Franklin Delano Roosevelt
GRU	Glavnoye Razvedyvatel'noye Upravleniye (Soviet military intelligence service)
HUAC	House Un-American Activities Committee
KGB	Komitet Gosudarstvennoy Bezopasnosti (Soviet intelligence and security agency)
MI6	British foreign intelligence service
MIT	Massachusetts Institute of Technology
NIS	Naval Investigative Service
NKVD	Narodnyy Komissariat Vnutrennikh Del (Soviet intelligence agency)

NSA National Security Agency

ONI Office of Naval Intelligence

OSS Office of Strategic Services

SCUBA Self-Contained Underwater Breathing Apparatus

UN United Nations

USSR Union of Soviet Socialist Republics

VPSF Volunteer Port Security Force

INTRODUCTION

Philadelphia's rightful claim as the cradle of American independence can obscure its heritage as the birthplace of the new government's intelligence activities. In the same buildings and taverns that the Founding Fathers debated the shape of a new nation, clandestine operations were planned and spies acquired secrets.

During the Revolutionary War, Philadelphia, then the largest city in the thirteen colonies, was occupied at different times by American patriots and British forces, making the city an intelligence center for both. Many residents, uncertain of the future, exhibited fluid loyalty, depending on which side controlled the city. Popular American history has judged one of Philadelphia's most infamous residents, Gen. Benedict Arnold, harshly as a traitor and spy who was disloyal to the patriot cause. By contrast, British major John André, a temporary Philadelphia resident who recruited Arnold, is depicted as a model of 18th-century military conduct, as he met his fate at the gallows with rare dignity.

When the Civil War erupted, Philadelphia was again caught between the two sides in a conflict. As a Northern city with numerous strong family and commercial ties to the Southern states, its citizens had divided loyalties. President-elect Abraham Lincoln arrived in Philadelphia en route to his inauguration with special security in place given rumors of his planned assassination. Yet the city remained loyal to the Union, and the Liberty Bell, one of America's icons, emerged during the Civil War as a powerful symbol of the abolitionist movement.

Philadelphia's manufacturing might was at the heart of America's World War I efforts. With factories operating at full capacity to turn out ships and war matériel, the city became a target for German espionage and sabotage. When social unrest during these years of radical politics brought anarchist bombings to the city, the federal government's reaction reached levels that seemed to threaten the liberties enshrined in the nation's founding documents.

After the 1917 communist victory in Russia, the Soviet government launched aggressive operations in the United States to recruit spies, assassinate defectors, and influence American politics. Students attracted to socialist and communist ideologies at Philadelphia's area universities were targets as well as left-leaning journalists and politicians. Some of those recruited as spies for the Soviet Union eventually held senior government positions during World War II, often escaping detection for decades.

When America entered World War II, the Office of Strategic Services (OSS) was established as a worldwide intelligence organization, and it recruited many prominent Philadelphians: bankers, scholars, and scientists. Others from the city's Main Line families with long-established ties in Europe and knowledge of foreign cultures, history, and languages became leaders of the OSS. As in World War I, German intelligence was active in the city.

Following World War II and the creation of the Central Intelligence Agency (CIA), Richard Helms, a native of Philadelphia, became a dominant figure in US intelligence for two decades during the Cold War, first as the CIA's deputy director of operations and subsequently as the director of Central Intelligence. Major CIA technical collection programs, including the Corona satellite and the *Hughes Glomar Explorer*, turned to engineering expertise and manufacturing capabilities in Philadelphia to design and build sophisticated platforms to operate secretly in distant space and the deep ocean.

Terrorism arose as a dominant intelligence issue in the 21st century. While Philadelphia has been spared from major attacks, some of its residents joined radical jihadists to become part of the international terrorist network. While this book captures significant bits of Philadelphia's spy history from 1775 to the present, in fact there is no final chapter. In the birthplace of American intelligence, spies remain always present.

1

FOUNDING FATHERS, CITIZEN SPIES

(1775–1783)

Philadelphia, the birthplace of freedom for the United States, was also the cradle of the American intelligence profession. Throughout the Revolutionary War, the city was filled with intrigue and operational bases for both patriot and British spies. Whispered secrets in the taverns, the coffeehouses, and the finest mansions, along with clandestine communications flowing in and out of the city, turned the tide of battles.

Only a few weeks after the Battles of Lexington and Concord, the Second Continental Congress convened in Philadelphia in May 1775. There would be no compromise or reconciliation with England. American colonists were entering into an armed conflict with the most powerful military force in the world, and their leaders understood the need for good intelligence and spies.

Preparing for an impending war, the Second Continental Congress voted to unite the scattered militias composed of citizen soldiers to form a continental army, appointing Virginia congressman George Washington as its commanding general. To support the new army, the Continental Congress created the Secret Committee by a resolution on September 18, 1775. Members of the committee included Benjamin Franklin, Robert Morris, Robert Livingston, John Dickinson, Thomas Willing, Thomas McKean, John Langdon, and Samuel Ward. The committee clandestinely contracted for arms and ammunition overseas, but as many of its records were intentionally destroyed to maintain secrecy, the full extent of its activities may never be known.

In November 1775, the Continental Congress set up a second committee, the Committee of Correspondence (soon renamed the Committee of Secret Correspondence and again in 1777 as the Committee on Foreign Affairs), with duties and five members that overlapped the Secret Committee. To prosecute the war, the new nation would use spies as well as an army. This required special organizations to enable the government to communicate secretly with the Committee of Correspondence in each of the thirteen colonies and to extend its reach across the Atlantic into Europe.

On July 4, 1776, the Continental Congress approved the final text of the Declaration of Independence, announcing to the world the thirteen colonies were independent of the British Empire.

Now formally at war with a powerful enemy, the Americans needed strategies that offered an advantage over a better-equipped and better-trained military. Among them they would heavily rely on espionage and clandestine operations, including running spies overseas and at home, establishing covert communications systems through courier networks, creating codes, and launching propaganda and deception operations. It was dangerous work. A bitter lesson of failure came early in the war with the execution of colonial spy Nathan Hale in New York City.

Nevertheless, Gen. George Washington believed secret operations were essential to victory. He took personal interest in the smallest details of tradecraft, offering advice to agents in the field while pushing for ever more timely intelligence from his networks of spies. He made this priority clear in a letter to Maj. Gen. William Heath of Massachusetts on September 5, 1776: "Everything, in a manner, depends upon obtaining intelligence."

Several other Founding Fathers also evidenced a special talent for espionage and intrigue. Benjamin Franklin proved himself a master of disinformation. The scientist, statesman, and publisher of *Poor Richard's Almanack* effectively navigated court intrigues of Europe and created successful disinformation campaigns designed to confound, mislead, and dishearten the enemy. John Jay, later the first chief justice of the Supreme Court, led counterintelligence efforts, while Thomas Jefferson and Alexander Hamilton also participated in secret operations.

■ 1. BIRTHPLACE OF AMERICAN INTELLIGENCE OPERATIONS

MAP I ➤ **Independence Hall:** 520 Chestnut Street

Construction of Independence Hall, originally built as the Pennsylvania State House, began in 1732 and was completed in 1749. During the Second Continental Congress in 1775, the building where the Declaration of Independence and US Constitution were signed also became the birthplace of America's first congressional foreign intelligence committees.

The priority the Founding Fathers placed on intelligence operations in the fight for independence can be seen in one of George Washington's first major expenditures after election as commander in chief of the Continental Army on June 19, 1775. Drawing on a secret account authorized by Congress, on July 15, Washington recorded payment of $333.33 (more than $100,000 in 2020 dollars) to travel to Boston and establish an intelligence network, according to volume 5 of *American Revolution: The Definitive Encyclopedia and Document Collection* by Spencer C. Tucker.

Independence Hall, where America's first spy organizations were created. Recognizing the need for spies in the inevitable war against England, the Founding Fathers devoted much time and energy to considerations of clandestine operations.

In June 1776 Congress created the Committee on Spies. Consisting of John Adams, Thomas Jefferson, Edward Rutledge, Robert Livingston, and James Wilson, the committee was charged with responsibility for strengthening the government's ability to detect and prosecute spies. Later that same month the Committee for Detecting and Defeating Conspiracies, chaired by John Jay, was established in New York and initiated espionage investigations. As a result, Jay has been called the Founding Father of US counterintelligence.

2. FOUNDING FATHERS AND THE FRENCH SPY

MAP I ➤ **Carpenters' Hall:** 320 Chestnut Street

In the two-story Carpenters' Hall some of the earliest clandestine meetings in our nation's history occurred between patriot leaders and an undercover French emissary in 1775.

Carpenters' Hall, site of the First Continental Congress, was also the location of one of the earliest and most important clandestine meetings in the nation's history. In December 1775, a French envoy, posing as an Antwerp merchant, arrived in Philadelphia. His contact, Francis Daymon, a native Parisian turned bookseller, worked part time at Benjamin Franklin's Library Company of Philadelphia, which was then located on the second floor of Carpenters' Hall. Sent as a secret emissary by France's foreign minister, the mission of 26-year-old Julien Achard de Bonvouloir was to meet with the American leadership and survey the viability of the colonial rebellion.

Both parties were suspicious of the proposed meeting. The patriots feared British spies were behind the visit, while France wanted to keep a cautious public distance from the colonial rebellion. Eventually, members of the Committee for Secret Correspondence, knowing they would need international support, agreed to meet the mysterious foreign visitor.

Between December 18 and 27, Bonvouloir conferred with Franklin, John Jay, and Thomas Jefferson three times on the second floor of Carpenters' Hall. Bonvouloir identified himself as a private individual with powerful connections

A FOUNDING FATHER OF AMERICAN CRYPTOGRAPHY

Although James Lovell was the son of a staunch Boston Loyalist, the young man grew into an ardent patriot. He graduated from Harvard, taught in his father's South Grammar School (today the Boston Latin School), and immersed himself in the colonists' cause. He was arrested as a spy by the British following the Battle of Bunker Hill/Breed's Hill and imprisoned in Halifax, Nova Scotia. In 1776 Lovell was exchanged for a British prisoner and, a year later, elected as a delegate to the Continental Congress.

James Lovell, cryptographer to the Founding Fathers, advocated the use of sophisticated codes for patriot communications and also decrypted British military codes.

While in Philadelphia, Lovell distinguished himself as a tireless worker and advocate for the use of secret codes in official communications. He served on the Committee for Foreign Affairs, where he decoded dispatches from overseas, specifically those from Swiss national and American ally Charles W. F. Dumas, who was living in the Netherlands. Lovell pressed the new government to use more sophisticated codes for correspondence and created a Vigenère-based cipher that substituted numbers for letters.

Lovell's most important contribution as a cryptologist, however, involved captured correspondence from British commanders. He correctly surmised that the British used a standard system, and he assembled the key for distribution to American commanders. In one instance, this enabled the deciphering of messages between British generals Charles Cornwallis and Henry Clinton. The resulting intelligence provided George Washington information about the deteriorating situation of the British fortress at Yorktown, Virginia, and contributed to a decisive patriot victory in the historic battle of 1781.

in France rather than as an official government envoy. The patriots asked if the French government would be open to selling desperately needed arms and ammunition. Bonvouloir warily offered no formal promises but hinted that weapons could possibly be made available from private firms. These secret meetings were the first tentative steps toward France's crucial assistance for the colonies' battle for freedom.

3. BUSINESSMAN, BANKER AND SPYMASTER

MAP I ➤ **Robert Morris statue:** Independence National Historical Park, bounded by Second and Sixth and Chestnut and Race streets.

Robert Morris, a signer of the Declaration of Independence and the US Constitution and a member of the Secret Committee of Correspondence, made his mark as a financier of the Revolutionary War. Often controversial and accused of profiteering, Morris used his extensive business contacts to spy on the British troops, to smuggle arms to patriot soldiers, and to finance General Washington's espionage operations.

Robert Morris, paymaster for America's earliest spies, is commemorated by a statue in Independence National Historic Park.

At a low point during the war, Washington wrote a letter dated December 30, 1776, to Robert Morris (displayed in *The Papers of George Washington*), in which Washington sought funds "[to] pay a certain set of people who are of particular use to us." With hard currency difficult to come by, Morris scraped together what he could on such short notice, sending Washington two bags filled with 410 Spanish dollars, two English Crowns, 10 shillings sixpence, and a French half crown. The modest sum was enough to keep the patriot spy operations afloat. Years later, Washington remembered the incident vividly, writing, "the time and circumstances of it being too remarkable ever to be forgotten by me."

Robert Morris—Declaration of Independence signer, Continental Congressman, American Senator, and United States Constitution signer—is buried in the churchyard of Philadelphia's historic Christ Episcopal Church.

In 1781 Morris was named superintendent of finance of the United States and again courted controversy when he refused to give up his business dealings while holding the position. Following the war, he bought the mansion on Sixth and Market Streets once occupied by Benedict Arnold and later, when the British held the city, by Gen. William Howe. George Washington subsequently used the residence as the Executive Mansion, and President Adams also occupied the mansion while overseeing the transfer of the federal government to Washington, DC.

Morris is buried at Christ Church, Second and Market Streets. A statue of the Founding Father stands in Independence National Historical Park, bounded by Chestnut and Walnut Streets.

GEORGE WASHINGTON'S INVISIBLE INK

Invisible ink, called sympathetic stain in the 18th century, was a vital piece of tradecraft for the colonies' spies. John Jay's physician brother, James, who was living in London during the war, kept Washington and his spies supplied with a secret compound. With hundreds of different formulas available at the time, it is difficult to determine the exact compound since apparently Jay did not write down his secret formula.

One formula that was prized by Washington employed a reagent called counter liquor that rendered the writing visible. One possible chemistry for the invisible ink, according to historians, is a mixture of 60 grains of gallic acid (a Chinese herb used by doctors as an anti-diarrheal but is also a common ingredient in ink) and 10 grains of gum arabic. The reagent would include 30 grains of ferrous sulfate (another common ingredient in ink) dissolved in eight ounces of water. Although these ingredients were not common at the time, James Jay would have had access to them as a medical doctor.

4. LYDIA DARRAGH: MOTHER, WIFE AND SECRET AGENT

MAP 8 ➤ **Rising Sun Tavern:** Corner of Germantown Avenue and Old York Road (site redeveloped)

While every school child knows about Paul Revere's famed ride from Charlestown to Lexington, Massachusetts, announcing the approach of British troops, less well known is a similar warning by Lydia Darragh of Pennsylvania. The mother of four was nearly 50 years old when she began eavesdropping on the conversations of British officers occupying her home at 177 South Second Street. She wrote what she heard on tiny scraps of paper and sewed them inside cloth buttons worn by her 14-year-old son, John. The young teen slipped through enemy lines to deliver the intelligence to his older brother, Charles, with the Second Pennsylvania Regiment.

The Rising Sun Tavern, where patriot Lydia Darragh warned Washington's spymaster of an impending British attack.

The grounds of the Religious Society of Friends Meeting House is the burial site of Lydia Darragh. Among the oldest houses of worship in Philadelphia, the structure was built between 1803 and 1805 on land donated by William Penn.

On December 2, 1777, Darragh overheard British officers planning a December 4 attack on George Washington's troops at nearby White Marsh. Since time was critical, the next day the Philadelphia housewife left town with an empty sack ostensibly to buy flour at the mill in Frankford, having hidden her intelligence in a small needlebook. She then walked three miles to her true objective, the Rising Sun Tavern, to deliver her information to Col. Elias Boudinot of the Continental Army.

"I was reconnoitering along the lines near the city of Philadelphia. I dined at a small post at the Rising Sun about three miles from the city. After dinner a little poor-looking insignificant old woman came in and solicited leave to go into the country to buy some flour. While we were asking some questions, she walked up to me and put into my hands a dirty old needlebook, with various pockets in it," Boudinot later wrote in his memoir. "Surprised at this, I told her to return, she should have an answer. On opening the needlebook, I could not find any thing till I got to the last pocket, where I found a piece of paper rolled up into the form of a pipe shank. On unrolling it I found that General Howe was coming out the next morning with 5000 men, 13 pieces of cannon, baggage wagons and 11 boats on wagon wheels."

A depiction of Lydia Darragh passing intelligence to a patriot soldier.

With Washington forewarned, the Battle of White Marsh ended in a series of indecisive skirmishes followed by General Howe's return to

Philadelphia and the Continental Army's strategic withdrawal to Valley Forge. The British were aware they had been betrayed, but Darragh confidently withstood questioning by the British officers.

5. MASTER OF PROPAGANDA AND DECEPTION

MAP I ➤ **Benjamin Franklin's residence:** 314–321 Market Street (Steel frame structure marks the spot where the three-story brick house once stood)

Benjamin Franklin was 70 years old when the American Revolution began. Suffering from gout and other ailments, the scientist, author of *Poor Richard's Almanack*, and bon vivant Founding Father seemed to relish espionage. As a member of the Secret Committee and Committee of Secret Correspondence, he was at the center of international intrigue at our nation's founding. Franklin was among the small group that met with France's secret envoy in Carpenters' Hall at the start of the War for Independence, and he later advised on overseas espionage operations.

Franklin's greater contribution may have been in disinformation operations. As a printer, publisher, and author, he understood the power of the written word and its value as a weapon in the fight for freedom. In one instance, he forged a letter from the German Count de Schamburgh to the commanding officer of Hessian troops in America, Baron Hohendorf, urging him to increase casualties among the German mercenaries to enhance payments from England. When made public, the letter prompted revulsion for both the purported German actions and the British policy.

Benjamin Franklin received a hero's welcome upon his return from Europe to Philadelphia in 1785. "My son-in-law came with a boat for us, we landed at Market Street wharf, where we were received by a crowd of people with huzzas, and accompanied with acclamations quite to my door. Found my family well," he recorded in his diary.

Although Benjamin Franklin's home no longer stands, a steel structure Ghost House stands in the courtyard of the Benjamin Franklin Museum.

Franklin also printed leaflets, which were cleverly folded to disguise them as tobacco pouches, that promised Hessian soldiers who deserted "all the rights, privileges and immunities of natives." According to numerous accounts, as many as 5,000 Hessian troops eventually deserted.

A masterpiece of Franklin's disinformation operations may have been an entire forged newspaper supplement purporting to report on war atrocities. The paper, printed as the *Boston Independent Chronicle*, dated 1782, included false ads for real estate and the announcement of a "stolen or stray Bay Horse." The primary content was a concocted letter from Capt. Samuel Gerrish of the New England militia, writing about captured British goods that included the scalps of men, women, and children taken by Native American allies of the British. The letter included gory details presented in dispassionate military style, such as "eight Packs of Scalps, cured, dried, hooped and painted, with all the Indian triumphal Marks." British newspapers fell for the hoax and reprinted the letter, outraging readers across England and draining public support for the war in the colonies.

"Tyranny is so generally established in the rest of the world that the prospect of an asylum in America for those who love liberty gives general joy, and our cause is estimated the cause of all mankind."

—Benjamin Franklin quoted in H. W. Brands, *The First American*

SPY FOR THE OTHER SIDE

Philadelphia-born William Franklin, the illegitimate son of Benjamin Franklin, was the last Royal Governor of the Colony of New Jersey. He left America for the United Kingdom following the decisive Battle of Yorktown.

As the last colonial governor of New Jersey, Benjamin Franklin's son, William, was an active Loyalist and spy. While he did not inherit his father's ambitions for American independence, the two did share an appetite for intrigue. William sent reports to the British about the First Continental Congress, held in Carpenters' Hall, 320 Chestnut Street, following a meeting in which all participants pledged an oath of secrecy. He also showed a knack for disinformation. In one instance, he proposed payment to the Loyalist writers Rev. Samuel Seabury and Rev. Jonathan Odell for placing "decent, well-meant essays" in Tory newspapers. After refusing to acknowledge the Provincial Congress of New Jersey, William lost his governorship of the state and was imprisoned during the Revolution. Following the war, he immigrated to England, never to reconcile with his father.

THE WASHINGTON FORGERIES

The British were equally adept at creating disinformation. In 1777 a pamphlet appeared in London that purported to be "letters from General Washington to several of his friends in the year 1776." The letters, which were said to be captured at Fort Lee (then known as Fort Constitution) in New Jersey, painted a portrait of a dispirited George Washington who was unsure of the cause of liberty and in hopeless discord with Congress. To the British public, the letters showed a half-hearted rebellion that would be quickly put down. When published in New York, the pamphlet was intended to persuade the public of the fruitlessness of the cause. What made the fraudulent pamphlet particularly effective was the use of accurate ancillary details, including references to Washington's Virginia estate. "I have seen a letter published in a handbill at New York, and extracts from it republished in a Philadelphia paper, said to be from me to Mrs. Washington, not one word of which did I ever write," Washington wrote to fellow Virginian and member of the Second Continental Congress Richard Henry Lee.

While the author of the letters remains a mystery, historians speculate that John Randolph, the last royal attorney general in Virginia and an early friend of Washington's, played a role in creating the forgery. Randolph, who was living in London at the time, would have known sufficient details about Washington's personality and life to make the letters sound authentic.

6. WALNUT STREET PRISON

MAP I ➤ Walnut and South Sixth Streets

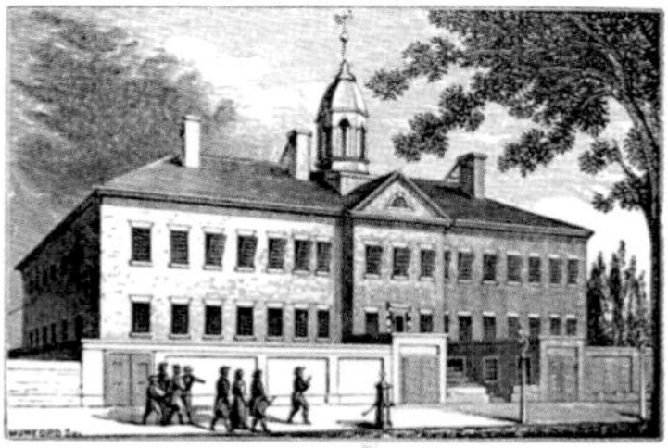

The notorious Walnut Street Prison was packed beyond capacity with captured patriot soldiers and suspected spies during the British occupation of the city.

The former buildings of the Penn Mutual Life Insurance Company now stand on the spot of one of the Revolutionary War's most notorious prisons. During the occupation of Philadelphia by the British from September 1777 to June 1778, the Walnut Street Prison at Walnut and South Sixth Streets at one time overflowed with more than 500 soldiers and accused spies, many from the Battle of Brandywine. The man in charge of the prison, Provost Marshal William Cunningham, had earned a reputation for cruelty and corruption when previously administering patriot prisoners in New York City. According to some reports, prisoners were crowded so tightly into cells they could not all lie down at the same time. Tales of men eating clay, cement, and even their own fingers were rampant.

7. TALE OF TWO TURNCOATS

MAP II ➤ **Parade Grounds at Valley Forge National Historical Park:** King of Prussia, Pennsylvania

George Washington recognized the threat that spies posed to the fight for independence and dealt severely with them, especially during the brutal winter of 1777–1778 while headquartered in Valley Forge. Morale among his troops was low, and at least a dozen Tory spies were executed on his orders in 1777. It was called the Year of the Hangman, in part because 777 resembled a trio of gallows.

The threat was real as the British enticed soldiers to switch sides or turn to spying. In one instance, the extraordinarily unlucky Thomas Shanks of the

British spies in the Continental Army were hanged in full view of former compatriots on Parade Grounds of Valley Forge, their dangling bodies a grim reminder of the price of treachery.

George Washington, accompanied by Marquis de Lafayette, reviews soldiers during the 1777–1778 winter encampment at Valley Forge that tested the patriots' will and resources.

10th Pennsylvania Regiment deserted and was recruited by the British to spy. The ill-fated Shanks had the fatal misfortune of encountering and confiding in a British soldier who was deserting to the patriot side. Brought before the

PRISON BREAK WIDOW

Little is recorded of Revolutionary War spy Elizabeth Burgin (sometimes spelled Bergen), except for a few surviving letters and some government records. Burgin was a New York City widow who, with accomplice George Higday, freed an estimated 200 American prisoners held by the British during the summer of 1779. According to what may be fanciful accounts, under the cover of doing charity work, Burgin rowed to the British prison ships anchored in New York Harbor and offered the guards drugged beer. When the guards became unconscious, the prisoners made their escape. More likely, she was involved with freeing captives from a prison in lower Manhattan. There, a hastily converted warehouse called the Sugar House was among the most notorious British prisons in New York.

After the British intercepted a letter from George Washington that mentioned Higday, Burgin's accomplice revealed her identity. A £200 bounty was offered for her capture, but Burgin made a hasty departure first to Connecticut and then to Philadelphia. She returned to New York in October under a "flag of truce" from the Board of War to retrieve her three children but had to forfeit her property. Destitute in Philadelphia, Burgin appealed to George Washington, who granted her rations that were typically only available to soldiers and their widows. In a 1781 letter to Congress, she again described her plight and asked for a job as seamstress in the Continental Army. The reply, which arrived a few months later, offered a pension of a little more than $50 a year. Records show she received the pension until 1787.

The HMS *Jersey* prison ship as moored at the Wallabout near Long Island, 1782. From *Capt. Thomas Dring,* Recollections of the Jersey Prison Ship

Board of General Officers, which included Maj. Gen. Benedict Arnold, he was found guilty and sentenced "to be hanged." After being hanged on the parade grounds, Shanks's body remained in full view of his former compatriots from morning until evening.

A MAN BEYOND REPROACH

Dr. Benjamin Church

The deceit of Dr. Benjamin Church provided an early and profound lesson in spying for early Americans. The Boston physician, whose loyalty seemed beyond question, was actually a long-standing British spy. In July 1775, while visiting Philadelphia to consult with the Continental Congress, Church was named director general and chief physician of the Medical Department of the Army. None of the Founding Fathers suspected that he was also actively spying for the Crown. Following his return to Boston, Church wrote a ciphered letter to a British officer in Newport, Rhode Island, that his mistress hand carried. Unfortunately for Church, she handed it to a former lover, assuming he, too, was a Tory and would deliver the missive as intended. Her assumption was wrong. The patriots acquired the letter, and when questioned, she implicated Church.

The Continental Army's chief physician was apprehended, court-martialed, found guilty, and sentenced to prison but could not be executed because Congress had not authorized the hanging of spies. The Continental Congress added a death penalty for espionage to the Articles of War in November 1775 and passed America's first espionage statute in 1776. Church was later released and exiled to Martinique in the West Indies. En route his ship was lost in a storm, and the spy never reached his final destination.

8. THE SPY FROM NEW YORK CITY

MAP 2 ➤ **Haym Salomon burial site:** Mikveh Israel Cemetery, South Eighth and Spruce Streets

A Jewish immigrant to New York City, Haym Salomon (sometimes spelled Saloman) was an early member of the Sons of Liberty. After George Washington's retreat from New York in 1776, Salomon remained in the city as a stay-behind agent, sheltering patriot spies and escaped prisoners in his home. Arrested and imprisoned by the British, he earned his release by working as an interpreter for Hessian mercenaries but was soon arrested again for

Haym Salomon

Captured and imprisoned twice as a spy in New York City, Haym Salomon eventually came to Philadelphia, became a behind-the-scenes financier for the American Revolution, and is buried in Philadelphia's Mikveh Israel Cemetery.

espionage and sentenced to death. Salomon escaped prison a second time by bribing a guard, and he eventually arrived in Philadelphia, where he continued working for the cause of freedom as a financier for the Revolution. Salomon died in 1785 and is buried at the Mikveh Israel Cemetery, South Eighth and Spruce Streets.

The historical marker at 44 North Fourth Street recognizes Haym Salomon's significance to the patriot cause.

9. SAFE HOUSE FOR THE LIBERTY BELL

MAP I ➤ **Liberty Bell Center:** 526 Market Street

Few symbols are closer to the hearts of Americans than the Liberty Bell. Yet the Liberty Bell's covert history remains virtually unknown. Following the victory at the Battle of Brandywine in September 1777, as the British Army was poised to occupy Philadelphia, patriots worked quickly to deny the British anything they could make use of in the city.

The copper and tin Liberty Bell, hanging in the steeple of the State House (Independence Hall) and weighing 2,080 pounds, posed a particularly difficult problem. To preclude the bell's being melted down and recast into cannons and other armaments, locals removed it from the steeple and transported it 60 miles by heavily guarded wagon to the Zion Reformed Church, 620 Hamilton Street, Allentown, Pennsylvania. The bell was hidden behind a false wall in the church until June 1778 when the British fled Philadelphia following France's entrance into the war. Afterward the bell was returned to Philadelphia.

With a British occupation of Philadelphia unavoidable, the patriots spirited the Liberty Bell to the Zion Reformed Church in Allentown, more than 60 miles away. The Liberty Bell later became a powerful symbol for the abolitionist movement. Its inscription reads, in part, "Proclaim liberty throughout all the land unto all the inhabitants thereof" (Leviticus 25:10).

YOU BROKE IT, YOU BOUGHT IT

The crack in the Liberty Bell occurred during its initial test in Philadelphia. The bell had been forged by the Lester and Pack Foundry, later known as the Whitechapel Bell Foundry, in London. The company stubbornly claimed well into the 20th century the fault was not in the craftsmanship but in the manner in which the bell was operated.

Liberty Bell

HOW THE LIBERTY BELL GOT ITS NAME

As Philadelphians were debating whether to melt down the Liberty Bell, then known as the State House Bell, for scrap in the 1800s, it was adopted as a symbol by the abolitionist movement in New York and Boston. In 1835 the Anti-Slavery Society's publication, the *Anti-Slavery Record*, referenced the Liberty Bell; then two years later, *Liberty*, another abolitionist publication, used its image as a frontispiece to a publication.

The first public use of the name Liberty Bell was in H. R. H. Moore's poem "The Liberty Bell," which appeared in 1844 in William Lloyd Garrison's abolitionist publication, *The Liberator*.

THE LIBERTY BELL

Ring loud that hallowed Bell!
Ring it long, ring it long;
Through the wide world let it tell
That Freedom's strong:
That the whole world shall be free—
The mighty crowd, the mighty crowd—
That the proud shall bend the knee,
The haughty proud.

Ring, ring the mighty Bell,
In the storm, in the storm!
Brothers! It shall herald well
Fair Freedom's form.
Ring it Southward, till its voice
For slavery toll, for slavery toll;
And Freedom's wakening touch rejoice
Both limb and soul.

Ring it o'er the negro's grave!
Ring it deep, ring it deep;
Its tones are sacred to the slave,
In Freedom's sleep.
Ring it, till its startling tones
Thrill young and old, young and old;
Till despots tremble on their thrones,
And their blood run cold.

Ring it, till the slave be free,
Wherever chained, wherever chained;
Till Universal Liberty
For aye be gained.
Ring it, till the young arise
To Freedom's fight, to Freedom's fight;
Spring gladly toward the kindling skies,
All clothed in light.

Ring it, till the bonds of sect
Be torn away, be torn away;
Till every man, as God's elect,
Kneel down to pray.
Ring it, till the world have heard,
And felt, at length, and felt, at length;
Till every living soul be stirred,
And clothed with strength.

10. THE FRENCH SPY IN PHILADELPHIA

MAP I ➤ **Slate Roof House:** Corner of South Second Street and Sansom Walk (now the site of Welcome Park)

A safe house used by French spy and baron Johann de Kalb was the "slate roof house," once home to William Penn.

Charles Willson Peale's portrait of Baron Johann de Kalb

German-born baron Johann de Kalb, who died as a hero of the American Revolution in 1780, first visited the colonies during the French and Indian War (1754–1763). Returning to Philadelphia in early 1768, de Kalb lodged with Mrs. Rachel Grayson at the "slate roof house" on the corner of Second Street and Norris Alley (now Sansom Walk). As a secret agent on behalf of France, his mission was to discern the mood of the colonists toward the British. He used disguises to travel throughout the colonies during the following year. Once caught by the British and accused of spying, he was eventually set free for lack of evidence.

De Kalb was impressed and sent reports in coded letters to his wife, who remained in France. He accurately observed that the land was filled with "flourishing industries, large fertile farms, and harbors barely able to hold the fishing and merchant fleets." His analysis was simply stated: "Whatever may be done in London, the country is growing to be too powerful to be governed at such a distance." His prediction that the colonials would not long suffer the heavy hand and taxation of British rule proved accurate.

When the colonies declared their independence, French general Marquis de Lafayette persuaded de Kalb to join him in America in July 1777. Commissioned as a major general, de Kalb joined General Washington's staff; in 1780 he took command of the Maryland and Delaware Continentals and moved south into North Carolina. He later became second in command to Gen. Horatio Gates and led his men toward a decisive battle in Camden, South Carolina. On August 16, with the Americans significantly outnumbered, de Kalb ordered a heroic bayonet charge that initially drove the British to retreat in confusion. However, after several British countercharges, the patriot forces were eventually driven back.

De Kalb made repeated efforts to rally his troops, placing himself in the thick of the battle, but the former French spy fell after being shot three times and bayonetted, sustaining eleven wounds. He died an American hero on August 19, 1780.

11. PAUL REVERE'S OTHER SECRET RIDE

MAP I ➤ **City Tavern:** 138 South Second Street

Paul Revere, best known for warning Boston's citizens of approaching British troops in 1775, made an earlier historic ride. In May 1774 he carried letters to Philadelphia announcing that Parliament had closed the port of Boston and containing requests from Boston's leading citizens for support of the revolutionary cause. Meeting in the "long room" of the City Tavern, Revere received a warm welcome. The next day a response was drafted that read, "We consider them [the citizens of Boston] as suffering in the general cause. . . . We recommend to them firmness, prudence and moderation, and . . . we shall continue to evince our firmness to the cause of American Liberty."

Paul Revere received a warm welcome at the City Tavern by American patriots when enlisting support for the Revolution.

The City Tavern, a favorite meeting place of Continental Congress members when they were not working, was torn down in the 1800s following a fire. A replica building now stands in its place.

12. FRUITS, VEGETABLES, AND ESPIONAGE

MAP I ➤ **The New Market:** South Second Street between Lombard and Pine Streets

Established in 1745, the New Market was a bustling center of Philadelphia commerce that stretched along South Second Street. The name distinguished the businesses from the "old" market across the street that did not have the stalls housed in a long shed; the New Market's merchants were protected from the elements.

During the British occupation, this 18th-century "shopping mall" became a center of espionage. Patriot farmers evaded roadblocks or bribed patrols to bring their goods to town, using their commercial activity as a cover for spying. An example was Jacob Levering—one of the so-called Green Boys, a loosely organized group of guerrilla fighters and spies—who disguised himself as a Quaker farmer and paddled a canoe loaded with produce down the Schuylkill River. Once inside the city, Levering collected intelligence and slipped out again. Washington's spymaster, Maj. John Clark Jr., provided other farmer-spies with stolen passes, allowing them to cross "legally" into British territory.

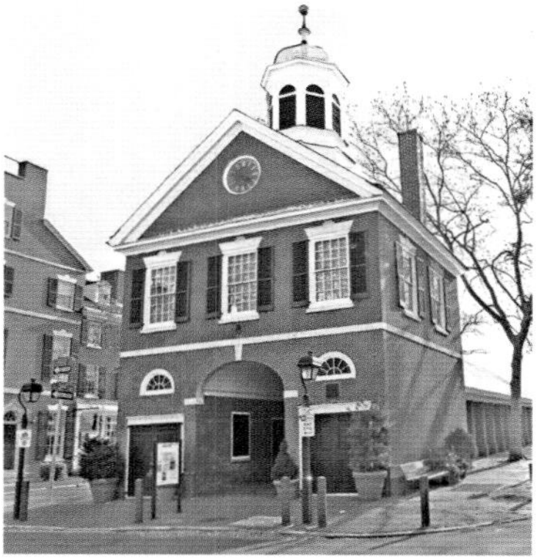

Philadelphia's center of commerce, the New Market, was a hotbed of espionage with spies using the marketplace as a clearinghouse of intelligence in and out of the city.

In another daring operation during the occupation, Mary Redmond, known by friends and family as the "Little Black-Eyed Rebel," developed an informal spy network to keep patriot husbands and sons in touch with their families. Working with a farm boy who visited the city to sell produce in the market, she received and passed to local women letters from their husbands and sons in the Continental Army. Redmond and her young courier ran their covert communications network until the British departed the city in June 1778.

13. WASHINGTON'S MASTER SPY

MAP 10 ➤ **John Clark operational headquarters:** 4111 Goshen Road, Newtown Square, Pennsylvania

One of George Washington's most valuable operatives was Maj. John Clark Jr., a young Connecticut-born lawyer. As an aide-de-camp to Gen. Nathan Greene in New York, Clark proved himself an expert in reconnoitering deep

Maj. John Clark Jr. conducted clandestine operations from the Humphreys' home and the nearby William Lewis farmhouse. A cautious spymaster, so tight was Clark's operational security that the identity of his agents remains unknown today.

CITIZEN SPIES IN OCCUPIED PHILADELPHIA

George Washington received advance notice the British, after holding Philadelphia for a year, planned to evacuate the city. One unlikely spy credited with providing intelligence in the matter was the elderly Thomas Coombe. The old man—the father of a Christ Church clergyman also named Thomas Coombe—made his way more than 20 miles from the city to the Continental Army's encampment in Valley Forge to report on the British withdrawal. "The old gentleman is come out to make his peace and take the oath," Lt. Col. John Laurens, Washington's aide-de-camp, later wrote. "He will be sent back to town with consolation for repentant sinners."

behind enemy lines before becoming a spymaster in Philadelphia. Despite suffering a severe wound at the Battle of Brandywine, he sent a constant flow of intelligence from Philadelphia to Washington's headquarters at Valley Forge, reporting on artillery emplacements, checkpoints, and infantry strengths as well as gossip picked up on the streets of the city. Clark ran operations out of the William Lewis farmhouse, 4111 Goshen Road, Newtown Square, Pennsylvania, and Continental congressman Charles Humphreys' home, Point Reading, 2713 Haverford Road, Havertown, Pennsylvania. A careful spy, Clark so assiduously protected the identity of his agents and couriers that most remain unidentified to this day.

In one imaginative operation, Clark conspired with Washington to provide false information on troop strengths and other pertinent intelligence to General Howe. Washington personally composed the fraudulent reports with Clark adding flourishes. In one letter Washington wrote that the Continental Army camped at Valley Forge had received some 8,000 replacements. Coming from the pen of the army's commanding officer, the British gave credibility to the information. Eventually Clark's failing health and an unhealed shoulder wound caused Washington to assign him to the job as auditor for the Continental Army.

■ 14. A TINY HOUSE THAT CHANGED HISTORY

MAP 11 ➤ **Washington's army headquarters:** Valley Forge National Historical Park, King of Prussia, Pennsylvania

Washington's headquarters during the winter of 1777 through the spring of 1778 was a small stone house in what is now Valley Forge National Historical Park. The two-story, four-room gabled farmhouse built in 1758 by Isaac Potts is only 22 feet wide and 27 feet deep. Less than 20 miles from Philadelphia, Washington suffered through the brutal winter in this simple dwelling while planning some of his most daring espionage operations of the war. They

Built by Isaac Potts in 1758, this farmhouse served as George Washington's headquarters in the winter of 1777–1778. Much of the structure is original.

John Honeyman, who lived in this modest home, remains at the center of a debate by espionage historians regarding his exploits as a spy. If the thrilling stories are true, he could be considered the American James Bond of the Revolutionary War.

included feeding British commanders a steady stream of disinformation about the size of his forces and receiving timely intelligence from his network of spies in Philadelphia and the surrounding area.

WHO WAS JOHN HONEYMAN?

According to legend, John Honeyman was one of George Washington's most artful and courageous spies. A onetime citizen of Philadelphia, Honeyman posed as a horse trader and a butcher to infiltrate enemy lines in preparation for Washington's surprise attack across the Delaware River at Trenton in late December 1777. Using a commercial cover of providing beef to the troops, he gathered information on Hessian mercenaries, while Washington publicly denounced him and called for his capture. When eventually "captured," Honeyman reported his findings to the general at Valley Forge; then he was allowed to escape and reported to the Hessians that Washington's army was unprepared to mount an attack.

The story portrayed a brilliant ploy by Washington and remarkable bravery by Honeyman. But did the Revolutionary War double agent actually exist? Maybe and maybe not. On the one hand, cautious historians note the first mention of Honeyman as a spy did not emerge until nearly 100 years after the war in an account written by a descendent in a New Jersey magazine called *Our Home*. After that, one author after another found the thrilling story too good to pass up. On the other hand, supporters of the Honeyman spy saga point to a precise time line that fits the tale and to the fact that Washington was known to employ spies posing as deserters. That no written documentation or other evidence survives does not deter Honeyman's supporters. After all, his mission was top secret.

"The necessity of procuring good Intelligence is apparent & need not be further urged—All that remains for me to add is, that you keep the whole matter as secret as possible. For upon Secrecy, Success depends in Most Enterprizes of the kind, and for want of it, they are generally defeated, however well planned & promising a favourable issue."

—Gen. George Washington, July 26, 1777

15. LAVISH LIFESTYLE OF A TRAITOR

MAP 5 ➤ **Benedict Arnold residence:** 3800 Mount Pleasant Drive

Before he became America's most despised traitor, Benedict Arnold was appointed military governor of Philadelphia following the British retreat in 1778. Possessing a taste for high living, Arnold resided in what was then called the Penn Mansion (later known as the President's House). An impressive three-and-a-half-story structure, the building stood on the south side of Market and Sixth Streets (now the site of the Liberty Bell Center). It had been home to British general Howe through the occupation of the city, and George Washington lived there during the 1787 Constitutional Convention.

Benedict Arnold

For Arnold, the grand house fit his personal style. He hired Joseph Stansbury—a china dealer, staunch Tory, and Loyalist poet—to help him furnish it. He entertained leading citizens of Philadelphia, Tory and patriot alike, including his future wife, the 18-year-old Margaret "Peggy" Shippen. The daughter of a prominent Tory family, the young Miss Shippen also caught the eye of a dashing young British intelligence officer, Maj. John André.

After Shippen accepted Arnold's hand in marriage, he made a grand gesture by purchasing Mount Pleasant, a Georgian mansion on 96 acres of property on the banks of the Schuylkill River (now listed at 3800 Mount Pleasant Drive). Barely a month after their wedding in April 1779 and perhaps with the

With his impending marriage to Margaret Shippen, Benedict Arnold purchased a grand home called Mount Pleasant.

assistance of his new wife, Arnold began spying for the British. Using his Tory interior decorator, Stansbury, as an intermediary, Arnold sent secret correspondence to Gen. Henry Clinton in New York City, mostly likely through André. The Arnold-André spy episode ended with André's arrest and execution on October 2, 1780, and Arnold's escaping to join the British in New York.

16. MRS. BENEDICT ARNOLD: SPY ACCOMPLICE?

MAP I ➤ **Margaret Shippen residence:** 218–220 South Fourth Street

As a teenager, Margaret "Peggy" Shippen dazzled Philadelphia society with her beauty and quick wit. Growing up in luxury in a house at 218–220 South Fourth Street, just below Walnut Street, her life was a whirlwind of high-society social events. George Washington dined at the Shippen home while the Continental Army held the town, and British officers later sat in the same chairs when they occupied the city. Courted by men from both sides, the 18-year-old Shippen eventually accepted the marriage proposal of 38-year-old

Before she was Mrs. Benedict Arnold, Margaret "Peggy" Shippen was admired by the dashing British intelligence officer Maj. John André. As a token of his affection for the young socialite, André sketched her likeness.

widower and war hero Gen. Benedict Arnold. They married on April 8, 1779.

The young wife's role in her husband's subsequent treason is still debated by historians, although letters in her handwriting contained secret writing in invisible ink (called sympathetic stain or white ink). "It was impossible not to have been touched with her situation. Everything affecting in female tears, or in the misfortunes of beauty; everything pathetic in the wounded tenderness of a wife, or in the apprehensive fondness of a mother . . . everything amiable in suffering innocence conspired to make her an object of sympathy to all who were present," Alexander Hamilton wrote in a widely published letter that skillfully skirted the issue of espionage.

Among the most sought-after young women in Philadelphia, Peggy Shippen grew up in comfort in this Fourth Street home.

Peggy Shippen's primary defense against charges of spying was that a woman and mother was simply not capable of such treachery. History has shown that to be preposterous. Immediately following the arrest of Major André and Benedict Arnold's sudden flight, the youthful woman launched into what has been described as the "Mad Scene." She ranted and cried hysterically at her home in West Point, where her husband was commanding officer of the Hudson River fortification. The sight of a woman in such apparent distress confounded even George Washington long enough that her husband could escape. Eventually cleared of the charges of spying, she was nonetheless forced from Philadelphia. She and her infant son eventually joined her husband in unhappy exile in London.

"It ought never to be forgotten, that a firm union of this country, under an efficient government, will probably be an increasing object of jealously to more than one nation of Europe."

—Alexander Hamilton

THE CASE AGAINST MRS. BENEDICT ARNOLD

After Benedict Arnold's betrayal, some of the public sentiment sided with his wife. The former Peggy Shippen was often seen as much of a victim of her husband's villainy as the patriot cause. "All the world here are cursing Arnold and pitying his wife," Founding Father John Jay wrote from Madrid.

However, the case against her is strong though still debated. Shippen came from a Tory household. Her father remained loyal to the British, even as he socialized with American leaders. It is also known that Arnold began spying for the British not long after his marriage to the young Philadelphian. His primary contact, Major André, was one of Shippen's former suitors. Many of her letters, as historians Stephen Case and Mark Jacob have noted, contradict the image of a frivolous young woman, showing her with a pragmatic command of the intricacies of financial matters.

If Shippen was a participant in Arnold's treason, her natural roles as an 18th-century mother and wife constituted a nearly ideal cover.

17. PLOTTING POETS

MAP I ➤ **Joseph Stansbury shop:** North Second Street (between Church and Filbert Streets, area redeveloped)

When Benedict Arnold decided to become a turncoat, he used Joseph Stansbury as his initial contact with British authorities. A local Philadelphia merchant operating under the code name J. STERLING, Stansbury owned a shop on

Christ Church cemetery is the final resting place of many notable Philadelphians from the Revolutionary War. Herbert Pullinger's sketch of old Christ Church was drawn in 1923.

Second Street, opposite Christ Church, featuring china, earthenware, linens, and other household items. A March 1776 invoice from Stansbury to George Washington lists a bill for cut glass vinegar cruets and four heavy saltcellars. Later Stansbury helped Arnold redecorate his mansion home at Sixth and Market Streets.

Stansbury must have been charming and incredibly wily or both. A known Philadelphia Loyalist who prospered when the British controlled the city, he was once arrested for singing "God Save the King" at a local tavern. Stansbury held an official position under British occupation yet remained safe in the city after the Americans retook it in 1778. As an amateur poet, he praised the British monarchy and military forces in Loyalist newspapers such as James Rivington's *Royal Gazette* in New York. His poem "A Welcome to Howe," written to commemorate the arrival of the British general commanding the occupying forces in New York, reads in part,

> He comes, he comes, the Hero comes:
> Sound, sound your Trumpets, beat your Drums:
> From Port to Port let Cannon roar
> Howe's welcome to this western Shore!

Stansbury agreed to assist Arnold's espionage, but the shopkeeper-poet was not the best of spies. Unable to find his way around New York City alone, he disclosed his mission to another amateur Tory poet who was also an Anglican minister and a New York doctor, Rev. Jonathan Odell. Together the poets contacted General Clinton's young intelligence officer Maj. John André. When the André-Arnold plot fell apart after the capture and execution of André, the Arnolds fled to London, and Odell took refuge in Canada. Stansbury, on the run, faded into obscurity. He worked for a New York insurance company until his death in 1809. He is buried in St. Paul's Chapel, Broadway and Fulton Street, New York City.

18. UNLUCKY IN ESPIONAGE

MAP 2 ➤ **James Molesworth execution site:** Centre Square at Market and 15th Streets

British-born James Molesworth had been clerk to two Philadelphia mayors prior to the start of the Revolution. In 1777, with the patriots holding the city and the position of mayor vacant, Molesworth was out of work. He went to New York City, where he struck a deal with British officers plotting to sabotage the Americans' defenses of Philadelphia. The ambitious operation to attack Philadelphia by water might have crushed the young rebellion. The British needed to find pilots willing to guide their warships up the Delaware River, and Molesworth agreed to help.

Taking a circuitous route back to Philadelphia, Molesworth first lodged with a supportive widow named Yarnall on Chestnut Street between South Second and Third Streets. Then he began arranging secret meetings with possible candidates for the mission at the safe house, the home of Abigail McCoy (sometimes spelled McKay). Unfortunately for Molesworth, two of the men he attempted to recruit reported the offer to the patriot authorities. Molesworth was arrested, tried, and found guilty. He was hanged on March 31, 1777, in front of a large crowd on the Commons in the area of Centre Square at Market and 15th Streets. Despite Molesworth's failed operation and execution, the British captured Philadelphia six months later.

19. WASHINGTON'S LOYAL SPYMASTER

MAP 5 ➤ **Joseph Reed burial site:** Laurel Hill Cemetery, 3822 Ridge Avenue

George Washington appointed Joseph Reed, a native of Trenton, New Jersey, as his first chief of intelligence in 1775. With the official title of secretary/adjutant general and quartermaster, Reed's duties included evaluating intelligence reports coming to Washington and outfitting spies with money and supplies. Reed—a lawyer by profession, a signer of Pennsylvania's Articles of Confederation, a member of the Pennsylvania General Assembly, and president of Pennsylvania's Supreme Executive Council, which is analogous to the modern office of governor of Pennsylvania—is remembered for refusing a British bribe of some £10,000 sterling, a fortune at the time. According to Washington's account, when approached by a British intermediary to purchase his influence in the war, Reed responded "that he was not worth purchasing, but such as he was, the King of Great Britain was not rich enough to do it." Reed is buried in Laurel Hill Cemetery, 3822 Ridge Avenue.

Joseph Reed

Joseph Reed, one of Washington's most effective and loyal spymasters, is buried in the historic Laurel Hill Cemetery. Offered a small fortune by the British to turn traitor, Reed adamantly refused.

20. 18TH-CENTURY JAMES BOND

MAP I ➤ **Surreptitious entry target:** Thomas McKean residence, 312 Chestnut Street (area redeveloped)

Portrait of Thomas McKean by Charles Willson Peale

The Continental Congress stored its secret records in the home of Thomas McKean, president of the Congress, at 312 Chestnut Street, just west of South Third Street. The papers included top-secret correspondence with France, details of disagreements among the delegates from the young states, and other sensitive material. The British, suspecting the records, if made public, would create an international scandal and perhaps cause irreparable damage to the young country, sent Lt. James Moody to steal them.

In Philadelphia, Moody; his brother, John; and a turncoat from New Jersey named Laurence Marr were betrayed by a fourth conspirator, Thomas Addison (sometimes referred to as Edison). James Moody barely escaped, while his brother and Marr were not so lucky. Both were captured and hanged as spies on November 11, 1781, but James Moody found his way to the British lines.

An experienced raider and spy, Moody previously was successful in pilfering patriot mail, directing sabotage, kidnapping Continental Army officers, and freeing Loyalist prisoners. Moody once used a double to deceive patriot troops into a wild goose chase and divert attention from his operation. In another instance in 1780, he escaped detention and eventual trial for the death of two patriots during a skirmish. Held first at West Point and then at George Washington's camp in New Jersey, Moody escaped despite a round-the-clock guard.

Lt. James Moody

Moody returned to England in 1782 and published his adventure-filled memoirs, *Lieut. James Moody's Narrative of His Exertions and Sufferings in the Cause of Government, since the Year 1776*. He then immigrated to Nova Scotia. Although he became a prominent shipbuilder until his death in 1809, Moody is better remembered for his harrowing adventures as an 18th-century James Bond.

21. THE TORY WAY

MAP 11 ➤ **James Galloway residence:** Trevose Manor (also known as Gen. James Wilkinson House and Joseph Growden House), 5408 Old Trevose Road, Bensalem, Pennsylvania

Joseph Galloway, at one time a close friend of Benjamin Franklin's and a member of the Pennsylvania House of Representatives and of the First Continental Congress, produced a plan in 1774 to keep the American colonies under British rule with additional freedoms. His measure, called a "Plan of a Proposed Union between Great Britain and the Colonies," was defeated by a single vote in the First Continental Congress.

Joseph Galloway, member of the Continental Congress of 1774

Joseph Galloway resided in Trevose Manor in Bensalem, Pennsylvania, prior to the war. After his proposal for a compromise with England was rejected by the First Continental Congress, he joined the British and ran a network of spies in Philadelphia.

Still loyal to the Crown and described as embittered following the defeat of his compromise, Galloway resigned his position in Congress and joined British general William Howe to prosecute the war. He accompanied Howe when British troops marched into Philadelphia and was appointed the superintendent-general of police and superintendent of ports. His force of two hundred men focused on patriot activities and potential plots. They compiled a census of the political leanings of every resident, administered oaths of loyalty, and controlled traffic in and out of the city. Galloway sent agents into Washington's camp at Valley Forge and formed bands of guerrilla fighters to disrupt the flow of supplies to his troops. By one estimate, Galloway's network included 80 spies among the patriot troops.

"A 'Tory' is defined as a thing whose head is in England and its body in America, and its neck out to be stretched."

—Popular saying during the Revolutionary War

Before the war, Galloway's property holdings included much of what is now Bensalem, Pennsylvania. His home was Trevose Manor (also known as the Gen. James Wilkinson House or the Joseph Growden House), 5408 Old Trevose Road, Bensalem. According to one unverified legend, after Galloway escaped to England following Washington's retaking the city, he opened his trunk to find his possessions had been replaced by a noose and a note paraphrasing a line from William Shakespeare's *Merchant of Venice*: "A halter gratis, and leave to hang yourself." In another version of the story, the noose and note were sent to him before he left Philadelphia.

■ 22. DOAN GANG OF SPIES

MAP II ➤ **Doan grave site:** Plumstead Friends Meeting House and Cemetery, 4914-A Pt. Pleasant Pike, Doylestown, Pennsylvania

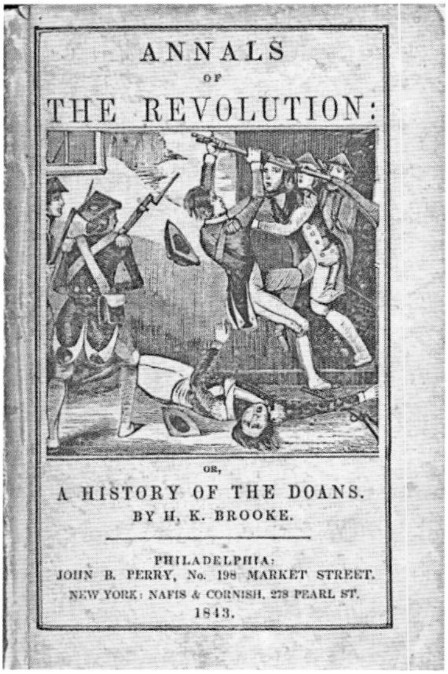
ANNALS OF THE REVOLUTION: OR, A HISTORY OF THE DOANS. BY H. K. BROOKE.

PHILADELPHIA: JOHN B. PERRY, No. 198 MARKET STREET. NEW YORK: NAFIS & CORNISH, 278 PEARL ST. 1843.

The Doan Gang was composed of brothers from a good Quaker family in Bucks County. By some accounts the family sought to remain neutral in the conflict until losing its land and possessions to patriot tax collectors. The embittered five brothers, led by Moses and Levi, turned to espionage, armed robbery, horse thievery, and murder. The Doans also volunteered their services as spies to the British commander, General Howe, and Moses took on the colorful nickname Eagle Spy. Over time, the Doans reportedly stole as many as 200 horses, which they sold to the Tories; robbed the Bucks County Treasury; and regularly informed the British about Washington's troop movements.

Possibly, however, the Doan Gang's most stunning piece of intelligence was ignored. According to popular legend, after observing patriot troops preparing to cross the Delaware River on December 25, 1776, Moses Doan reached

Hessian headquarters near Trenton to warn of the impending surprise attack. However, the garrison commander, Col. Johann Gottlieb Rall (sometimes spelled Rahl), was playing cards and left orders that he was not to be disturbed. Doan supposedly scribbled a hasty note to the Hessian colonel that went unread. That night Washington crossed the Delaware for the decisive victory at the Battle of Trenton. Doan's note, it is said, was later found in the dead Hessian colonel's pocket.

Two members of the Doan Gang who worked with the British during the Revolutionary War are buried at the Plumstead Friends Meeting House cemetery. Their outlaw exploits became local legends.

A roadside marker along the Point Pleasant Pike in Gardenville near the Friends Meeting House marks the exploits of the Doan Gang. Moses Doan was eventually killed while surrendering to authorities and buried in an unmarked grave. Mahlon Doan escaped jail and went to New York City, while Joseph Jr. evaded capture, changed his name, and settled in New Jersey before eventually fleeing to Canada. Levi Doan and his cousin, Abraham, were hanged in Philadelphia in 1788 and buried at the Plumstead Friends Meeting House cemetery at 4914-A Pt. Pleasant Pike, Doylestown, Pennsylvania.

23. THE BATTLE OF THE KEGS

MAP I ➤ **Delaware River Piers:** Independence Seaport Museum

On January 5, 1778, the Americans launched an operation that would become known as the Battle of the Kegs. A floating wooden keg, packed with gunpowder and a spring-lock igniting mechanism, was the 18th-century version of a sea mine and the brainchild of Connecticut inventor David Bushnell. A year prior, Bushnell launched the first submersible, called the *Turtle*, off the southern tip of Manhattan in an unsuccessful operation to sink a British warship

Francis Hopkinson, signer of the Declaration of Independence, may be better known for writing the Revolutionary War ballad "The Battle of the Kegs."

Battle of the Kegs engraving from John Gilmary Shea's *A Child's History of the United States*

anchored nearby. Now he floated a small fleet of explosive kegs down the Delaware River for a secret night attack against British ships at anchor.

Because Bushnell miscalculated the river's current, the kegs did not arrive at their targets until morning. Two boys, spotting a keg in the river, rowed out to it and were inadvertently blown up. Seeing the danger, British troops lined the banks of the Delaware River and wharves in the harbor and throughout the day fired on the remaining sea mines, successfully destroying them. Rumors spread that General Howe dispatched a ship to London with news claiming victory over the kegs.

Although the operation failed, Francis Hopkinson, a signer of the Declaration of Independence, was inspired to compose a satirical ballad poem commemorating the effort, thereby turning Bushnell's failed attack into a public relations victory. "The Battle of the Kegs" became a popular propaganda song of the Revolution and succeeded where the kegs failed.

THE BATTLE OF THE KEGS

Gallants attend and hear a friend
Trill forth harmonious ditty,
Strange things I'll tell which late befell
In Philadelphia city.
'Twas early day, as poets say,
Just when the sun was rising,
A soldier stood on a log of wood,
And saw a thing surprising.
As in amaze he stood to gaze,
The truth can't be denied, sir,
He spied a score of kegs or more
Come floating down the tide, sir.
A sailor too in jerkin blue,
This strange appearance viewing,
First damned his eyes, in great surprise,
Then said, "Some mischief's brewing.
"These kegs, I'm told, the rebels hold,
Packed up like pickled herring;
And they're come down to attack the town,
In this new way of ferrying."
The soldier flew, the sailor too,
And scared almost to death, sir,
Wore out their shoes, to spread the news,
And ran till out of breath, sir.
Now up and down throughout the town,
Most frantic scenes were acted;

And some ran here, and others there,
Like men almost distracted.
Some fire cried, which some denied,
But said the earth had quaked;
And girls and boys, with hideous noise,
Ran through the streets half naked.
Sir William he, snug as a flea,
Lay all this time a snoring,
Nor dreamed of harm as he lay warm,
In bed with Mrs. Loring.
Now in a fright, he starts upright,
Awaked by such a clatter;
He rubs both eyes, and boldly cries,
"For God's sake, what's the matter?"
At his bedside he then espied,
Sir Erskine at command, sir,
Upon one foot he had one boot,
And th' other in his hand, sir.
"Arise, arise," Sir Erskine cries,
"The rebels—more's the pity,
Without a boat are all afloat,
And ranged before the city.
"The motley crew, in vessels new,
With Satan for their guide, sir,
Packed up in bags, or wooden kegs,
Come driving down the tide, sir.
"Therefore prepare for bloody war;
These kegs must all be routed,
Or surely we despised shall be,
And British courage doubted."
The royal band now ready stand
All ranged in dread array, sir,
With stomach' stout to see it out,
And make a bloody day, sir.
The cannons roar from shore to shore.
The small arms make a rattle;
Since wars began I'm sure no man
E'er saw so strange a battle.
The rebel dales, the rebel vales,
With rebel trees surrounded,
The distant woods, the hills and floods,
With rebel echoes sounded.

The fish below swam to and fro,
Attacked from every quarter;
Why sure, thought they, the devil's to pay,
'Mongst folks above the water.
The kegs, 'tis said, though strongly made,
Of rebel staves and hoops, sir,
Could not oppose their powerful foes,
The conquering British troops, sir.
From morn to night these men of might
Displayed amazing courage;
And when the sun was fairly down,
Retired to sup their porridge.
A hundred men with each a pen,
Or more upon my word, sir,
It is most true would be too few,
Their valor to record, sir.
Such feats did they perform that day,
Against these wicked kegs, sir,
That years to come: if they get home,
They'll make their boasts and brags, sir.

24. A MAESTRO OF DISINFORMATION

MAP 8 ➤ **Elias Boudinot residence:** Rosehill and East Cambria Streets (site redeveloped)

Elias Boudinot

At first a British Loyalist, Philadelphia native Elias Boudinot eventually sided with the patriots. As commissioner of prisoners, he interrogated captured British soldiers for intelligence, but his true talent was disinformation operations. At a low point in the war in 1776, with Washington's troops down to fewer than 4,000 men at the winter encampment in Morristown, New Jersey, Boudinot ordered soldiers to disperse throughout the town and the surrounding area to give the appearance of an enormous army. In another deception operation, Boudinot allowed a known British spy, who posed as a local merchant, to see troop status reports that Boudinot inflated by 75 percent. The spy copied the false numbers and sent them to the British as authoritative reports.

Following the war, Boudinot lived on his estate Rose Hill, Rosehill and East Cambria Streets, and maintained a second residence at 218 Arch Street (neither of them remain). He served six years in the House of Representatives, and in 1795 President Washington appointed him director of the US Mint, an office he held until 1805. Boudinot, a founder of the American Bible Society, died in 1821 at age 81 and is buried in the Saint Mary's Episcopal Churchyard, 145 West Broad Street, Burlington, New Jersey.

25. THE "STAY-BEHIND" AGENT AND WIFE

MAP 5 ➤ **Rebecca Shoemaker home:** Laurel Hill, 7201 North Randolph Drive

As the wife of a wealthy Tory merchant and former mayor of Philadelphia, Rebecca Shoemaker remained a staunch Loyalist during the Revolutionary War. When patriot troops marched into the area, they confiscated her country home, a Georgian-style mansion called Laurel Hill, 7201 North Randolph Drive (now East Fairmount Park), that she had inherited from her first husband. After her second husband was found guilty of treason for his Tory views and fled to British-occupied New York City, Rebecca remained in the family home on the north side of Arch Street between Front and North Second Streets. From there she acted as a stay-behind agent, secretly inserting bits of intelligence into letters to her husband.

The Laurel Hill mansion was home to Rebecca Shoemaker, a loyal agent for the British in Philadelphia. Although confiscated by the patriots, the home was eventually returned to Shoemaker.

Eventually she was suspected of spying, and the Shoemaker home was raided in March 1780. Rebecca's personal journal detailing support for the British, including unspecified assistance to prisoners held by the patriots, was discovered. Rather than jail the wife and mother of three, however, the patriots granted her request to join her husband in New York. Following the war, she regained ownership of the Laurel Hill property.

26. KNIT ONE, PURL TWO, SPY THREE

MAP 5 ➤ **Rinker's Rock:** Fairmount Park, 4231 North Concourse Drive

Molly "Mom" Rinker was a Pennsylvania tavern keeper and patriot. According to legend, she perched herself on a flat rock along the Wissahickon Creek not far from the Walnut Lane Bridge and knitted. A passerby would see only a middle-aged woman quietly working away with yarn and needles. However, from time to time, the wily Rinker would drop a ball of yarn with a written message wrapped in its center; the messages contained intelligence that she collected from Tory conversations she overheard in her family's tavern and inn. The Green Boys, a Patriot guerrilla band, retrieved and couriered the yarn balls to Washington's Valley Forge headquarters.

Today a marble statue of a Quaker man known as *Toleration*, a tribute to religious and political tolerance, stands in Fairmount Park near Rinker's Rock.

Ma Rinker would sit on this rock ledge, appearing to pass the time knitting, an activity that served as cover for dropping messages to the band of patriot guerrilla fighters known as the Green Boys.

■ 27. WASHINGTON'S INTELLIGENCE PLANNER

MAP 12 ➤ **Thomas Mifflin burial site:** Holy Trinity Lutheran Churchyard, 31 South Duke Street, Lancaster, Pennsylvania

As George Washington considered the possibility that British forces would occupy Philadelphia in 1777, he issued written orders to Thomas Mifflin, then quartermaster general of the Continental Army: "The spies are to remain among them under the mask of friendship. I would have some of those in Bucks County, some in Philadelphia, and others below Philadelphia about Chester. . . . I would therefore have you set about this work immediately, and give the persons you pitch upon, proper lessons."

Mifflin delegated the execution of the order to Maj. John Clark Jr., Col. Elias Boudinot, Capt. Charles Craig, and Maj. Allan McLane. As a result of

Grave site of Thomas Mifflin, spy master for George Washington and president of the Continental Congress

Thomas Mifflin

the planning, by the time the British marched into Philadelphia in September, a network of reliable citizen spies was in place. Almost immediately after the British occupied the area, Mifflin's clandestine network, now directed by Major Clark, began its reporting. Although the identities of these citizen spies have been lost to history, the intelligence they supplied is reported to have been of high value.

Following the war, Mifflin, then president of the Continental Congress, accepted George Washington's resignation as commander in chief of the Continental Army on December 23, 1783. Mifflin, a native of Philadelphia, became the first governor of Pennsylvania in 1790 and served until 1799. He died the following year and is buried at the Holy Trinity Lutheran Churchyard, 31 South Duke Street, Lancaster, Pennsylvania.

28. SPY AND GUERRILLA WARRIOR

MAP 8 ➤ **Allan McLane headquarters:** Jolly Post, 4606 Frankford Avenue (site redeveloped)

Born in Philadelphia in 1746 and raised in Delaware, Maj. Allan McLane used much of his considerable personal fortune to outfit the patriot soldiers under his command. He proved himself in the Battles of Trenton, White Plains, and Long Island, but his greatest successes were in guerrilla warfare, which included the use of disguises to operate behind enemy lines.

McLane's lone missions and artful deceptions became legendary. In one tale, he acquired the codebook of British flag signals, giving allied French warships an advantage over the British Navy. In another, he posed as a merchant and sold beef to British troops at inflated prices to help finance the war effort. The "beef" had been cut from British horses that had fallen in combat. During the winter of 1777, McLane and his men became so adept at

Maj. Allan McLane launched daring intelligence missions from his headquarters at the Jolly Post tavern and inn.

disrupting the flow of supplies into British-controlled Philadelphia, they became known as the Market Stoppers.

McLane's fighters made their headquarters at the Jolly Post tavern and inn on Frankford Avenue just above Orthodox Street, Frankford, Pennsylvania. McLane, nearly impoverished following the war, was appointed the first US marshal for Delaware and subsequently became the collector of customs for the Port of Wilmington until his death in 1829. The Jolly Post itself was demolished in 1911.

Encounter between Capt. (later Maj.) Allan McLane and a British dragoon at Frankford, now part of Philadelphia

WHAT HAPPENS IN PHILADELPHIA STAYS IN PHILADELPHIA

During the nine-month British occupation of Philadelphia from September 1777 to June 1778, discipline among British officers eroded. With a winter lull in the fighting, parties, drinking, and gambling were favorite pastimes. The commanding officer, Gen. Sir William Howe, was seen squiring his married mistress, Mrs. Elizabeth Loring, around town. Even Tories took note of Howe's behavior, circulating a song that included the lines:

Awake, arouse, Sir Billy
There's forage on the plain.
Ah, leave your little filly,
And open the campaign!

Benjamin Franklin, no stranger to a good time, wrote, "General Howe has not taken Philadelphia—Philadelphia has taken General Howe."

With Howe scheduled to leave Philadelphia and North America in the spring of 1778, the British staged an over-the-top social event. Called the *Meschianza* (from the Italian word *mescolanza*, meaning "mixture" or "medley"), the festivities were planned to the last detail by Maj. John André and included a regatta down the Delaware River, fireworks, a display of mock jousting, numerous bands, and banquets.

A month later, on June 18, 1778, Allan McLane led a small group of patriots into the city to determine the state of the British departure. According to reports, he was able to capture several British officers who were still occupied by their paramours.

29. LEAKING SECRETS

MAP 2 ➤ **London Coffee House:** Front and Market Streets (demolished), Thomas Paine Plaza, 1401 John F. Kennedy Boulevard

Thomas Paine's *Common Sense*, published in January 1776, inspired many Americans to join the Revolution. The small pamphlet caused a sensation throughout the colonies, becoming a best seller of the day. Those who did not buy it could hear its inflammatory passages read aloud in coffeehouses and taverns. Its well-reasoned, passionate message was written in language the common man could understand.

For Paine, who lived near the popular London Coffee House at Front and Market Streets, the pamphlet, although published anonymously, made him an instant celebrity and hero of the revolutionary cause. However, while working as the secretary of the Committee of Foreign Affairs in 1779, Paine also published stories in the local paper *Pennsylvania Packet* under the headline "Common Sense to the Public on Mr. Deane's Affairs." The two pieces accused American diplomat and spymaster Silas Deane of fraud in his purchases of needed supplies of weaponry and thereby exposed a vital clandestine network.

The network was run by Silas Deane, who coordinated the American side, and Pierre-Augustin Caron de Beaumarchais, a colorful Parisian adventurer, self-promoter, inventor of miniature timepieces, and playwright whose works included *The Barber of Seville* and *The Marriage of Figaro*, both later turned

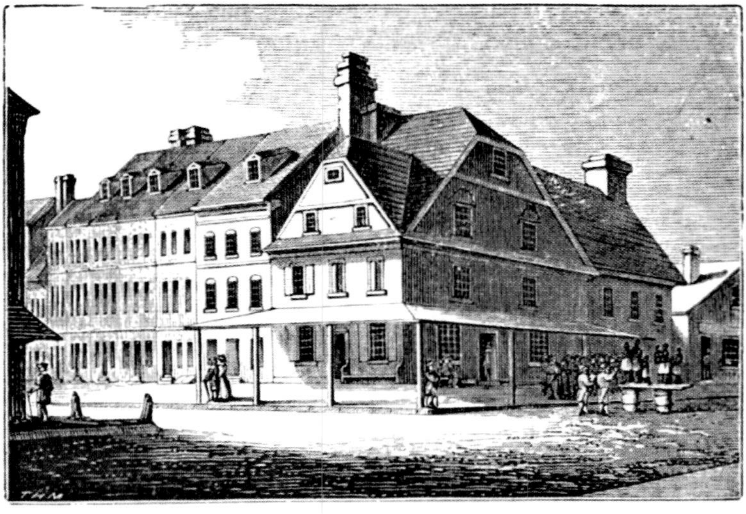

A popular meeting place for Philadelphians, the London Coffee House was one of Thomas Paine's haunts while writing his revolutionary pamphlet *Common Sense*.

"Volumes have been written on the subject of the struggle between England and America. Men of all ranks have embarked in the controversy, from different motives, and with various designs; but all have been ineffectual, and the period of debate is closed. Arms, as the last resource, decide the contest; the appeal was the choice of the king, and the continent hath accepted the challenge."

—Thomas Paine, *Common Sense*

into operas. Beaumarchais set up a commercial cover under the Spanish name Roderigue Hortalez and Company to funnel desperately needed supplies to the colonists. Its exposure by Paine, who helped fuel the Revolution in its early days, ignited an international scandal. Given the press leak, Paine was dismissed from his duties with the Committee of Foreign Affairs and ordered to turn over all official papers. Congress moved quickly, sending letters of apology and thankfulness to Beaumarchais that eventually smoothed over the diplomatic flap.

30. THE ART OF ESPIONAGE

MAP 13 ➤ **Patience Wright residence:** 100 Farnsworth Avenue, Bordentown, New Jersey

Born in Oyster Bay, New York, in 1725 and growing up 30 miles from Philadelphia, Patience Wright married and lived at 100 Farnsworth Avenue in Bordentown, New Jersey. In her forties, she was widowed with four children and moved to Philadelphia to live with her widowed sister, Rachel Wells. With few prospects for income, Wright turned her hobby of sculpting, once used to amuse her children with putty and dough, into a career. Working in wax, she created uncanny likenesses that were exhibited in studios in Philadelphia and New York City.

A 1782 portrait of Patience Wright by Robert Edge Pine

In 1772 she moved to London and there, using letters of introduction from Benjamin Franklin, established a waxworks museum in the West End. Her popular exhibition eventually

Built in 1700, this house was home to Revolutionary War spy Patricia Wright and her wax sculptures.

gained her commissions among Great Britain's elite, including Prime Minister Lord North, Lord Chatham, and King George III.

Wright was seen as an eccentric artist and something of a harmless novelty by the British. Frequently disheveled in appearance, she broke the strict rules of 18th-century British propriety by calling members of royalty by their first names. During sittings she used her body heat to maintain the malleability of the wax, pulling needed amounts from under her clothing.

Wright's demeanor relaxed her subjects' inhibitions, and as they gossiped, the sculptor-spy elicited information. Wary that her letters would be opened and read by authorities, she concealed her information inside the sculpted heads that were shipped back to her sister in Philadelphia.

Exactly when Wright became a spy remains vague, but one possible clue may be found in her 1772 last will and testament, which she executed before she sailed for London. Preparing wills was a standard practice for those making what could be a perilous sea journey, and a witness to Wright's document was Hercules Mulligan, an active member of the Sons of Liberty in New York. A tailor by trade, Mulligan elicited information from British patrons when they came in for fittings, and he passed it along to the colonial spy network. Wright's New York gallery-studio on Queen Street (today Pine Street) was on the same street as Mulligan's tailor shop. That Wright's spying was inspired by Mulligan seems possible.

31. THE GINGERBREAD MAN

MAP 7 ➤ **Christopher Ludwick grave site:** Saint Michael's Lutheran Church, 6671 Germantown Avenue

German immigrant and baker Christopher Ludwick (sometimes Ludwig) had spent time in London and other parts of Europe prior to opening a gingerbread and fancy pastries shop on Laetitia Court (sometimes Letitia Court) in the 1750s. With profits from his prosperous business, he moved into a home at the corner of Race and Fourth Streets and, in

Rations for soldiers in George Washington's patriot army included gingerbread baked in these molds.

time, acquired numerous rental properties and farms in Germantown and Lancaster County.

A friend of George Washington's, Ludwick was an ardent supporter of the American Revolution and became a member of the Philadelphia Committee of Correspondence in May 1774. He was also active in rallying fellow German immigrants to the cause and supplied gunpowder to patriot troops, transporting it to Fort Ticonderoga. Just where he obtained the gunpowder remains a mystery, though he seems to have advertised for a supplier. In the local German-language newspaper *Philadelphische Staatsbote*, he placed an ad for someone "who knows how to get saltpeter and make gunpowder from it."

At one point in 1776, at the age of 56, he took up arms, traveling to New York to help defend the city from British occupation. He was appointed the superintendent of bakers and the director of baking for the Continental Army in May 1777.

Ludwick became involved with intelligence through a committee to conduct psychological operations aimed at Hessian troops. On August 9, 1776, the Continental Congress passed the resolution: "Resolved That a committee of three be appointed, to devise a plan for encouraging the Hessians, and other foreigners, employed by the King of Great Britain, and sent to America for the purpose of subjugating these States, to quit that iniquitous service."

Members of the committee were James Wilson, Thomas Jefferson, and Richard Stockton. Benjamin Franklin, an able propagandist, joined a short time later. Ludwick's plan, presented to the committee, was simple: captured Hessians would be given to him for a tour of Philadelphia. "Let us take them to Philadelphia," he wrote, "and there show them our fine German churches. Let them see how our tradesmen eat good beef, drink out of silver cups every day, and ride out in chairs every afternoon; and then let us send them back to their countrymen, and they will all soon run away, and come and settle in our city and be as good whigs as any of us."

The committee approved the plan in early 1777, and the first group of captured Hessians arrived in Philadelphia a short time later. They were placed, not in prisons, but under Ludwick's supervision with German families in the outlying areas of the city, including Lancaster County, and given jobs making shoes and clothing for the Continental Army. A March 8, 1777, report that Ludwick sent to the Continental Congress showed the hospitality worked as planned. He wrote, "Many of the Hessians and Waldekish Prisoners of War, especially single men, are so well pleased with this country and the way of its Inhabitants that at all events they would rather prefer to settle here than to return to the dreary abodes of Bondage from whence they came."

Following the war, Ludwick returned to his business. He died in 1801 and is buried in the churchyard at the now-closed Saint Michael's Lutheran Church, 6671 Germantown Avenue.

FIRST TRANSLATION

Many German immigrants were supporters of the patriots' cause during the Revolutionary War. Among the most prominent was John Henry Miller. A printer and publisher by profession, Miller worked for Benjamin Franklin and William Bradford before striking out on his own to publish the German-language newspaper *Philadelphische Staatsbote*. On July 9, 1776, Miller published the entire Declaration of Independence in German for easier reading by the large immigrant population, thus creating the first translation of the historic document into a foreign language.

32. JAMES RIVINGTON: PUBLISHER SPY

MAP I ➤ **Slate Roof House:** South Second Street and Sansom Walk

James Rivington, a publisher and bookseller, arrived in Philadelphia from England in 1760. The scion of a respectable publishing family, he was aggressive and successful at business and just as aggressive, though largely unsuccessful, at gambling. Reportedly prior to emigrating, he went bankrupt by wagering at Newmarket Racecourse in Suffolk.

James Rivington

Rivington first opened a bookshop on South Second Street and later relocated to the corner of Market and Front Streets. He lived in a mansion-turned-boardinghouse on Second Street north of Walnut known as the Slate Roof House (demolished in 1868).

Later, moving to New York, Rivington posed as a Loyalist publisher of *The Royal Gazette* and a self-described "Printer to the King's Most Excellent Majesty." Even by the freewheeling standards of the day, Rivington's publication was extreme. Among the news items published were false tales of George Washington's fathering illegitimate children and France's King Louis XVI plotting with the colonists to turn the country Catholic under French rule. So inflammatory were the stories that a mob of patriots attacked his building in lower Manhattan.

Unknown, except to a select few, was Rivington's secret affiliation with General Washington's Culper spy ring. Because Rivington was trusted by British soldiers who patronized his shop, which featured hard-to-get delicacies, the spy collected a steady stream of intelligence from customers that he relayed from New York to Washington's headquarters.

To what extent Rivington's views on the American Revolution were influenced by his time in Philadelphia is open to debate. He was acquainted with Alexander Graydon, another boarder at the Slate Roof House. An early member of the colonists' cause, Graydon was commissioned as a captain by the Continental Congress, raised troops, and saw combat in the Battle of Harlem Heights, where he was taken prisoner. In *Memoirs of a Life, Chiefly Passed in Pennsylvania, within the Last Sixty Years,* Graydon fondly remembered Rivington. "This gentleman's manners and appearance were sufficiently dignified, and he kept the best company," Graydon wrote. "He was an everlasting dabbler in theatrical heroics."

■ 33. THE TRAGEDY OF MAJOR ANDRÉ

MAP I ➤ **British major John André residence (during occupation):** Franklin Court, 314–321 Market Street

Maj. John André became a notable figure of Revolutionary War espionage by accident and poor tradecraft. Witty, charming, handsome, and described as

Captured in civilian clothing following his meeting with Benedict Arnold and carrying incriminating documents, Maj. John André was treated as a spy.

FRANKLIN'S TRAVELING PORTRAIT

British troops occupied Philadelphia from September 1777 through June 1778, with officers residing in some of the finest homes in the city. Maj. John André occupied Benjamin Franklin's handsome three-story brick home while Franklin was in France. Leaving the city as American troops advanced, British officers loaded all they could manage into commandeered wagons. Reportedly the wagons carried Major André's possessions and items looted from the house, such as books, musical instruments, scientific devices, and a portrait of Franklin. The painting, which André later presented to his superior officer, Maj. Gen. Charles Grey, was eventually sent to England. Grey's descendant, Albert Grey, Fourth Earl Grey and the governor general of Canada, returned the portrait to the United States in 1906, the bicentenary of Franklin's birth. The painting hung in the White House.

possessing a "shining spirit," he was fluent in English, French, German, and Italian; a skilled amateur painter; and able to carry a tune or write amusing verse. In 1775 André was captured at Fort Saint-Jean by Gen. Richard Montgomery during an American incursion into Canada. Shipped to Lancaster, Pennsylvania, the British soldier pledged, as an officer and gentleman, not to attempt an escape. That enabled André to roam freely, without guard, prior to a prisoner exchange and his return to active duty with the British Army.

During the British occupation of Philadelphia, André lived in Benjamin Franklin's stately brick home, Franklin Court, 314–321 Market Street, where he entertained in style and became a fixture at the dinners and balls hosted by the Tory elite. Admired by both men and women, he was among the most eligible bachelors in the city and at one time was attracted to Peggy Shippen, a debutante who would eventually marry patriot-officer-turned-traitor Benedict Arnold.

In short, André was everything a British officer should hope to achieve, both professionally and personally. As an 18th-century case officer, André ran a number of effective spies, notably Ann Bates, a Philadelphia schoolteacher and wife of a British field artillery repairman. Bates knew armaments and military terminology better than most soldiers and, using the alias Mrs. Barnes, infiltrated American troop encampments disguised as a peddler.

André's ambitious recruitment of Benedict Arnold, however, ended badly. During a secret meeting behind colonial lines with Arnold, then the commander of the American fortifications at West Point, New York, André negotiated the handover of the strategic fort in exchange for awarding Arnold a British commission as a brigadier general, a lifetime pension, and several thousand pounds. While attempting to return to his headquarters, André was captured

THE SHOW MUST GO ON!

The Southwark Theatre, the first permanent theater in colonial America, opened in November 1766 on the corner of South and Leithgow Streets. During the British occupation of Philadelphia, redcoats acted in the productions of plays that were often written by officers. Maj. John André not only acted in the performances but also painted the scenery for some of the productions, signing his name in bold lettering. His artistic work survived the war, and in 1807, a play based on his capture featured scenes done by the ill-fated spy thirty years earlier. The Southwark Theatre closed in 1821 and was replaced by a distillery, which was demolished in 1912.

British officers were playwrights and actors, as well as patrons, for performances in this famed theater during their 1777 occupation of Philadelphia.

by local robbers and detained at a patriot checkpoint. When documents were found concealed in his boots, he was held prisoner. André was in serious trouble because he was not in uniform when captured, making him a spy. At his trial before a military court, he was found guilty of spying and sentenced to death. George Washington was willing to trade André for the turncoat Arnold, but the British were unwilling to sell out their prized agent.

André was denied the benefit of a soldier's death by firing squad. The 29-year-old was hanged on October 2, 1780, in Tappan, New York. According to eyewitness accounts, the young André was calm when he tied the handkerchief for a blindfold. "Only this, gentlemen, that you all bear witness that I meet my fate like a brave man," were his reported last words.

His body was buried in Tappan near the gallows until 1821, when the remains were returned to England and reinterred in London's Westminster Abbey. "Never perhaps did any man suffer death with more justice, or deserve it less," Alexander Hamilton later wrote of him.

34. HAVANA'S MAN IN PHILADELPHIA

MAP I ➤ **Don Juan de Miralles residence:** 242 South Third Street

Although Spain was officially neutral during the American Revolution, it firmly allied with France against Britain. To assess the state of the Revolution and governance in the American colonies, Spain sent the spy Don Juan de Miralles, a Spanish-born businessman living in Cuba, to Philadelphia in 1778. Miralles posed as a merchant whose ship encountered problems on the way to Spain and was forced to land in Charleston, South Carolina.

The cover story allowed Miralles to make his way up the coast by sea and land to Philadelphia, where he became acquainted with many of the Founding Fathers. George Washington found him to be "a Spanish gentleman of distinction and amiable character." Entertaining lavishly and dispensing Havana cigars freely, he became a local society favorite, eventually purchasing a fashionable house at 242 South Third Street.

The Spanish spy Don Juan de Miralles lived in grand style while in Philadelphia, where he socialized with some of the city's leading citizens.

During his time in Philadelphia, Miralles dispatched hundreds of secret reports to Spain through the governor of Cuba, Don Diego Joseph Navarro García de Valladares. His optimistic reports of the American Revolution moved Spain somewhat in the direction of siding with the colonists. Functioning, albeit unofficially, as something of a diplomat, he soon became friends with France's first official ambassador to the colonies, Conrad Alexandre Gérard de Rayneval, who arrived in Philadelphia at about the same time.

Miralles also forged ties with the banker William Morris, and the pair formed a private shipping venture to Cuba. Miralles funded the enterprise, while Morris saw to the details of ships and cargoes that included beef, pork, and soap in exchange for fruits, rum, and sugar. Whether the colonists recognized that Miralles was also functioning as a spy for Spain is uncertain.

Miralles died from a fever on April 28, 1780, while visiting George Washington's headquarters in Morristown, New Jersey. Initially buried in Morristown, the Spaniard's body was returned to Cuba following the war.

35. GENERAL WASHINGTON'S TEMPORARY HEADQUARTERS

MAP II ➤ **Summerseat:** Clymer and North Morris Avenues, Morrisville, Pennsylvania

Summerseat in Morrisville, Pennsylvania, served as General Washington's headquarters from December 8 to December 14, 1776. Although his stay was short, those few days would prove critical to the war. After arriving at

The basement of the stately Summerseat was a prison for two British spies before their execution by hanging on the banks of the nearby Delaware River.

the stately home and finding prospects for military victory grim, Washington decided not to defend Philadelphia against attack by the British. Rather, on December 25th he would cross the Delaware River with his men and engage the Hessian troops garrisoned at Trenton. The surprise attack, known as the Battle of Trenton, resulted in few losses on the American side and nearly two thirds of the Hessian troops captured. The decisive victory not only increased morale among Washington's men but also bolstered the Continental Congress's faith in the general and served to increase enlistments.

Summerseat reentered the pages of history in 1781. As the war dragged on, morale among American troops was low. The men suffered from inadequate food, clothing, and pay. On New Year's Day 1781, 2,400 soldiers of the beleaguered army under Gen. Anthony Wayne at Morristown, New Jersey, threatened to strike over the conditions and elected a negotiating committee of sergeants for meetings in Princeton.

As the troops assembled to debate their options, John Mason, an agent provocateur from British general Henry Clinton's staff, dressed in civilian clothes and circulated copies of prepared proposals exhorting the soldiers to strike. The pamphlets proclaimed the soldiers' positions were reasonable and that unless they were met, the war could not come to a peaceful end. The propaganda so blatantly supported the British that the soldiers recognized its source and intent immediately. They were unanimous and had no intention of "turning Arnold," referring to traitor Gen. Benedict Arnold, who earlier had switched to the British side.

Mason and a companion named James Ogden were arrested and brought before Governor Reed of Pennsylvania. The pair were convicted as British spies at a military trial held at Summerseat House on January 10, 1781. The trial was brief after Mason foolishly admitted to one of the sergeants he was a spy and implicated Ogden as well. Mason tried to save his life by revealing another plot to kidnap General Washington, but the court was unimpressed. The two were imprisoned in the basement of Summerseat House before being hanged the next morning at Colvin's Ferry, near what today is the intersection of South Delmorr Avenue and Green Street in Morrisville.

Summerseat is also significant as the home of two signers of the Declaration of Independence and the US Constitution—George Clymer and Robert Morris. Designated a National Historic Landmark, it is open to the public and offers a wide variety of events throughout the year.

National
"WE NEVER SLEEP."
Agency

2

FROM EDGAR ALLAN POE THROUGH THE CIVIL WAR

(1837–1865)

The Civil War pitted American spies against American spies. Two nations with a shared history, a common language, and a 2,000-mile porous border minimized many of the security and cultural challenges typically faced by wartime spies. For the Union side at the beginning of the war, the army was devoid of a formal intelligence apparatus. The Secret Service, not established until 1865, mostly concerned itself with catching counterfeiters. Union commanders did not seem to possess George Washington's sense for espionage and battlefield intelligence.

The Confederate generals enjoyed some advantages in intelligence collection. Rebel sympathizers held positions of trust throughout the US government, including in the War Department and in the White House. Formal spy rings were quickly established, such as the one under the command of Col. Thomas Jordan, the roommate of Ulysses S. Grant at the US Military Academy, West Point, New York. Jordan's network provided an early, steady flow of information to the Confederate leaders.

Not until Philadelphia-born major general George B. McClellan, known affectionately as "Little Mac" by his troops, established an intelligence component did the US Army attempt to build a formal intelligence capability. Even that effort was haphazard, with Gen. Winfield Scott (Old Fuss and Feathers) also setting up a separate intelligence organization and with Maj. Gen. Joseph "Joe" Hooker appointing Col. George H. Sharpe as his head of military intelligence. General Grant retained Sharpe, while President Abraham Lincoln personally hired spies outside the military. The ensuing organizational confusion not only was predictable but also took time to sort out. By the end of the war, however, Union spies were providing timely and valuable intelligence to generals in the field.

Emerging 19th-century technologies changed the practice of espionage in the Civil War. The telegraph, also used in Europe's Crimean War, produced communication speeds unavailable to previous generations, while the lines themselves became a target for intelligence gathering through taps and intercepts. The emerging field of photography created permanent, indisputable after-battle accounts of the war for commanders and counterintelligence officers. More precise maps with accurate topography could be created following major battles. Balloons rising hundreds of feet offered troops aerial battlefield surveillance for the first time in America.

The Civil War also produced celebrity spies. After the war, Pauline Cushman, Lafayette C. Baker, Rose O'Neal Greenhow, and Loreta Janeta Velázquez became famous, discovering that readers on both sides of the conflict were eager for their tales of clandestine heroism. Memoirs and lectures attracted large audiences that seemed unconcerned that the storytellers often strayed far from the truth in recounting dramatic tales of adventure, courage, and danger.

As the nearest major Northern city to the Confederate-held territory beyond Washington, Philadelphia's seaport, railroads, and manufacturing were critical to the Union's military. Yet even within a city that officially remained a staunch supporter of the Union, prominent citizens maintained long-established personal and business relationships to the South that offered opportunities for espionage. Shadowy intrigues and rumors of conspiracies flourished during the war years. In May 1865, a month following the end of hostilities, reports of a plot to burn Philadelphia and other northern cities appeared in the *Philadelphia Inquirer*. News articles, derived largely from rumors, asserted as many as 800 would-be arsonists were involved in the conspiracy. In this instance, such fears may not have been completely unfounded. Confederate saboteurs had attempted to burn New York City several months earlier by lighting small fires in hotels and other buildings in Manhattan. That plot failed largely because of the arsonists' incompetence, but the lingering threat of Southern armed resistance extended to Philadelphia.

36. FROM CRYPTS TO CRYPTOGRAPHY

MAP 4 ➤ **Edgar Allan Poe residence:** 532 North Seventh Street

Of Poe's multiple residences during the six years he spent in Philadelphia, only the house on North Seventh Street survives and is designated a National Historic Landmark.

Frequently cited as the first detective story, Edgar Allan Poe's "The Gold-Bug" is also significant to the discipline of cryptography. Submitted to a writing contest, the story was first published in two installments beginning in June 1843 in Philadelphia's *Dollar Newspaper*, a subsidiary publication of the *Public Ledger*, then located at Third and Chestnut Streets. An instant success and the winner of the paper's $100 prize, the tale was reprinted in the *Saturday Courier* and again in the *Dollar Newspaper*. Pirated reprints appeared in Europe, and a short time later Philadelphia-based playwright Silas S. Steele turned it into a drama. The play, staged at the Walnut Street Theatre, Ninth and Walnut Streets, opened on August 18, 1843, and closed not long afterward.

An illustration from "The Gold-Bug." Edgar Allan Poe's classic tale inspired generations of cryptographers with its portrayal of codes and code breaking.

According to cryptography historian David Kahn, author of *The Codebreakers*, Poe's story "glamorized cryptology" and revealed the mechanics behind what was widely viewed as a mysterious discipline. Cryptographer William Friedman, who helped break the Japanese Purple Code prior to the attack on Pearl Harbor, became fascinated with code breaking after reading the story as a youth. Lectures he later gave at the National Security Agency referenced Poe's story.

Poe's interest in cryptography was previously exhibited in essays he wrote for various publications such as *Alexander's Weekly Messenger* (December 18, 1839) and *Graham's Magazine* (July, August, October, and December 1841). In the December 18, 1839, edition of *Alexander's Weekly*, Poe's article "Enigmatical and Conundrum-ical" issued his famous challenge to readers to create a cipher he could not crack. Readers sent in ciphers, and Poe claimed to have solved all of them—some 100 entries—by May 1840. He then added two additional ciphers attributed to W. B. Tyler, whom some speculate was Poe himself.

FAMED INMATES OF MOYAMENSING PRISON

Edgar Allan Poe spent one night in Philadelphia's Moyamensing Prison for public drunkenness in 1849. Only Poe's single account of his stay in the prison exists. The prison also held the abolitionist Passmore Williamson and America's first serial killer, H. H. Holmes, who was executed at the facility on May 7, 1896. More recently, poet and author Charles Bukowski served time at the facility in 1944 on suspicion of draft evasion, though psychological tests found him unfit for military duty.

He launched a similar promotion in August 1841 in *Graham's Magazine*, which he was editing at the time. This challenge involved a cryptonym devised by a friend named Dr. Frailey, with a prize of a year's free subscription "to any person, or rather to the first person who shall read us this riddle."

Literary scholars assess the time Poe lived in Philadelphia, 1837–1844, as among the most productive years of his career. During that period, he wrote "The Gold-Bug," "The Tell-Tale Heart," and "The Murders in the Rue Morgue." Although he lived in numerous houses in Philadelphia, only one remains, a red-brick house at 532 North Seventh Street. Now a National Historic Landmark, it is open to the public and maintained by the National Park Service.

37. DETECTIVE WORK IS WOMAN'S WORK

MAP I ➤ **Pinkerton's National Detective Agency office:** 45 South Third Street

Allan Pinkerton ca. 1861

Allan Pinkerton, Chicago's first police detective, formed a private detective agency in 1850, and his clients included some of the nation's most prominent railroads. While the agency's purpose was to curtail theft and maintain order among employees, the organization eventually gained a fearsome reputation as strikebreakers. Although that reputation follows the Pinkerton name to this day, Allan Pinkerton was also a staunch abolitionist

Kate Warne, an employee of the Pinkerton Agency, has been described as America's first female detective.

The famed Pinkerton's Detective Agency maintained a branch office on South Third Street during its early years.

and supporter of the Union cause. With an already established reputation for his support of Lincoln and the Union, the government would turn to the experienced detective in wartime.

In 1860 Pinkerton assigned five agents to investigate threats against the Philadelphia, Wilmington, and Baltimore Railroad by secessionist sympathizers from Maryland. Among the Pinkerton agents was Kate Warne, possibly America's first female detective. In early 1861, using the aliases of Mrs. Cherry and Mrs. M. B. Barley, Warne infiltrated the Baltimore secessionist movement under the cover story of a visiting Southern lady. With a thick Southern accent complementing a readiness to flirt and a mischievous twinkle in her eye, she was welcomed into secessionist social gatherings. The combined work of Warne and other Pinkerton agents uncovered a plot to assassinate President-elect Abraham Lincoln during his trip to Washington for his inauguration.

As Lincoln's train rolled from Philadelphia to Baltimore to Washington on the night of February 22, 1861, Warne did not sleep a wink. She remained in Baltimore as a precaution while watching the president's train depart for the capital. According to legend, Pinkerton came up with the slogan for his agency "We Never Sleep" as a result of Warne's sleepless night guarding Lincoln.

Pinkerton later said it was not the custom to employ women detectives, but Warne had presented her case eloquently by arguing women are "most useful in worming out secrets in many places which would be impossible for a male detective. A Woman would be able to befriend the wives and girlfriends of suspected criminals and gain their confidence. Men become braggarts when they are around women who encourage them to boast. Women have an eye for detail and are excellent observers."

When the Civil War ended, Pinkerton opened offices for the Chicago-based Pinkerton's National Detective Agency throughout the country, including a Philadelphia office at 45 South Third Street. Warne, his superintendent of detectives, was promoted to head the Female Detective Bureau. However, at the young age of 38, she caught pneumonia and died in 1868 with Pinkerton at her side. She was buried in the Pinkerton family plot at Graceland Cemetery, Chicago.

In his memoirs Allan Pinkerton named Warne one of the five greatest detectives he ever employed. Into the 21st century, the Pinkerton legacy remains in operation under the name Securitas Critical Infrastructure Services.

38. CATCHING THE TRAIN WITH ABRAHAM LINCOLN

MAP 6 ➤ **West train depot:** North 32nd and Market Streets

Deserving of the honor or not, Allan Pinkerton claimed he saved President-elect Lincoln's life. National political tension ran high in the winter of 1860–1861. The issue of slavery divided Northern and Southern states. With open talk of assassination abounding, the president-elect was warned of the potential danger as he traveled from Springfield, Illinois, to Washington, DC, for his inauguration. After providing Lincoln with information of the plot, Pinkerton received the go-ahead to provide security along Honest Abe's train route to Washington, but only if he worked around the president-elect's schedule. With the admission of

President-elect Abraham Lincoln boarded a Southern and Western Railroad car at the Broad Street station at Broad and Prime Streets for the overnight trip to Washington, DC, and his inauguration.

Kansas to the Union as a free state on January 29, 1861, Lincoln had committed to raising the Kansas flag at Independence Hall the morning of February 22—George Washington's birthday—and to giving a speech at a banquet in Harrisburg before the General Assembly of Pennsylvania.

Despite the possible danger, Lincoln insisted on attending these events, though he agreed that when he reached Baltimore he would forgo traveling to Washington by carriage and continue on a more secure train car. After the Harrisburg speech, a Pinkerton operative disabled the telegraph wires leading out of the city, while another operative put Lincoln and his former law partner, Ward H. Lamon, on a train to the West Philadelphia train depot at 32nd and Market Streets. Reports differ, but the president-elect was likely in disguise when he arrived in Philadelphia from Harrisburg. One description depicted Lincoln in a wide-brimmed "Scotch" or kossuth hat, which Lincoln later said was presented to him in Harrisburg, and an overcoat draped across his shoulders as a cape. He was observed to have stooped over as he walked to conceal his noticeable height.

Met by Allan Pinkerton in Philadelphia, Lincoln and Lamon were ferried by closed carriage a short distance to the Southern and Western Railroad station on the northwest corner of Broad and Prime Streets (now Washington Avenue). There, Pinkerton's famed female detective, Kate Warne, had hired a rear sleeper car on the Washington-bound train for her "sick brother." Pinkerton operatives were stationed along the route to ensure Lincoln's safety, signaling one another with lights.

For the operation, Pinkerton used the code name PLUMS and gave Lincoln the unfortunate code name NUTS. The train arrived in Washington as scheduled at six o'clock the following morning. After successfully escorting the president-elect to the city, Pinkerton checked into the Willard Hotel and is said to have sent a telegram to his operatives: "Plums arrived with Nuts this morning."

Fifty months later, President Lincoln passed through Philadelphia for the final time as his funeral train moved slowly along tracks lined with mourners. The Civil War was won and the Union preserved but at the cost of one of America's greatest presidents.

39. THE UNION'S COUNTERSPY

MAP 4 ➤ **Lafayette C. Baker residence:** 1737 Coates Street (later renamed Fairmount Avenue)

Colorful and tirelessly self-promoting, Lafayette C. Baker may have been, in his own assessment, the most effective counterintelligence officer of the Civil War. Hired by Gen. Winfield Scott in 1861, Baker is credited with capturing famed Confederate spy Isabella "Belle" Boyd along with dozens of Southern sympathizers lurking in the nation's capital. In one exploit, Baker adopted

Lafayette C. Baker

the cover of an itinerant photographer and an alias—Sam Munson, the son of a Knoxville judge—to go behind enemy lines to Richmond, Virginia. Toting a broken camera and no photographic plates, Baker was first arrested by Union troops, then by the Confederacy, and eventually returned to Washington, where he reported on what he observed in the Confederate capital. Secretary of War Edwin M. Stanton brought Baker into the War Department first as a special agent and then as a special provost marshal.

In this later role, Baker seemed to have operated outside the law, hauling in and questioning suspects without benefit of warrants. During this period, Baker's own honesty came into question with rumors abounding that he was profiting from corruption in the nation's capital.

Baker eventually ran afoul of Stanton and was demoted for suspicion of tapping the secretary's telegraph line. One of Baker's men was assigned to guard President Lincoln during that fateful April 14, 1865, night at Ford's Theatre, but following the murder, Baker was called to track down the assassin John Wilkes Booth. Baker's work eventually earned him a portion of the reward money.

In his book *History of the United States Secret Service* published in 1867, Baker stretched the truth to absurdly bolster his wartime exploits and enhance his reputation. Retiring to his Philadelphia home at 1737 Coates Street (later renamed Fairmount Avenue), he reportedly died of meningitis on July 3, 1868. Originally buried in the Mutual Family Cemetery at Tenth Street and Washington Avenue in Philadelphia, his remains were moved when the cemetery was closed. His final resting place is an unmarked grave at Forest Hills Memorial Park (also known as Somerton Hills Cemetery), 101 Byberry Road, Huntingdon Valley, Montgomery County, Pennsylvania.

"In the early stages of the war, before any police organization of the Government had been perfected or set in operation, and before blockade restrictions had been established, the whole North was flooded by a class of southern spies, correspondents, and incendiaries."

—Lafayette C. Baker, *History of the United States Secret Service*

40. BLACK SPY IN THE CONFEDERATE WHITE HOUSE

MAP 2 ➤ **Quaker School for Negroes:** Southeast corner of Locust and South Hutchinson Streets (site redeveloped)

Mary Elizabeth Bowser, born into slavery in the John and Elizabeth Van Lew family of Richmond, Virginia, acquired the reputation of a daring Civil War spy. Following John Van Lew's death in 1843, his wife freed the family's slaves, but Bowser remained as a paid servant in the Van Lew household. A staunch abolitionist and Quaker, Van Lew recognized Bowser's exceptional intelligence coupled with a near-photographic memory and arranged for her education at the Quaker School for Negroes in Philadelphia.

In 1861 Bowser graduated and returned to Richmond to marry a free black man. She remained in contact with the Van Lews' daughter, Elizabeth, who, despite her abolitionist beliefs, was prominent in Richmond society and aided prisoners who escaped from Richmond's hellish Libby Prison. At times, escapees were hidden in secret rooms in the Van Lew mansion.

Many records describe the two women working together to conduct espionage operations. In one of the more daring tales, Bowser was placed in the Confederate White House as a servant to Varina Davis, wife of Confederate president Jefferson Davis. Using the alias Ellen Bond, Bowser played the role of dim-witted servant while feeding Van Lew a steady stream of information through Thomas McNiven, a baker who made regular deliveries to the Davis household.

Black, female Union spy Mary Bowser is believed to have been educated at the Quaker School that once stood at Locust and Hutchinson Streets.

According to the account, Jefferson Davis determined that information was leaking from his household and suspected a spy in his midst. When McNiven was identified as the source of the information, suspicion also fell upon Bowser, who fled Richmond but not before unsuccessfully attempting to set fire to the Confederate White House.

Paucity of verifiable documentation about Bowser's activities, however, causes historians, such as Douglas Waller in *Lincoln's Spies*, to question many of the dramatic elements of her espionage. Such caution is understandable since embellishment of the exploits of spies on both sides is common in the postwar writings by the participants as well as the observers. In Bowser's case, a key document, the journal she wrote chronicling her wartime experiences, was mistakenly discarded by her dependents in 1952, leaving much of her life shrouded in mystery. Nevertheless, Bowser received official recognition for her Civil War spying when inducted into the Military Intelligence Corps Hall of Fame in Fort Huachuca, Arizona, in 1995.

HOOPSKIRTS AND CROSS-DRESSING

Spy memoirs flourished following the Revolutionary and Civil wars. Spies discovered a good living could be made by penning details of their exploits and entertaining packed audiences eager for wartime adventure. If the stories weren't 100 percent accurate, nobody seemed to mind.

One feature of memoirs that consistently proved a crowd pleaser was transgressing taboos of the day. Benjamin Franklin Stringfellow was said not only to have hidden under a hoopskirt but also in another case to have disguised himself as a woman to attend a formal ball in honor of George Washington's birthday in the nation's capital. Union spy Sarah Emma Edmonds reportedly assumed a number of male disguises and aliases, including that of Franklin Thompson and another of a Southern gentleman, James Mayberry. Cuban-born adventuress Loreta Janeta Velázquez went one better by wearing male clothing enhanced with a sophisticated wiring to give her a male physique. Actress Pauline Cushman performed to packed houses dressed in a Union uniform, complete with a sword.

Exigent circumstances to break social norms combined with daring escapades are recurring themes in spy fiction. One explanation for this attraction is offered by academic Jacques Barzun in a 1965 essay "Findings: Meditations on the Literature of Spying" in *The American Scholar*. He observed, "The soul of the spy is somehow the model of our own; his actions and his trappings fulfill our unsatisfied desires. How else explain the stir caused, also this past summer, by the death of Ian Fleming?"

41. UNDERGROUND RAILROAD INTELLIGENCE

MAP 5 ➤ **Belmont Mansion:** 2000 Belmont Mansion Drive

The beautiful Belmont Mansion in Fairmount Park now houses the Underground Railroad Museum.

Runaway slaves moving north through the Underground Railroad were valuable sources of Civil War intelligence for the Union. Called contraband informants because of their status in Southern states as property, the runaways provided Union generals, such as Joseph Hooker and George McClellan, with first-person information about the South. Intelligence provided by the newly free slaves was called black dispatches. Confederate general Robert E. Lee recognized the value of their intelligence when he wrote, "The chief source of information to the enemy is through our Negroes. They are easily deceived by proper caution."

An important safe house or station for the escaping slaves along the Underground Railroad in Philadelphia was the Belmont Mansion, 2000 Belmont Mansion Drive. The mansion was built in 1745 and previously hosted many of the Founding Fathers, including George Washington, John Adams, Thomas Jefferson, and James Madison. It is now home to the Underground Railroad Museum.

Only relatively recently have the contributions of African Americans to Civil War intelligence efforts come to public attention. Among those whose stories

John Scobell, a freed slave from Mississippi, posed as a servant while working with Allan Pinkerton's organization.

have gained wider recognition is Mary Touvestre, a freed slave who worked in Norfolk, Virginia, as a housekeeper for an engineer. After overhearing conversations regarding the retrofit of the USS *Merrimack* into an ironclad capable of breaking the Union blockade, she stole the technical plans and delivered them to military officials in Washington.

Another example is John Scobell, a freed slave from Mississippi who posed as a servant while working with Allan Pinkerton's operatives Timothy Webster and Hattie (sometimes Carrie) Lawton. Scobell elicited intelligence information through his access and acceptance to black communities that would have been impossible for his white counterparts to obtain.

42. THE PRICE OF BAD INTELLIGENCE I

MAP I ➤ **Maj. Gen. George B. McClellan birthplace:** 248 Walnut Street (near the corner of redeveloped Walnut and South Seventh Streets)

Criticized often by Civil War historians for a lack of aggressive tactics on the battlefield, Philadelphia native Maj. Gen. George B. McClellan excelled at organizational strategy and at raising and training an army to fight Southern secessionists. He assembled the Army of the Potomac early in the war and briefly served as the general in chief of the Union Army.

Philadelphia native Maj. Gen. George B. McClellan graduated second in his class at West Point but came under harsh criticism for timidity in combat. A statuary tribute to the general by Henry Jackson Ellicott stands at City Hall's North Plaza.

As commander of the Army of the Potomac, McClellan employed Allan Pinkerton as his chief of secret service, directing him to conduct spying operations for the 1862 Peninsula Campaign. Unfortunately, Pinkerton's battlefield operations were the product of inexperience and characterized by flawed information. Intelligence arrived late, and inaccurate reporting, sometimes from frightened runaway slaves, was often taken at face value. Pinkerton may have intentionally manipulated figures and bent facts to suit McClellan's preconceptions. In one instance, Pinkerton's report inflated Confederate troop strength by more than 100 percent.

"Pinkerton's idea of military intelligence was to count the noses of the opposing troops and then to count them again to be sure the first figure was right."

—Allen Dulles, *The Craft of Intelligence*

"From every available field the facts were gleaned. From prisoners of war, contrabands [freed slaves], loyal Southerners, deserters, blockade-runners and from actual observations by trustworthy scouts, my estimates were made."

—Allan Pinkerton

The intelligence failings were disastrous for the Peninsula Campaign when McClellan failed to mount an attack against Confederate troops of inferior numbers. Confederate general Joseph E. Johnston was pleasantly surprised. "Nobody but McClellan could have hesitated to attack," Johnston later wrote. President Lincoln was even harsher in his criticism: "If General McClellan does not want to use the Army, I would like to borrow it for a time, provided I could see how it could be made to do something."

43. THE PRICE OF BAD INTELLIGENCE II

MAP I ➤ **Union Navy Yard:** Federal Street, Southwark neighborhood from Front Street to the Delaware River

Fear of Confederate attacks on Philadelphia early in the Civil War was fueled by unconfirmed intelligence reports. Union agent Lafayette C. Baker, who later became the provost marshal and the head of the National Detective Bureau, reported he received a communication dated December 26, 1861, from one of his agents in Philadelphia that painted a grim scenario for the city's security. "He [Baker's agent] says that as soon as the advance is made upon the lines at

Although Philadelphia saw no combat during the Civil War, rumors of a Confederate attack proved stubbornly persistent, including one against the Union Navy Yard.

"False intelligence may prove worse than none."

—Gen. George Washington

Joseph Hooker, commander of the Union's First Corps, debunked the dire warnings of an impending Confederate attack on Philadelphia.

Washington, a party here, now numbering over five thousand in this city together with thrice that number in the adjoining counties will seize the Navy Yard arsenal in the Southwark neighborhood, at Federal Street to Front Street and Delaware River."

The attack never came. Despite Lee's retreat after the Battle of Antietam, rumors of impending danger to Philadelphia continued. During the fall of 1862, word spread that unspecified Confederate troops were planning to invade Pennsylvania and march on Philadelphia. Union intelligence placed the number of rebel troops at 120,000. Either the result of an intentional misinformation campaign by Gen. Robert E. Lee or of speculative rumors in Union barracks, the information started a panic. Pennsylvania governor Andrew Curtin ordered the mobilization of 80,000 militia soldiers, and citizen committees appealed to Washington for additional protection. Clearly, should Confederate forces capture Philadelphia, the Union would be dealt a severe blow. However, Joseph Hooker, commander of the Union's First Corps, recognized the exaggerated Confederate number and wrote to his headquarters, "It is satisfactory to my mind that the rebels have no more intention of going to Harrisburg than they have of going to heaven. It is only in the United States that atrocities like this are entertained."

44. NO KIDDING, I REALLY AM A SPY

MAP 3 ➤ **William Crawford temporary residence:** Moyamensing Prison (demolished in 1960s), South Tenth and Reed Streets

William Crawford, employed by Union major general John Dix, was no doubt a brave operative. He went undercover into the heart of enemy territory numerous times, but the intelligence he delivered could not be fully trusted. Once his observations overestimated troop strength by ten times and in another instance by 35 percent.

Possibly his most stunning intelligence failure took place in Philadelphia. Assuming the role of a smuggler seeking to sell goods in the South, Crawford

Spies, criminals, poets, and authors were inmates of Philadelphia's Moyamensing Prison. Edgar Allan Poe spent a night there, as did Charles Bukowski decades later.

Chief of Detectives Ben Franklin

built a cover by talking openly about traveling to the South and about the "inexhaustible resources of the Rebels." Apparently, he proved a little too believable and was arrested by the Philadelphia Police Department's chief of detectives Benjamin Franklin. In Crawford's possessions were percussion caps and a supply of Confederate money; while necessary to support his cover, they also persuaded Franklin that he had a criminal in custody.

Most likely taken to the Moyamensing Prison, Tenth and Reed Streets, Crawford broke cover and declared himself an undercover operative for the Union. However, neither Crawford's admission of his espionage activities nor the passes he carried from Union generals Dix and Robert Schenck convinced the Philadelphia lawman. Franklin conferred with the War Department, then he shipped the spy to Washington. Crawford was held in the Old Capitol Prison until General Dix finally sprung him, calling the spy "a tried and trusted agent . . . who swam rivers, waded swamps, at the risk of his life to give . . . the most important information."

KNIGHTS OF THE BLUE GAUNTLET

Philadelphia, one of the major Union cities that is geographically close to the South, was a potential source of supplies and intelligence for the secessionist states in need of everything from arms to medical supplies. The holder of a bullet mold patent was offered $30,000 by Virginia's governor John Letcher for the mold. The patent holder rejected the offer, but others with weapons or equipment needed by the Confederacy were tempted to deal in what was called contraband. As the war progressed, Philadelphia officials confiscated large quantities of rifles, kegs of powder, percussion caps, and other items headed for Southern states. Fearing damage to their reputation, businesses rumored of dealing in contraband regularly took out ads in local papers denying the charges.

Safety committees and vigilante groups were formed to root out Confederate spies, sympathizers, and collaborators. According to reports in the *Philadelphia Inquirer* and *Philadelphia Press*, in some instances the spies were covered in molasses and raw cotton before being banished from town. A letter sent to one suspected Confederate spy, an actor performing in Philadelphia, offered fair warning:

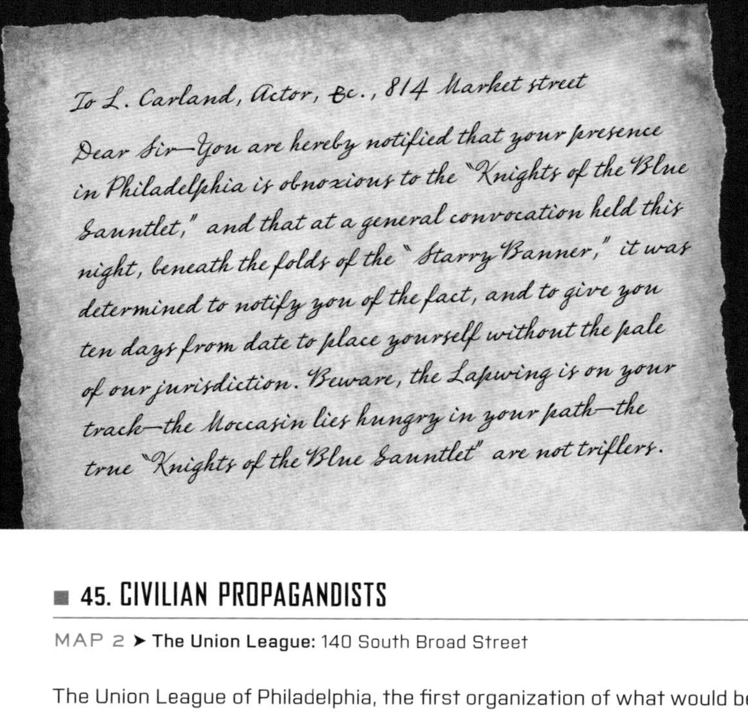
To L. Carland, Actor, &c., 814 Market street

Dear Sir—You are hereby notified that your presence in Philadelphia is obnoxious to the "Knights of the Blue Gauntlet," and that at a general convocation held this night, beneath the folds of the "Starry Banner," it was determined to notify you of the fact, and to give you ten days from date to place yourself without the pale of our jurisdiction. Beware, the Lapwing is on your track—the Moccasin lies hungry in your path—the true "Knights of the Blue Gauntlet" are not triflers.

■ 45. CIVILIAN PROPAGANDISTS

MAP 2 ➤ **The Union League:** 140 South Broad Street

The Union League of Philadelphia, the first organization of what would become a nationwide movement, was established in 1862 to oppose the Confederacy and promote loyalty to the Union. Meetings were held at 1208 Walnut Street before the organization moved a year later to 1118 Chestnut Street. Among its

Founded in 1862 to oppose the Confederacy and promote loyalty to the Union, the Union League was housed in multiple locations before settling into its Broad Street address.

Civil War efforts was a particularly clever periodical, *The Planter's Almanac for 1864*, designed for circulation among Rebel troops with the hope of promoting desertion. Inserted between charts of the phases of the moon, planting tables, and a recipe for "Beer in Small Quantities" were speeches by Abraham Lincoln, letters from government officials advocating the Union cause, and promises of fair treatment for those who abandoned the Confederacy.

The Union League of Philadelphia is housed in a stately building at South 140 Broad Street and continues to abide by its founding motto, "Love of Country Leads." The network of Union League clubs, which include New York City and Chicago, continues today. Although primarily social organizations, the clubs maintain strong civic ties and sponsor current affairs forums and speaker programs.

46. UP, UP, AND AWAY

MAP II ➤ **Thaddeus S. C. Lowe House:** 823 West Main Street, Norristown, Pennsylvania

He can be called the father of military aerial reconnaissance. Professor Thaddeus Sobieski Coulincourt Lowe acquired a reputation as an "aeronaut" for ballooning in 1860 when a group of prominent citizens associated with the Franklin Institute lured him to Philadelphia with a promise of financial support for his aeronautical research. Professor John C. Cresson, then president of the Philadelphia Gas Works, promised an adequate supply of gas from the Point

Breeze Gas Works, then located on Passyunk Avenue near the Schuylkill River, for the balloon. Lowe's ambition was to launch a balloon, called an aerostat, that could cross the Atlantic Ocean to Europe.

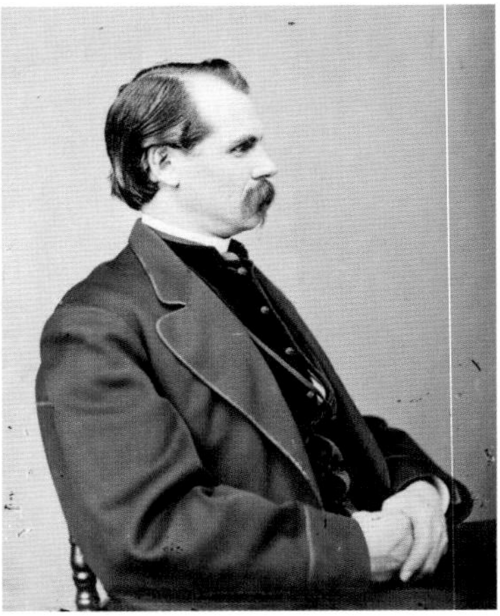

Thaddeus S. C. Lowe

Some members of the press were skeptical of the endeavor. "Prof. T.S.C. Lowe is in Philadelphia, and has actually persuaded some of the citizens to advance him funds so that he may undertake his long-promised balloon trip to Europe," the *New York Times* sneered on July 23, 1860. "He is to be accompanied by an astronomer, a historian, a sea-captain and an artist."

During this period, Lowe lived in Chester County on a farm that bordered Pickering Creek. His balloon, named the *Great Western*, was said to be the largest ever made. It weighed some two tons and required 400,000 cubic feet of helium. A test flight on June 28, 1860, carried Lowe and several passengers, including a reporter from the *Philadelphia Inquirer*, to Atlantic City and back. Although the trip was deemed a success, an Atlantic crossing was still seen as too risky, and funding dried up. Undeterred, Lowe launched a less ambitious flight, this time from Cincinnati, Ohio, to the East Coast, but blown off course, he landed in South Carolina. Fort Sumter had fallen to Confederate forces a week prior, and Lowe was arrested as a spy.

Civil War scientist Thaddeus S. C. Lowe created what is arguably the first aircraft carrier by outfitting a former coal barge as a balloon launching pad.

Eventually released, Lowe went to Washington, eager to put his aeronautical know-how to work for the war effort. With a presidential authorization of $250, Lowe went aloft in Washington on June 11, 1861, in a balloon called the *Enterprise*. Rising to a height of 500 feet above the National Mall and trailing a telegraph wire, the telegrapher sent a message: "This point of observation commands an area nearly 50 miles in diameter. The city, with its girdle of encampments, presents a superb scene. I have the pleasure of sending you the first dispatch ever telegraphed from an aerial station and in acknowledging indebtedness to your encouragement for the opportunity of demonstrating the availability of the science of aeronautics in the military service of the country. T.S.C. Lowe."

Several days later, on June 24, Professor Lowe observed Confederate cavalry from the balloon platform, now moved to Falls Church, Virginia, marking the first combat aerial reconnaissance in our nation's history. Historical records show Lincoln appointed Lowe as the chief aeronaut of the US Balloon Corps of the Potomac in July 1861. As a civilian employee, Lowe was paid $10 a day in gold, and the Balloon Corps made some 3,000 flights during a three-year period before it was disbanded.

Following the war, Lowe returned to the Philadelphia area and lived at 823 West Main Street, Norristown, Pennsylvania. He continued to innovate and invent, patenting what is said to be the first ice-making machine, the Compression Ice Machine, in 1865 and a new gas technology for lighting homes. Lowe eventually moved to California and died in 1913.

FIRST AIRCRAFT CARRIER?

Thaddeus S. C. Lowe, ever the innovator, outfitted the coal barge USS *George Washington Parke Custis* with gas-generating equipment. By launching a balloon from the deck, he was able to observe Confederate forces several miles away during the Battle of Seven Pines near Richmond, Virginia, and relayed reports on May 31 and June 1, 1862. In doing so, Lowe created what could arguably be called the nation's first aircraft carrier.

47. THE POWER OF THE PRESS

MAP I ➤ ***Philadelphia Inquirer***: 304 Chestnut Street

Public sources have always been a staple of information for intelligence professionals. During the Civil War, as telegraph communications enabled newspaper reports to become more timely, Confederate general Robert E. Lee was said to favor the reporting of the *Philadelphia Inquirer*, 304 Chestnut Street, as a source of reliable intelligence. Lee expressed a

Philadelphia's leading newspaper of the day, the *Philadelphia Inquirer*, made no effort to conceal its pro-Union sympathies. In the 20th century, socialist journalist and Soviet spy I. F. Stone began his career at the same newspaper.

Maj. Gen. George Gordon Meade

preference for certain reporters, saying of one of the *Inquirer's* correspondents, "He knew what he reported and reported what he knew."

Although the *Inquirer* was fervently pro-Union, its reports of the war often caused controversy. Following the First Battle of Bull Run, when many papers proclaimed a Union victory, the *Inquirer's* accurate report of the Union's defeat caused a near riot. When *Inquirer* reporter Edward Crapsey wrote a story in 1864 that described Ulysses S. Grant as a brilliant strategist, it so angered Maj. Gen. George Gordon Meade that he made the reporter mount a mule backward, wear a sign reading "Libeler of the Press" around his neck, and parade the camp to the tune of "The Rogue's March."

48. THE CONSPIRACY THAT NEVER WAS

MAP I ➤ ***Philadelphia's Daily News***: 74 South Third Street

In the mid-1850s a mysterious and secret organization emerged called the Knights of the Golden Circle. Its avowed purposed was to expand the number of American slave states by conquering Mexico, Central America, parts of South America, Cuba, and portions of the Caribbean. As impractical as the idea seemed, the concept took hold following the Dred Scott decision in 1857, and chapters, called Castles, formed throughout the Midwest and the South.

Col. John P. Sanderson

The organization came to the attention of Maj. Gen. William Rosecrans and Col. John P. Sanderson, stationed in Missouri, in 1864. Sanderson, a Philadelphia lawyer and state politician who once edited the *Daily News*, 74 South Third Street, previously served as the chief clerk of the War

CAPTURED IN PHILADELPHIA

Among the Confederacy's most daring spies was Pennsylvania native John Burke. Born in 1830 and orphaned at an early age, he made his way to New York City and then to Texas. He learned the profession of cobbler and became a Texas lawyer. An early volunteer to the Confederate cause, Burke was one of General Lee's trusted spies and scouts, reportedly playing a critical role in the Confederate victory at the First Battle of Bull Run.

Adept at disguise, Burke's Northern accent, acquired from his time spent in New York and Philadelphia, allowed him to move freely behind Union lines. It was said that he changed the color of his glass eye, replaced it with a patch, or appeared with an empty socket to disguise his appearance. In one instance, he donned a Union officer's uniform to infiltrate government facilities around Washington. Captured in Philadelphia in 1864 and en route to Washington for trial, he escaped by jumping from a train into a river. A few days following his escape, he presented himself to General Lee outside Richmond, Virginia. By then the spy was exhausted. Burke returned to Texas, where his brother-in-law governor Pendleton Murrah appointed him the state's adjutant general.

Few official records remain of Burke's exploits, yet legends grew around his escapades as a spy. He was said to have hidden himself in the feather bed of a proper Southern belle. In another tale, he took refuge from Union soldiers under the billowing hoopskirt of another Southern lady. Other examples of his daring include having a thoroughbred horse shot out from under him in a high-speed chase and concealing himself on a narrow crossbeam as Union soldiers searched a barn. As with many post–Civil War accounts by both Northern and Southern spies, accuracy remains elusive.

Following the defeat of the Confederacy, Burke first went to Mexico. Then he returned to Jefferson, Texas, where he became a prominent criminal defense attorney and practiced law until his death in 1871.

Department. Assigned to investigate the organization, he paid informants and spies to infiltrate the mysterious group and its affiliated organizations. The underground rebel groups reputedly had thousands, if not tens of thousands, of members; required loyalty oaths; performed rituals; and maintained secret signals to recognize a fellow knight. The password for the Knights of the Golden Circle was "Nu-Oh-Lac" (Calhoun spelled backward).

As sinister and extensive as it sounded, the organization was primarily a scam conceived by George W. L. Bickley. Largely unsuccessful in past ventures, which included a failed literary magazine, a brief and scandal-plagued career impersonating a medical doctor, and a short-lived plan for mounting an exhibition military drill team, Bickley thought he had a winner with the Knights of the Golden Circle. In addition to secret oaths and signals, membership required a fee of either $5 or $10, depending on circumstances. Bickley, not one to waste a failure, repurposed the uniforms from the unsuccessful drill team venture and solicited funds from wealthy Southerners.

The organization made a few ill-advised incursions into Mexico and may have burned down a building that housed a pro-Union newspaper in Texas. However, the membership was never close in the numbers or the activity that Bickley promoted in the numerous press interviews touting his secret society. Sanderson's investigation was plagued by rumormongers who saw an opportunity to be on the government payroll. A report prepared by Sanderson and Rosecrans was rejected by both Lincoln and the War Department. Then Sanderson, using his experience as a Philadelphia newspaperman, decided the best way to neutralize the dangers of the knights was to publicize it. Sensational stories began appearing, asserting Philadelphia as well as New York City were targets of terrorism planned by the secret society. Politicians began openly accusing each other of membership in the organization. Hucksters, seizing an opportunity, sold tickets at a dollar apiece throughout Lancaster County that allegedly guaranteed to save their farms from seizure by the organization.

The knights finally collapsed when Bickley was drafted into the Confederacy in 1863 as a surgeon. Promptly deserting, he was quickly captured as a spy and spent the remainder of the war in prison. He died in obscurity in 1867.

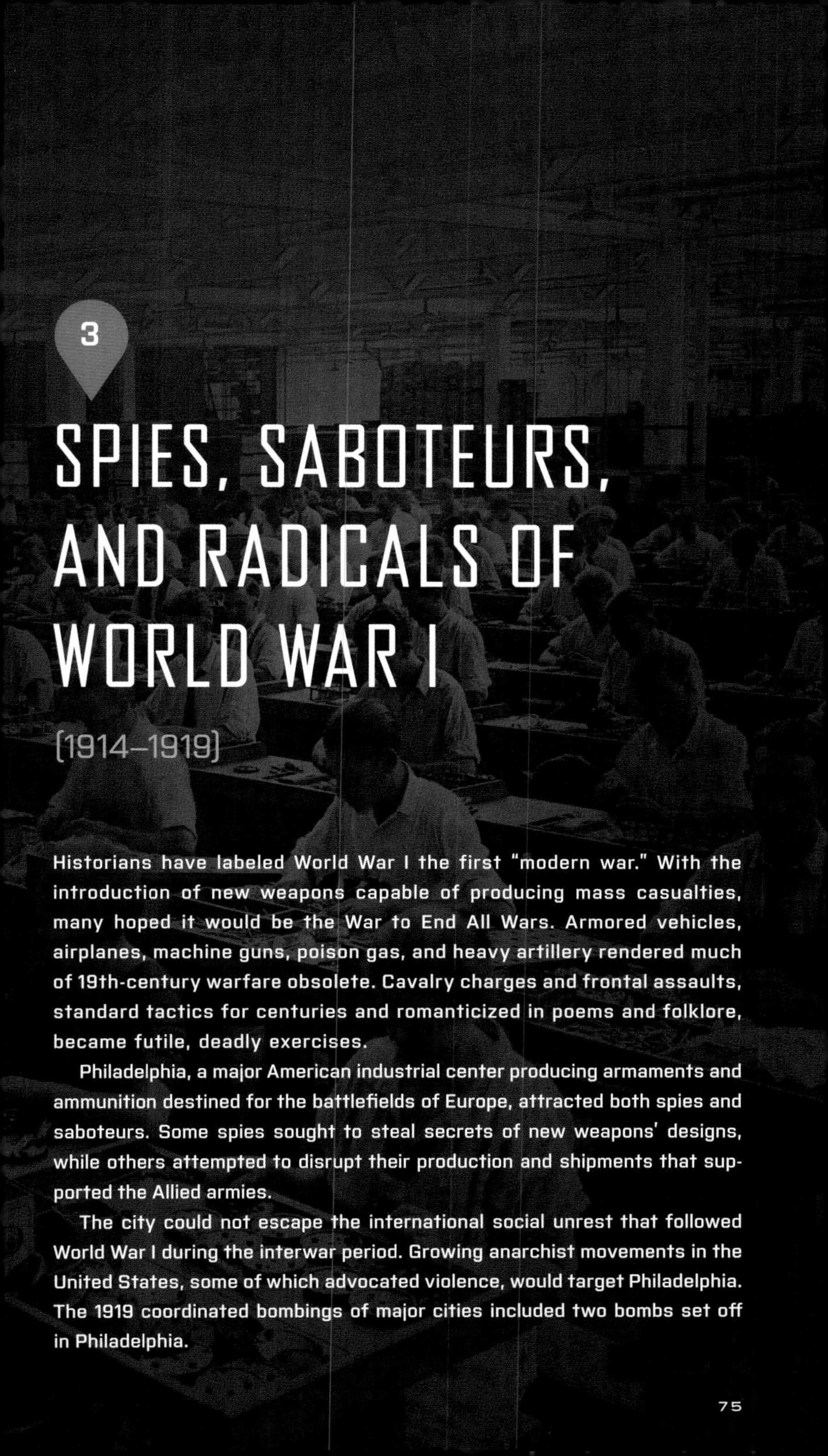

3

SPIES, SABOTEURS, AND RADICALS OF WORLD WAR I

(1914–1919)

Historians have labeled World War I the first "modern war." With the introduction of new weapons capable of producing mass casualties, many hoped it would be the War to End All Wars. Armored vehicles, airplanes, machine guns, poison gas, and heavy artillery rendered much of 19th-century warfare obsolete. Cavalry charges and frontal assaults, standard tactics for centuries and romanticized in poems and folklore, became futile, deadly exercises.

Philadelphia, a major American industrial center producing armaments and ammunition destined for the battlefields of Europe, attracted both spies and saboteurs. Some spies sought to steal secrets of new weapons' designs, while others attempted to disrupt their production and shipments that supported the Allied armies.

The city could not escape the international social unrest that followed World War I during the interwar period. Growing anarchist movements in the United States, some of which advocated violence, would target Philadelphia. The 1919 coordinated bombings of major cities included two bombs set off in Philadelphia.

49. PUTTING ON THE RITZ

MAP 2 ➤ **Ritz-Carlton Hotel:** 211 South Broad Street (now site of Daniel J. Terra Building)

In April 1915 Paul Hilken, the son of a successful Baltimore businessman, met German diplomat-turned-spymaster Franz von Rintelen in the writing room of Philadelphia's Ritz-Carlton Hotel, 211 South Broad Street (today the Daniel J. Terra Building). A resident of Baltimore, Hilken was born in the United States of German immigrant parents, attended Lehigh University and the Massachusetts Institute of Technology (MIT), and, like his father, seemed destined for a career with the North German Lloyd shipping company. Those ambitions came to an end, however, with World War I.

German spy Paul Hilken

The meeting with Rintelen, arranged through a customs broker named Friedrich Henjes (sometimes Henjez), offered a different opportunity. What the spy Rintelen needed at the moment was a businessman to keep the books and launder money for his operations. Hilken could become a clandestine paymaster.

Respected in the Baltimore financial community, the Hilken family's business operated under the name Albert Schumacher and Company as a tobacco exporter and agent for Lloyd. As a result, local bankers would likely not ask questions about a family member's transactions or probe too deeply into those financial affairs. Hilken later confessed German funds were laundered through accounts of legitimate businesses.

Paul Hilken was recruited by German spymaster Franz von Rintelen in the writing room of Philadelphia's Ritz-Carlton Hotel, 211 South Broad Street. Today it is the Daniel J. Terra Building.

As a paymaster, Hilken's fluency in German added a level of trust from members of Rintelen's clandestine cell. By the time America entered the war, Hilken had moved funds to finance the July 30, 1916, ground-shaking explosion at Black Tom Island and several other smaller operations. In one case, he arranged for the German national and spy ring courier Karl Thummel, using the alias Charles Thorne, to become the assistant employment manager at the Canadian Car and Foundry factory in Kingsland, New Jersey. Thummel/Thorne then hired the arsonist Theodore Wozniak to clean shell casings, giving Wozniak the opportunity to set the factory on fire on January 11, 1917. Hilken also laundered funds to pay Anton Dilger, who headed a germ warfare operation out of Washington, DC, that sought to infect horses with diseases prior to their shipment to European allies.

DEBATING THE EVIDENCE

A key piece of evidence presented during the Mixed Claims Commission hearing was the January 1917 issue of the pulp magazine *Blue Book*. Paul Hilken, the paymaster for the sabotage operation, testified secret writing was used on four pages where the story "The Yukon Trail" by the British-born author of westerns, William MacLeod Raine, appeared. The validity of Hilken's testimony that would affect tens of millions of dollars of claims depended on an old copy of a magazine that originally sold for 15 cents.

The authenticity of the magazine and its secret message immediately came into question. German lawyers asserted an operative would not have used such a simplistic lemon juice–based formula for secret writing along with pinpricked pages that spelled out names. They further contended the magazine was recently purchased at a store in Manhattan. Hilken countered that he recovered the magazine from his estranged wife's home. When a detailed forensic analysis of the paper, ink, and handwriting confirmed the writer was that of German operative Fred Hermann (sometimes spelled Herrmann), the commission ruled that the Black Tom Island explosion was the work of German saboteurs.

Secret writing in a popular magazine was crucial evidence in establishing the Germans' responsibility for sabotage in the United States prior to its entrance into World War I.

Hilken's involvement in espionage was said to have ceased in April 1917 when America officially entered the war. The years following the war were not kind to the former clandestine paymaster. His marriage ended, and multiple business ventures failed, including a trucking company. He moved to New York, where he lived modestly at 135 West 185th Street in the Bronx and worked as a wholesale paint salesman.

Although questioned by law enforcement about his role in the sabotage operations, Hilken was never charged. Later, he was tracked down by investigators for the German-American Mixed Claims Commission in the 1930s and granted immunity from prosecution to testify. He then confessed to supporting sabotage operations and bolstered his testimony with a copy of the popular pulp magazine *Blue Book*, which contained coded secret writing, as well as a diary he kept during his time working for Rintelen. The German defendants challenged the claim, but the court found in favor of US interests, awarding $50 million in compensation to the corporations for losses suffered.

50. EXPLOSIVE "DIABOLICAL PLOT"

MAP 10 ➤ **Unidentified Victims Memorial:** Chester Rural Cemetery, 412 West 15th Street, Chester, Pennsylvania

The small industrial town of Eddystone was the site of one of America's deadliest acts of sabotage. At approximately 10:00 a.m. on April 10, 1917, an explosion ripped through the Eddystone Ammunition Corporation's F Building, where nearly 400 women were loading shells with black powder. The explosion claimed more than 130 victims just days after America entered World War I. One official characterized the destruction as "the result of a diabolical plot conceived in the degenerate brain of a demon in human guise."

Sidney "Ace of Spies" Reilly

An exhaustive investigation never assigned responsibility for the explosion, but there was no shortage of suspects. A sailor on a German ship, radical socialists, Leon Trotsky, and others fell under suspicion. Even the famed Sidney "Ace of Spies" Reilly, who was in the process of suing Eddystone for $500,000, was added to the suspect list. The newly formed government of the Union of Soviet Socialist Republics (USSR) came under suspicion due to a telegram sent by Russian inspectors who were at the plant overseeing shipments of armaments for their army. There was also a report from a Trenton, New Jersey, woman who claimed she found an envelope with an incriminating letter and the initials "N.K." at the Broad Street train station in Philadelphia.

The investigation, which included a mix of local law enforcement, Department of Justice investigators, and private investigators, followed leads for months. In the end, they turned out to be dead ends, though sabotage seemed to be the final conclusion. Pressed to resume production by the demands of World War I and despite the damage, the plant was operational again within a month after the explosion.

The Eddystone explosion was one of the most destructive acts of sabotage in our nation's history. Unidentified victims of the explosion and resulting fire are buried beneath a simple stone in the Chester Rural Cemetery.

The remains of more than fifty victims who could not be individually identified were buried in the Chester Rural Cemetery, 412 West 15th Street, Chester, Pennsylvania. A simple stone monument commemorates their memory.

51. RECRUITING IRISH RADICALS

MAP 6 ➤ **Joseph McGarrity residence:** 5412 Springfield Avenue

During World War I, Germany sought Irish nationalists inside America who were willing to conduct sabotage operations. One of those identified, Joseph McGarrity, was an Irish immigrant who made a fortune as a bar owner, a wholesaler, and a distiller in Philadelphia. A prominent figure in Clan na Gael, a sister organization to the Irish Republican Brotherhood, McGarrity was well placed to organize and direct sabotage operations against British-bound wartime supplies and manufacturing facilities in the still-neutral United States.

Joseph McGarrity

An encrypted January 24, 1915, telegram to Franz von Papen, Germany's military attaché in Washington, instructed him to recruit a number of Irish

One of Philadelphia's prominent distillers, Joseph McGarrity was a passionate supporter of the Irish Republican Brotherhood during and after World War I.

Americans for sabotage operations. At the top of the list was "Joseph Mac Garrity *[sic]* 5412 Springfield [Avenue] Philadelphia." The telegram described McGarrity as "completely reliable and discreet." McGarrity and his saboteurs, the directive stated, should be instructed to target factories producing munitions and war matériel. In return for the Irish Americans' assistance, Germany would provide guns and other armaments to fight the British in Ireland.

The plan fizzled. Papen reported in a telegram sent on March 17, 1915, that the Irish as well as German workers had been fired from munitions factories, and critical targets were under heavy guard. He also noted the presence of British spies in the United States who were intent on uncovering conspiracies.

Papen further noted in his memoirs, "The atmosphere in the United States at this time made it impossible to risk exacerbating public opinion by any acts of sabotage." His caution and assessment were well founded. Two years later, the Zimmermann Telegram was decrypted by British intelligence, exposing Germany's proposed alliance with Mexico and offer of assistance in a war with the United States. When news of the telegram was leaked, it inflamed American opinion in favor of entering the war in Europe.

McGarrity, meanwhile, remained committed to Irish independence and was said to have provided a large portion of the funding as well as arms for the 1916 Easter Rising in Dublin. He died August 5, 1940, and was buried in the Holy Cross Cemetery, 626 Baily Road, Yeadon, Pennsylvania.

52. ARTISTS AT WAR

MAP 2 ➤ **Pennsylvania Academy of the Fine Arts:** 118–128 North Broad Street

Not all of Germany's World War I intelligence operations in the United States involved explosives and sabotage. In the years prior to 1917, Imperial Germany invested significant amounts of money to influence America's perception of the European war. Concern about the success of German messaging is evident in that one week after the United States formally declared itself at war, President Woodrow Wilson issued Executive Order 2594 on April 13, 1917, creating the Committee on Public Information (CPI) to reshape public attitudes toward Germany.

Unapologetically a propaganda organization, the CPI was headed by a civilian, George Creel, who was also a joke writer, journalist, former Denver police

During World War I, artists from Philadelphia worked with the US Committee on Public Information to build public support for the war effort. The artist H. Devitt Welsh was a former student at the Pennsylvania Academy of the Fine Arts.

commissioner, and political operative. Creel created 14 CPI divisions, whose work ranged from motion pictures to retail window displays. The most well-known group was the Division of Pictorial Publicity. This unit sought to harness the power of art and advertising for the war effort by enlisting the assistance of America's most creative artists.

"Even in the rush of the first days, when we were calling writers and speakers and photographers into service, I had the conviction that the poster must play a great part in the fight for public opinion," Creel wrote in his wartime memoir, *How We Advertised America*. "The printed word might not be read, people might not choose to attend meetings or to watch motion pictures, but the billboard was something that caught even the most indifferent eye."

H. Devitt Welsh and Joseph Pennell, two of CPI's artists and both native Philadelphians, would play major roles in CPI's Division of Pictorial Publicity. Welsh, a member of the Philadelphia Sketch Club and former student of the Pennsylvania Academy of the Fine Arts, 118–128 North Broad Street, acted as the liaison between US government officials and the artists seeking to stretch the boundaries of creativity.

Pennell, who was born at 603 South Ninth Street on July 4, 1857, but grew up on 819 Lombard Street, came to CPI with a well-established reputation in fine arts. Pennell's artwork expanded beyond what is commonly thought of as propaganda by depicting some of the most closely guarded sites around Philadelphia, including shipyards and munitions factories. The lithographs he created formed the basis of his classic book, *Joseph Pennell's Pictures of War*

Work in America. Pennell, a religious Quaker who disdained the war, stood in awe of the modern factories he visited. He wrote, "It is the working of the great machinery in the great mills which I find so inspiring. . . . If only the engines turned out were engines of peace—how much better would the world be."

WHERE IS *THE SPIRIT OF '76*?

During the years George Creel and the Committee on Public Information were producing documentary films such as *Pershing's Crusaders* (1918) and *Under Four Flags* (1918), Robert Goldstein, a costume supplier from California, produced a very different kind of movie. Called *The Spirit of '76*, the 1917 film was a big budget (approximately $200,000) extravaganza and unabashedly anti-British. Set in Philadelphia, Valley Forge, and other locales of the American Revolution, the film featured scenes of British soldiers bayonetting a baby and sexually assaulting women. King George III also was shown sucker punching an elderly Benjamin Franklin.

Chicago's Film Review Board, headed by Metellus Lucullus Cicero Funkhouser (also known as Maj. M. L. C. Funkhouser), ordered Goldstein to remove the more inflammatory content from the film prior to its Chicago premier in May 1917, a little more than a month after America entered World War I. However, by its November opening in Los Angeles, the offending content was back in the film, and Goldstein was prosecuted under the Espionage Act of 1917. Amid rumors of connections to German intelligence, he received a 10-year sentence and a fine of $5,000. In March 1919 President Wilson waived the fine and commuted Goldstein's sentence to three years.

The film had a brief revival in the summer of 1921 with a showing at New York City's Town Hall. The effort was funded by the All-American Film Company, which appeared to be a hastily established front company associated with All-American Brokers, Inc., an insurance company that also published the *Sein Feiner* weekly magazine.

"It [All-American Film] is a $50,000 corporation, with Goldstein owning half the stock and I the other half, but Goldstein is not an officer of the company," James S. Keily, an officer of the insurance concern, told the *New York Times* on July 14, 1921. "He is known as the producing director. I am the whole bag of works here, and I will do the talking."

The film's second debut did not overwhelm reviewers. "As for the picture itself—it is safe saying that it lacks everything a picture ought to have besides good taste," wrote Harriette Underhill, the *New York Tribune* reviewer.

Goldstein, the would-be filmmaker, left for Europe upon his release and failed in his attempts to make more movies. By the mid-1930s he was in Germany, though by 1938 he was said to have returned to the United States. Today, no copies of the film are known to exist. The only traces marking the existence of the once-controversial saga are court records, newspaper accounts, and a poster.

53. HERE TODAY, GONE TOMORROW

MAP 7 ➤ **Vernon Park:** 5818 Germantown Avenue

A statue commemorating the 1683 founding of Germantown by Francis Daniel Pastorius, an early abolitionist, poet, and naturalist, has an uneasy history. With anti-German sentiment rampant as America entered World War I in 1917, the approximately 30-foot-tall monument created by German sculptor Albert Jaegers was crated and put into storage before its formal dedication.

A monument to early German immigrant Francis Daniel Pastorius is located in a small park on Germantown Avenue. German intelligence appropriated the name "Pastorius" during World War II as a code name for an infiltration and sabotage operation.

Officially erected in Vernon Park in 1920, the marble monument was again crated and hidden in a secret location at the beginning of World War II when anti-German tensions reemerged. Pastorius's name was appropriated by the German intelligence service, the Abwehr, as the code name for a World War II sabotage mission that included targets around Philadelphia. The statue was moved back to its Vernon Park, 5818 Germantown Avenue, location following the war.

54. A TREASURE TROVE OF CRYPTOGRAPHIC HISTORY

MAP 6 ➤ **University of Pennsylvania, Van Pelt Library:** 3420 Walnut Street

One of the largest collections of rare and antiquarian books on cryptography resides in the University of Pennsylvania Library. The books, pamphlets, and other writings were a donation from Charles J. Mendelsohn, a cryptographer of note whose work is not well known. The son of a rabbi from Wilmington, North Carolina, Mendelsohn attended the Episcopal Academy of Philadelphia, then located at Locust and Juniper Streets, before enrolling in the University of Pennsylvania and earning a PhD in classics in 1904.

Memorial marker of cryptologist Charles J. Mendelsohn, a World War I military code breaker who was called back to government service at the beginning of World War II. His untimely death in 1939 deprived the US government of his exceptional talent.

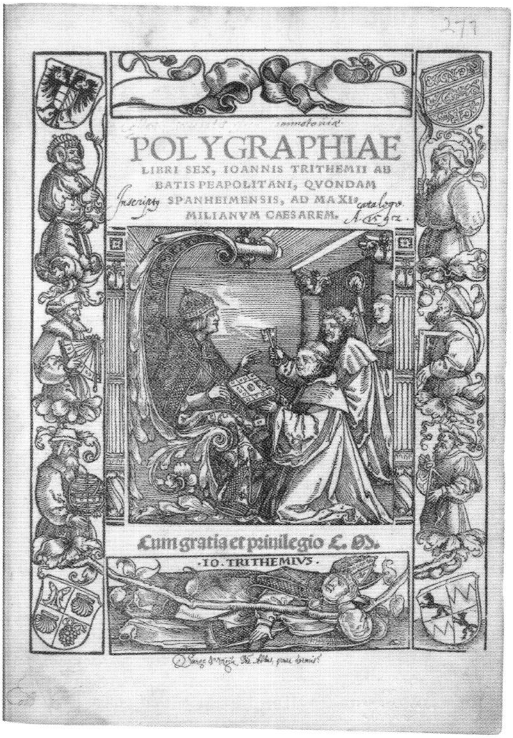

Johannes Trithemius's *Polygraphiae* (1518), an investigation of writing systems, may be the first printed book of cryptology. The woodcut on its title page shows Trithemius presenting his book to its dedicatee, Emperor Maximilian I, while a monk offers a set of keys, suggesting that this book contains secret knowledge.

While teaching at the College of the City of New York, he joined the Censorship Division of the US Post Office during World War I. From there he was recruited into Military Intelligence, Section 8 (also known as MI-8), the US Army's code-breaking division. Whether it was his training in the classics or his innate talent, Mendelsohn proved himself an exceptional cryptographer, breaking numerous diplomatic German codes.

At war's end, with the need for a peacetime code-breaking capability apparent, Herbert Yardley founded the Cipher Bureau. Unofficially known as the Black Chamber, the nickname is more historical than sinister, being derived from the 16th-century French term *cabinet noir*—a secret facility where European royalty garnered intelligence from intercepted letters.

Working part-time at the Cipher Bureau's commercially covered office in New York City, Mendelsohn collaborated on a number of business codebooks with Yardley. The books sustained the facility's commercial cover and sold well to businesses that wanted to keep their telegraphic correspondence secret as well as reduce their costs by using acronyms for long, often-used business phrases. Despite its value as an intelligence source, President Herbert Hoover's secretary of state Henry Stimson shuttered the operation in 1929, reportedly justifying the closure with the oft-quoted line, "Gentlemen do not read each other's mail."

Through the 1930s, Mendelsohn continued his love of cryptography, published papers on classic codes, and collected rare texts on the subject. He was called back to government service as World War II loomed but died on September 27, 1939, just a few days prior to reporting for active duty.

55. MILITARY INTELLIGENCE ON MARKET STREET

MAP 2 ➤ **Arcade Building:** 1428–1434 Market Street (demolished)

Three months after the US Army established the Military Intelligence Section (later known as the Military Intelligence Branch, then as the Military Intelligence Division) in May 1917, a branch of the operation opened in Philadelphia under John W. Geary Jr. Geary's father, John White Geary, once served as the postmaster and mayor of San Francisco, as the governor of the Kansas Territory, and then two terms as the governor of Pennsylvania. The younger Geary was born in the governor's mansion in Harrisburg.

Commissioned as an army captain, Geary occupied Room 2032 of the now-demolished Commercial Trust Building (also known as the Arcade Building), 14th and Market Streets. The organization soon expanded to occupy the entire 20th floor with more than 100 personnel. Working with the Pennsylvania State Constabulary as well as the Office of Naval Intelligence, the Philadelphia jurisdiction reached west to Pittsburgh and included all of Delaware and New Jersey.

The Philadelphia branch of the US Army's Military Intelligence Section had offices in the Arcade Building on Market Street during World War I.

Philadelphia branch members of the US Army's Military Intelligence Division.

Geary's organization investigated serious threats. The Black Tom Island, New Jersey, explosion in 1916 demonstrated just how far saboteurs would go to halt the flow of armaments to Europe. With Philadelphia and the surrounding region a wartime manufacturing center, an effective counterintelligence force was essential. The Philadelphia branch was closed on February 28, 1919, following the war, and Geary joined the brokerage firm of W. H. Newbold's Son and Company, 511 Chestnut Street.

56. ADVANCING AERIAL PHOTOGRAPHY

MAP 4 ➤ **Arthur Brock Jr. Headquarters:** 533 North Eleventh Street (site redeveloped)

Above-the-battlefield photography was not entirely new at the start of World War I. Images taken from balloons and dirigibles were already seen as valued sources for military cartographers and intelligence organizations. However, the introduction of airplanes and the recognition of the valuable intelligence that could be acquired advanced aerial photographic technology. In the United States, Eastman Kodak of Rochester, New York, and two Philadelphia companies, G. E. M. Engineering and Arthur Brock Jr., all made significant contributions to Allied aerial capabilities.

The American companies improved and deployed cameras originally developed by European nations, including the de Ram unit created by Lt. G. de Ram of the French Air Service. The camera, powered by a small propeller mounted in the slipstream outside the aircraft, could capture an image on a 7-inch by 9.5-inch photographic plate and move it into storage before loading another plate. With its capacity of 50 plates, the bulky automated unit weighed upward of 100 pounds.

American companies, such as Brock—headquartered in the now-demolished Bullitt Building, 131 South Fourth Street, with a manufacturing plant at 533 North Eleventh Street—improved on existing photographic technology by minimizing

Brock Manufacturing was one of a handful of US companies with the expertise to produce cameras suitable for early aerial photography.

The French-designed de Ram camera (lens pointed downward as it would be mounted on the side of an aircraft) used for World War I aerial surveillance was manufactured in Philadelphia.

the effects of vibration, increasing the reliability of the shutter mechanism, and mitigating space constraints of already crowded cockpits of the era's biplanes. By the end of the war, cameras using lightweight flexible film stock were capable of holding 100 exposures. When the armistice arrived, more than 1,100 US planes were outfitted with photographic equipment.

57. ESPIONAGE BY DESIGN

MAP 12 ➤ **Anna Wagner Keichline birthplace:** Bellefonte, Pennsylvania

Anna Wagner Keichline, born in 1899 in Bellefonte, Pennsylvania, showed a talent for design from an early age. At 14 she won first prize in a contest at the Centre County Fair for a card table and walnut chest she designed and built; then she stated her intention of making design her profession. True to her word, Keichline attended Cornell University for architecture, and when the school balked at granting her a diploma because she was a woman, fellow students staged a protest. As a result she received her degree in architecture and a short time later became Pennsylvania's first certified woman architect in 1920. A strong supporter of the women's suffrage movement, Keichline also led a march in Bellefonte on July 4, 1913.

In 1918, the last year of World War I, Keichline volunteered to become a spy. Writing to Capt. Harry A. Taylor of the US Army's Military Intelligence Division, she offered her service, though she eschewed a clerical role. The list of qualifications she presented included fluency in German and owning a car that

Anna Wagner Keichline

she was also able to repair herself, a rarity for a woman at the time. Taylor accepted her offer and assigned her to infiltrate German groups in munition factories and attend socialist meetings throughout the Washington, DC, area. No record of her intelligence work remains.

Keichline resigned at the end of the war, returned to Bellefonte, and built a thriving architectural practice, whose projects included churches, private homes, and commercial buildings throughout the area. During her lifetime of design, she was granted six patents, including one for the K-brick, a clay block for hollow wall construction.

58. A SPY AT THE FRANKLIN INSTITUTE

MAP 2 ➤ **Franklin Institute:** 222 North 20th Street

The prestigious Franklin Institute, 222 North 20th Street, was once headed by a decorated spy. A World War I British intelligence officer, graduate of Sandhurst, and recipient of the Order of the British Empire, Maj. Thomas Coulson served in the Tripoli Campaign and the First Balkan War before joining Britain's secret service. He immigrated to the United States in 1929 and was first employed by the Victor Talking Machine Company, of Camden, New Jersey, the predecessor company of RCA Victor. He then joined the Franklin Institute's staff in 1934, eventually rising to become acting director from 1958 to 1960.

Thomas Coulson, 1950

The Franklin Institute

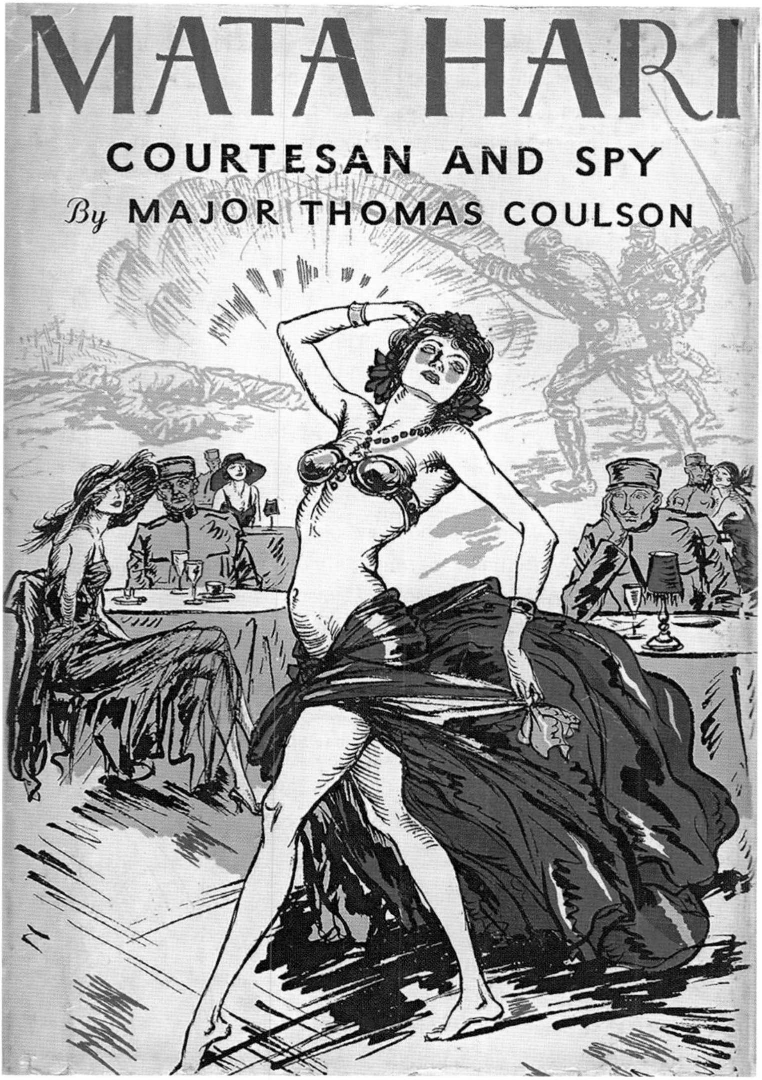

Thomas Coulson's *Mata Hari* fueled the legend of the dancer as a femme fatale of early 20th-century espionage.

During his time at the Franklin Institute, Coulson was a popular lecturer on espionage and criminology, sometimes surprising audiences at the start of a presentation by having an accomplice fire blanks at him and flee the room. "Now, I'm dead," he would announce. "Describe the assailant!" The roomful of witnesses would then inevitably provide less than reliable eywitness testimony by offering contradictory descriptions of the assailant.

Coulson reveled in telling stories of espionage, revealing that at one point during World War I he managed to insert bogus German newspapers containing pro-British stories into the wrapping of armaments in Zurich. The propaganda effort worked until the local German consul became aware of the operation and sabotaged the printing operation with inferior ink that turned "sickly gray."

Coulson may be best known, however, for claiming he helped capture World War I spy Mata Hari. According to his 1930 book, *Mata Hari: Courtesan and Spy*, Coulson was moved to pursue the ill-fated spy after a fellow soldier named Hogg died in his arms with the last words, "If only we could find that damned dancer."

Pursue her he did, at least according to his book. "Like her favorite reptile, the serpent," Coulson wrote, "the slime of her writhing body, coiled from one city to another, leaving its track of debauchery and treacherous betrayal." Although scholars have questioned elements of Coulson's tale, and no meeting occurred between the doomed femme fatale and Sidney "The Ace of Spies" Reilly, the book was a best seller and the basis of the 1931 film *Mata Hari* starring Greta Garbo. "Her kiss sent thousands to their death," the movie's trailer proclaimed, keeping with the overwrought style of Coulson's book.

For much of his time in Philadelphia, Coulson lived at 50 LaCross (sometimes LaCrosse) Avenue, Lansdowne, Pennsylvania. He died in 1971.

59. THE DAY JOHN REED SHOOK PHILADELPHIA

MAP 4 ➤ **Moose Hall of the Loyal Order of Moose Lodge 54:** 1314 North Broad Street

John Reed, one of America's first journalists to embrace Vladimir Lenin's version of communism, was viewed as extreme, even among leftists. While traveling in Russia in November 1917, he was indicted under America's new Espionage Act for an anti-war article he had written for the *New Masses*. Six months after the war ended, Reed returned to the United States, and upon arrival in New York, he was detained, his possessions searched, and his body examined for secret writing. Then he was released.

A riot erupted at the Moose Lodge on North Broad Street when the audience attending a John Reed lecture attacked police officers.

Once seriously considered for a Soviet consul general position in New York, Reed's undeclared mission in the United States was that of a Bolshevik propagandist. His wife, Louise Bryant, was supportive and published a series of

John Reed

nationally syndicated, high-profile pieces on the Russian Revolution that appeared in Philadelphia's *Public Ledger* in 1918.

On May 31, 1918, Reed was scheduled to address a meeting sponsored by the Socialist Party, 1326 Arch Street, at the Moose Hall of the Loyal Order of Moose Lodge 54, 1314 North Broad Street. A permit initially granted for the gathering was revoked, and when police moved in to disperse the crowd, a riot broke out. Some of the audience attacked the police, and Reed was arrested but later acquitted of the charges. Reed published *Ten Days That Shook the World* (1919), which offered his account of the Russian Revolution. Still a true believer in communism, he returned to Russia, where he died of typhus in Moscow in 1920 and is buried just outside the Kremlin's walls.

The widowed Bryant married diplomat William C. Bullitt Jr. in 1924. Bullitt shared his new wife's admiration for her first husband, and Reed makes a thinly veiled appearance as the character Raoul, a devoted communist, in Bullitt's 1926 novel, *It's Not Done*. The couple divorced in 1930, and President Franklin Roosevelt appointed Bullitt the first US ambassador to the Soviet Union (1933–1936).

60. PRIVATE SPIES IN AMERICA'S BIRTHPLACE

MAP 2 ➤ **End of the American Protective League:** Bellevue-Stratford Hotel, 200 South Broad Street

The American Protective League (APL) was the creation of advertising executive Albert M. Briggs, widely known as A. M. Briggs. With passage of the Selective Service Act in 1917, law enforcement agencies—including the Bureau of Investigation (BOI), the predecessor to the Federal Bureau of Investigation (FBI)—became overwhelmed by wartime security demands. That's when Briggs and the APL stepped in.

Attorney General Thomas Gregory permitted Briggs's APL, a private, national group of volunteers, to undertake some quasi-official counterintelligence and law enforcement functions. The group's letterhead and other official documents noted that it was "organized with the Approval and Operating under the Direction of the United States Department of Justice, Bureau of Investigation." Members were issued a badge and an identification card, and

The American Protective League held a closing banquet for its Philadelphia members at the Bellevue-Stratford Hotel as the organization disbanded in 1919.

they often worked closely with military units, local police, and federal law enforcement but received little training to hunt for wartime spies or draft dodgers. At its height, during 1918, APL had an estimated 250,000 members in 600 cities. By contrast, the BOI had only 219 agents in its offices around the country, none of whom had federal authority to carry weapons or make arrests.

The APL also sought to counteract the activities of radicals, anarchists, and anti-war activists, as well as left-wing labor and political organizations. APL members' lack of training in enforcement and investigations did not lessen their unbounded enthusiasm for the perceived task. They illegally opened mail, made surreptitious office searches, and reported "word of mouth propaganda."

The Philadelphia-based APL, headed by Mahlon R. Kline, who previously conducted investigations for the Philadelphia Rapid Transit Company, grew to include more than 3,400 members and encompassed some local police work, such as supplementing the vice squad. The league conducted security surveillance on munitions plants and launched a series of high-profile raids to identify "slackers," men of draft age who had not registered. In July 1918 APL members, along with a contingent of military personnel, descended on the red-light district of nearby Chester, raiding pool halls, gambling dens, saloons, and houses of ill repute. "Such places make the Mexican border look like a Sunday School picnic," one APL member told the *Philadelphia Inquirer*. In all, some 150 men without draft cards were taken into custody along with an assortment of bootleggers and other criminals.

A few weeks later, APL representatives raided the now-defunct Woodside Park Amusement Park, inside Fairmount Park, stopping and questioning an estimated 2,000 men, 300 of whom were detained. Another raid, this one on Shibe Park, today known as Connie Mack Stadium, garnered more men accused of slacking.

The most ambitious raid of the Philadelphia APL occurred on August 15, 1918, when a caravan of 85 cars filled with APL members and federal agents drove to Atlantic City. Joining forces with local police, the contingent raided the boardwalk's amusement piers, including Steeplechase, Steel, and Young's Ocean and Million Dollar Piers. The men sealed off the piers and escorted suspected slackers to the entrances, where they were questioned. Some 700 men were taken into custody and held at the Morris Guards Armory, 10–12 South New York Avenue (today redeveloped). Though only 60 were deemed genuine slackers, press reports at the time based on APL claims placed the number stopped and questioned at an estimated 60,000 men.

The Philadelphia raids made news throughout 1918. In November, 40 Philadelphia police officers and 125 APL members raided Philadelphia's Olympia Athletic Club, 720 South Broad Street, during a boxing match between Jack Dempsey and King (Kingfish) Levinsky. The crowd of more than 8,000 fight fans included 36 draft evaders.

Despite glowing local press reports of the APL's successes, opinion began to turn against the organization as World War I ended. Excesses that accompanied some of the larger raids, such as those in New York City, drew the public's ire. Some saw the organization as thinly veiled vigilantism. By early 1919, not quite two years after its formation, APL's Philadelphia branch was disbanded. Local papers reported the branch had conducted more than 18,000 investigations.

"The time has passed, however, for one man to spy on his neighbor and the league's work is therefore finished," the *Philadelphia Inquirer* noted. "Such organizations would be perfectly at home in the Bolshevik regime in Russia, say the directors, but for the United States—never."

A final banquet was held on February 5, 1919, at the Bellevue-Stratford Hotel for the Philadelphia members of the APL, who were told they could keep their badges and identification cards as mementos of their service.

61. 1919 BOMBING PLOT

MAP 6 ➤ **Bombing target:** Our Lady of Victory Catholic Church (now St. Joseph Baptist Church), 5412 Vine Street

In June 1919 coordinated bombing attacks terrorized citizens in American cities from Boston to Cleveland to Washington, DC. Among the Philadelphia targets was Our Lady of Victory, a Catholic church (today the St. Joseph Baptist

William J. Flynn

Luigi Galleani

A Philadelphia church was a target of anarchists in a 1919 nationwide bombing spree.

Among the targets of the 1919 anarchist bombings was the home of the jeweler Louis Jajieky on South 57th Street.

Church) at 5412 Vine Street, where two bombs were placed under the porch leading to the rectory. Less than a mile away, another powerful bomb exploded outside the home of the jeweler Louis Jajieky, 244 South 57th Street. Another bomb placed near the Washington, DC, home of US attorney general A. Mitchell Palmer exploded prematurely, killing the unlucky bomber.

The BOI, predecessor to the FBI, recovered little of the bomber himself but discovered clues pointing to a Philadelphia connection. The presumed bomber's hat had the label of a Philadelphia store DeLucca Brothers of 919 South Eighth Street. A ticket stub showed that he boarded a Washington-bound train in Philadelphia at the Baltimore and Ohio Railroad station at 24th and Chestnut Streets (demolished in the early 1960s). In Philadelphia a stolen car resembling one seen driving away from the church after the bombings was found abandoned in the city's Fairmount Park section.

Philadelphia then became the focus of the investigation. Known radicals and union leaders were placed under surveillance. William J. Flynn, the BOI's acting director, moved to the city to oversee the investigation. The careless bomber was identified as Carlo Valdinoci, an Italian immigrant in his mid-20s with anarchist ties and a history of publishing leftist literature.

Suspicion eventually fell on the followers, called Galleanists, of anarchist Luigi Galleani, who advocated a warped philosophy of "propaganda by deed" to bring about social change. Attorney General Palmer ordered a nationwide series of roundups of radicals that became known as the Palmer Raids, but the culprits responsible for the bombings were never identified or apprehended.

62. THE FIRST RED SCARE

MAP I ➤ **Nest of Radicals:** Technical School to Aid Soviet Russia, 259 North Sixth Street (demolished, area redeveloped)

Following the coordinated nationwide bombings by anarchist groups in June 1919, Attorney General A. Mitchell Palmer created the General Intelligence Division in the Bureau of Investigation (the FBI's predecessor organization). The division, headed by J. Edgar Hoover, was assigned responsibility for collecting intelligence on subversive groups and arresting individuals deemed particularly dangerous.

A. Mitchell Palmer, once a rising star in American politics, lost public support for what was considered his overzealous response to the anarchist bombings of 1919.

Palmer was particularly sensitive to the threat since he had been the target of a bomb that destroyed the front of his Washington, DC, home a few months earlier. He was also aware of the civil liberties issues raised by the actions of semi-official citizen organizations that conducted so-called Slacker Raids, which were directed against young men who failed to register for the draft during World War I.

Palmer, who turned down the position of secretary of war because of his Quaker faith, was born in Moosehead, Pennsylvania; graduated from Swarthmore College; and began his legal career with a practice in Stroudsburg, Pennsylvania. He served in the US House of Representatives from 1909 to 1915. Despite a failed bid for the US Senate, he was still viewed as a rising political star in the Democratic Party as the attorney general under President Wilson.

Now, with the new division in place, Palmer sought to bring the task of controlling dangerous radicals to a more professional level. However, the subsequent nationwide raids on suspected organizations by federal officials caused more controversy. In early November 1919, officials rounded up dozens of suspected radicals in Philadelphia, and another series of raids followed in January 1920 with more people detained. Among the offices raided was the Technical School to Aid Soviet Russia, 259 North Sixth Street.

Both Philadelphia raids netted dozens of suspected radicals and significant caches of radical literature, but they yielded no clues as to the culprits behind the 1919 bombings. When seemingly credible threats of a May Day attack in 1920 did not materialize, public opinion shifted against Palmer and the program, putting an end to the raids and Palmer's political career. Critics alleged the raids were poorly planned, that arrests were made without warrants, and that individuals were held without access to legal counsel or their families.

Palmer made a failed bid for the presidential nomination at the 1920 Democratic National Convention. Afterward he returned to private law practice, first in Washington, DC, and then in Stroudsburg.

63. PROTOCOLS OF THE LEARNED ELDERS OF ZION

MAP I ➤ ***Public Ledger***: Chestnut and South Sixth Streets, southwest corner (building demolished)

The anti-Semitic tract known as the *Protocols of the Learned Elders of Zion* has a strange history in the United States. Created in the early years of the 20th century in Russia, the fraudulent document purports to be an account of Jewish leaders plotting world domination. Fueled by then existing anti-Semitism, the tract remains one of the most persistent and effective pieces of propaganda ever created.

Likely originated by the czarist secret police, the Okhrana, the tract was said to have arrived in the United States with a White Russian in 1918 and given to Dr. Harris Ayres Houghton, a military intelligence officer stationed on Governors Island, New York. Using his own funds, Houghton paid for an English translation of the Russian text and began circulating copies. Brig. Gen. Marlborough Churchill, then head of military intelligence, assigned Capt. John B. Trevor to analyze the text; he concluded the *Protocols* was a sham. "The material contained in the subject gives me the impression it might have been prepared by an Agent Provocateur of the former regime in Russia," he wrote in his report.

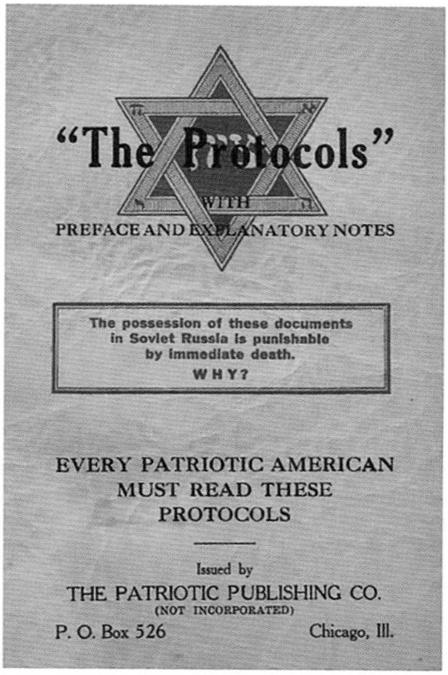

Despite being a decades-old hoax, the anti-Semitic tract *The Protocols of the Learned Elders of Zion* received major attention in the United States when the *Public Ledger* printed a translation of it in 1919.

Despite repeated debunking, the *Protocols* took on a life of its own. The first widespread publicity the tract received in America was in Philadelphia's *Public Ledger*, one of the largest daily newspapers in the city, then located at Chestnut and South Sixth Streets. On October 27 and 28, 1919, the paper published a two-part series about the book headlined "The Red Bible." Written and edited by Carl W. Ackerman, later head of the Journalism Department at Columbia University, the series recast the "Jewish conspiracy" as a Bolshevist manifesto. "A prominent American diplomat today placed at my disposal a Russian document which bears every evidence of being the guide book of the world revolutionists," Ackerman wrote. "It is a booklet of 24 protocols, written by one of the leaders of the Bolshevist movement for the guidance of the secret council of the society, and was brought to the United States recently by an American intelligence officer who has been in Moscow and Petrograd."

Ackerman's story caused a sensation during America's first Red Scare and the violent bombings of anarchists. His story, which was picked up by newspapers across the country, was eventually forgotten as the anarchists' cause faded. Other editions of the *Protocols*, however, reinstated its anti-Semitic elements.

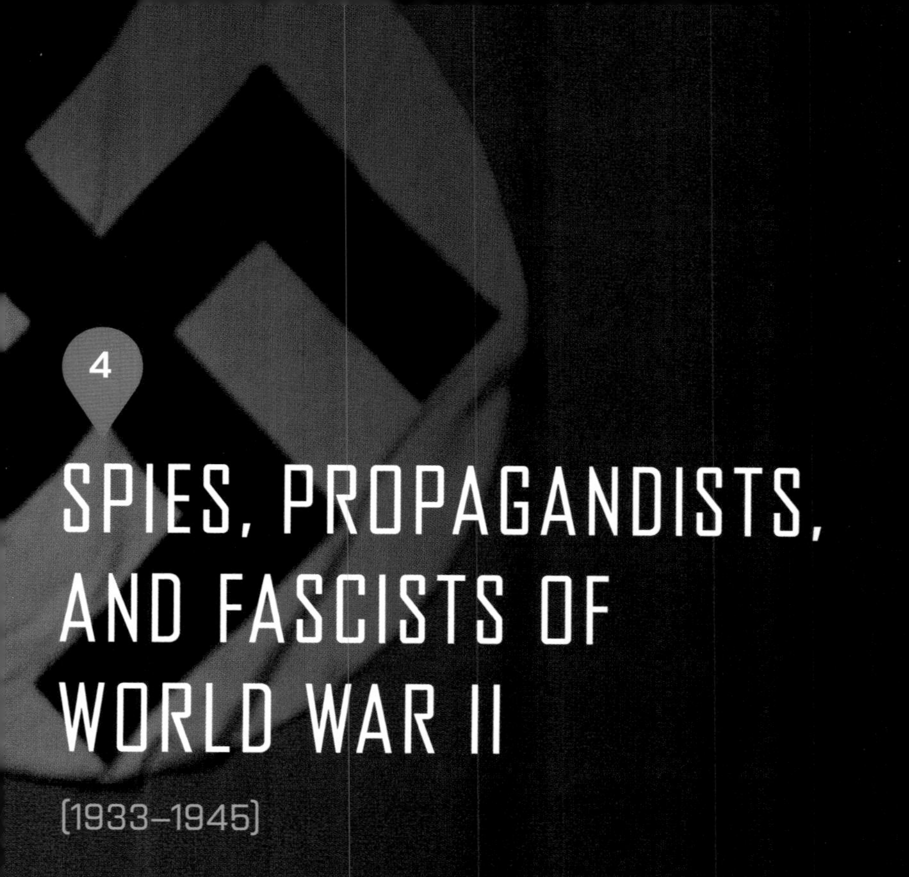

4

SPIES, PROPAGANDISTS, AND FASCISTS OF WORLD WAR II

(1933–1945)

Philadelphia once again became a clandestine battlefield, primarily contested by Britain, Germany, and the Soviet Union, during the years immediately preceding World War II. As a critical manufacturing center, the city attracted both spies and saboteurs. The city's newspapers drew the attention of German propagandists who praised Adolf Hitler as a strong and effective leader and who worked to influence public opinion in favor of an isolationist foreign policy. With the United States officially neutral in the European conflict and the horrors of the Nazi regime largely hidden from public awareness, the level of the country's future involvement was uncertain and undecided.

Philadelphia's large German American population, combined with that of the surrounding region, made the area a seemingly vulnerable target. Playing on ancestral loyalties and traditions, German agents sought to recruit sympathizers to the cause of Nazi Germany. Raucous rallies attracted large crowds, and propaganda efforts found a sympathetic audience. Once the United States entered the war, the noisy pro-fascist voices were largely silenced,

but German intelligence continued to operate a network of couriers and clandestine agents collecting intelligence and threatening sabotage.

In response, the US government strengthened the FBI, created the Office of Strategic Services, and worked with the British Security Coordination (BSC) to conduct operations and recruit officers from nearby institutions, such as the University of Pennsylvania. The FBI, which had grown in size, experience, and authorities since World War I, had the lead role in combating Axis and Soviet espionage along the mid-Atlantic coast.

64. PASTOR OR SPY?

MAP I ➤ **Nazi mail drop site:** Old Zion Church, South Fourth and Cherry Streets (razed in 1972)

In 1929 Rev. Kurt E. B. Molzahn, a World War I veteran of the German army, became pastor of the German-speaking congregation at Philadelphia's Old Zion Church, South Fourth and Cherry Streets. The pastor of the oldest German Lutheran congregation in the United States joined the German Society of Pennsylvania and encouraged his congregation to support the emerging Nazi Party in Germany. Later Molzahn nurtured personal contact with officials in Berlin through the German consul in Philadelphia and allowed the parsonage to become a non-alerting mail drop for messages to Berlin. German intelligence gave the pastor an agent cover number of 2320. In late 1940, Molzahn extended his international activities when he became involved with Count Anastase Andreyevich Vonsiatsky, a naturalized US citizen and leader of the Russian National Revolutionary Labor and Workers Peasant Party of Fascists, which he founded in 1933.

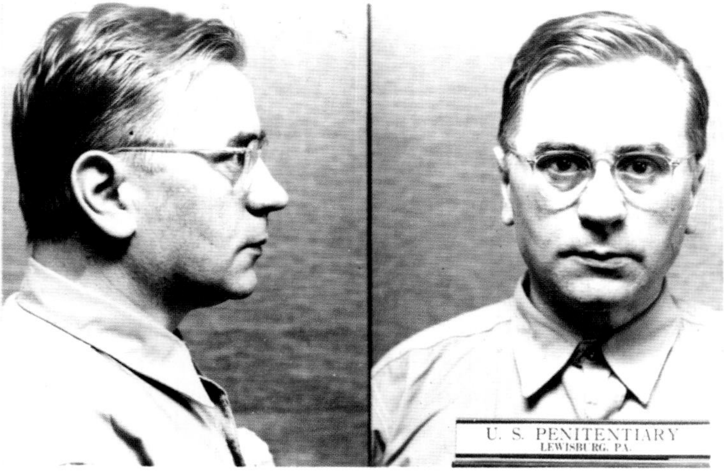

Rev. Kurt E. B. Molzahn

The two agreed on a plan to sabotage US military fortifications and allegedly delivered sensitive information about military fortifications to the German Embassy. The pair's operations came to a halt when Vonsiatsky confided plans to a supposedly reliable fascist priest, Alexei Pelypenko, who was actually an FBI informant. This led to a federal grand jury indictment of Molzahn and others on June 10, 1942. Although three of his codefendants pleaded guilty "to conspiracy to transmit to Germany and Japan information relating to the national defense," Molzahn did not. He was tried, found guilty, and sentenced to a 10-year prison term.

The Old Zion Lutheran Church in the heart of Philadelphia was pastored by Rev. Kurt E. B. Molzahn, a World War I veteran of the German army who was arrested for being a German intelligence agent in 1942.

Molzahn was released in June 1945, having been pardoned by President Harry Truman for unspecified reasons and subsequently unconditionally pardoned by President Dwight Eisenhower in 1956. After prison, he returned to the pastorate; published an autobiography, *Prisoner of War*, in 1962; and died in Philadelphia in 1979.

65. FASHION FORWARD FASCIST

MAP 8 ➤ **Khaki Shirts of America headquarters:** 4430 North Broad Street

Formed in 1932 and headquartered in Philadelphia, the Khaki Shirts of America was the creation of Arthur J. Smith. Claiming his inspiration came from Hitler's "brown shirts," Smith managed to gain some followers in the depths of the Great Depression. Unlike the German American Bund, which was financed and directed by Nazi Germany, the Khaki Shirts of America was a homegrown fascist organization with a convoluted ideology. Based on a philosophy of populist fascism, Smith's political platform included establishing an old age government pension, reducing the workweek's hours, and repealing Prohibition along with advocating for the violent overthrow of the government, spreading virulent anti-Semitism, and installing a dictator in place of an elected president.

Smith, who claimed to have fought in various conflicts as a soldier of fortune and who worked as a policeman in St. Louis, was seen by much of the public as either a crackpot or a huckster. The purchase of a shirt and cap uniform—at the cost of $1.25 and $0.75, respectively—was required to join the organization. The press called it a "shirt-selling racket."

At various times Smith boasted that he commanded between 5 million and 10 million followers. "We have a tank corps, artillery, machinery gun units, cavalry, and regiments of shock troopers," Smith told the *Shamokin (PA) Daily News*, "and outnumber the regular army by four to one. I guess we might even out-maneuver them, if it came to a showdown."

When the day arrived for a march on Washington in 1934, a few hundred followers and curious onlookers gathered at the group's headquarters at 4430 North Broad Street. Smith, who had not provided transportation to the nation's capital, ducked out the back door, taking the group's funds with him. Eventually apprehended, he was brought to trial in New York for perjury in an earlier case, convicted, and sentenced to prison.

66. HITLER'S SHADOW OVER PHILADELPHIA

MAP 8 ➤ **Gerhard Kunze residence:** 6501 North Smedley Street

Flag of the German American Bund

Nazi agent Gerhard Wilhelm Kunze once lived at this North Smedley Street address.

The German American Bund, or German American Federation, was a US-based organization established in the 1930s to promote a favorable view of Nazi Germany. The Bund held rallies with Nazi regalia, used the Hitler salute, and attacked the administration of President Roosevelt, Jewish groups, communists, trade unions, and American boycotts of German goods. The organization also asserted its loyalty to the United States by displaying the American flag at Bund meetings and declared George Washington "the first Fascist" who did not believe democracy would work.

In 1936 the Bund elected German-born American citizen Fritz Julius Kuhn, a veteran of the Bavarian

The reputed headquarters of the German Bund was in Philadelphia's West Erie residential neighborhood.

infantry during World War I, as its leader. Kuhn would later be replaced by Gerhard Wilhelm Kunze, a Philadelphia native living at 6501 North Smedley Street. Kunze also served as an agent of German intelligence, traveled to Germany several times, and maintained contact with Berlin through diplomats at the German Embassy. As the United States prepared to enter the war in late 1941, Kunze obtained funds from Anastase A. Vonsiatsky, leader of the Russian National Revolutionary Labor and Workers Peasant Party of Fascists, for an escape to Germany via Mexico. Kunze crossed into Mexico on November 4, 1941, and got as far as Chihuahua before being arrested by Mexican authorities and deported to the United States.

Members of the German Bund were issued a special medallion on September 2–4, 1939.

Following the Japanese bombing of Pearl Harbor and the US declaration of war on Germany, the Bund withered away. A federal grand jury at Hartford, Connecticut, indicted German sympathizers Vonsiatsky, Kunze, and Rev. Kurt E. B. Molzahn on June 10, 1942, for conspiracy to violate the Espionage Act. Molzahn professed his innocence but was found guilty at trial. Vonsiatsky was declared mentally ill, while Kunze pleaded guilty and received a 15-year sentence for subversive activities.

67. "HITLER WILL LICK THE WHOLE OF EUROPE"

MAP 11 ➤ **Deutschhorst Country Club:** Sellersville, Pennsylvania (site redeveloped)

During the 1930s, the German American Bund built a network of country retreats across the United States, including Camp Siegfried in Yaphank on Long Island, New York; Camp Nordland in Sussex County, New Jersey; Camp Hindenburg in Grafton, Wisconsin; Camp Sutter outside of Los Angeles; and Camp Bergwald in Bloomingdale, New Jersey. One of the larger camps—located on a 130 acre–property in West Rockhill Township just outside the city limits of Sellersville, Pennsylvania—was called the Deutschhorst Country Club. To obscure the intended use of the site, the land was purchased in 1934 through a company called the Rockhill Realty Association Inc., and designated a "country club," which inspired images

Fritz Julius Kuhn

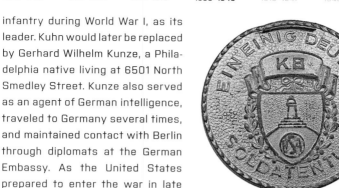

of golf and tennis.

In addition to paramilitary training for visitors, Bund leaders Fritz Julius Kuhn and Gerhard Wilhelm Kunze both led rallies at the property. On September 3, 1939, Kuhn attracted more than 2,000 followers, many in full Nazi uniforms. "Hitler will lick the whole of Europe," he proclaimed to an enthusiastic crowd.

Plans to build hundreds of cottages and create a "racially pure" community on the property never materialized, and almost from the start the camp drew the ire of local residents. There were acts of vandalism, and groups such as the American Legion and Veterans of Foreign Wars spoke out forcefully against the facility. The controversy concluded on March 31, 1943, with the dissolution of the corporation that owned the property. American Legion Post No. 255 in Sellersville purchased the old mill on the property, and the remaining acreage eventually was turned into tracts of ranch-style homes.

IT ENDED IN KRUMSVILLE

Fritz Julius Kuhn's career as America's foremost Nazi ended on the evening of May 25, 1939, in Krumsville, Pennsylvania. Under investigation for fraud by New York City authorities and surveilled by New York Police Department detectives, Kuhn was arrested at a gas station café on Route 22 in Krumsville within hours after a warrant was issued for his arrest. The 12-count indictment accused the Bund leader of stealing nearly $15,000 from the organization and carried a potential sentence of more than 50 years of jail time.

Kuhn was returned to New York, and the high-profile trial exposed his lavish lifestyle and included public readings of love letters written to a mistress. Found guilty, he was released after serving three and a half years but was rearrested as an enemy agent. He was interned in a Texas facility for the duration of the war; then he was deported to Germany, where he died in obscurity in 1951.

68. OPERATION PASTORIUS

MAP 11 ➤ **Sabotage target:** Philadelphia Salt Manufacturing Company's Cryolite Plant (now Waterside neighborhood development), 2375 State Road, Bensalem, Pennsylvania

By mid-1942 American factories were working at full capacity, building the warships, planes, and tanks needed to defeat the Axis powers in World War II. To disrupt US military supplies, Hitler and his generals planned to bring the war to American soil by sending their agents to sabotage US war production plants. Designated OPERATION PASTORIUS, the plan was named for the first German settlement in America near Philadelphia.

Just after midnight on June 13, 1942, a team of four Germans from the submarine *U-202* infiltrated Long Island near Amagansett, New York. The saboteurs were led by George John Dasch and included Ernest Peter Berger, Heinrich Farm Heinck, and Richard Quirin. They dragged explosives, primers, and incendiary devices onto the shore and carried more than $175,000 in cash to support a planned two years of sabotage and mayhem.

Among the targets of German World War II saboteurs was the Philadelphia Salt Manufacturing Company's Cryolite Plant. Cryolite is essential in the production of aluminum.

Four days after the New York team landed, the second phase of OPERATION PASTORIUS was initiated when *U-584* delivered a similarly equipped group to Ponte Vedra Beach near Jacksonville, Florida. All members of the New York and Florida teams were German nationals who had spent significant time in the United States.

Among the strategic targets assigned to the New York team was the cryolite factory operated by the Pennsylvania Salt Manufacturing Company in Andalusia at 2375 State Road, Bensalem, Pennsylvania. Cryolite, a critical mineral for the nation's war effort, was essential to the production of aluminum, which was used in almost every phase of war production, particularly for airplanes. The Pennsylvania Salt Manufacturing Company's plant was the only cryolite facility of its kind in the country.

Another Pennsylvania target assigned to the saboteurs was the famous horseshoe curve of the Pennsylvania Railroad at Altoona. The scenic mountainside spot was among the busiest east–west lines of the railroad, with dozens of fast freight trains roaring across the inclined rails every day. Because of the track configuration at that point, and the importance of the line, the curve was one of the most heavily patrolled sections of railroad in the United States.

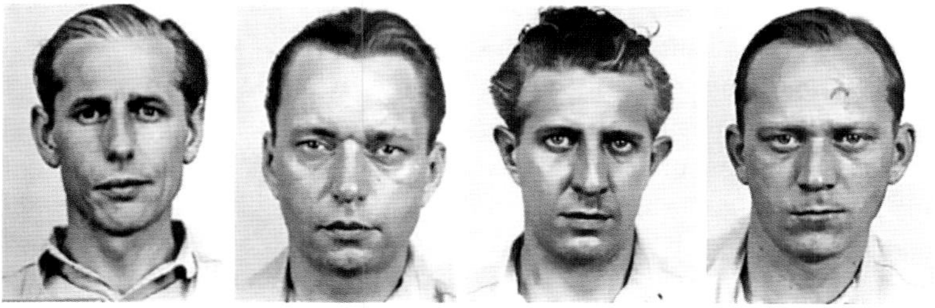

From left to right: George Dasch and Ernest Berger, two of four saboteurs of OPERATION Pastorius who infiltrated via a beach landing on Long Island, New York, cooperated with the US government and were sentenced to jail. The other two, Richard Quirin and Henrich Heinck, were executed.

After only one night in New York, however, Dasch lost his nerve, took a train to Washington, DC, and reported the plot to the FBI. Within two weeks, all the would-be saboteurs were in federal custody. All eight received the death sentence, and six were executed. Dasch and Berger's sentences were commuted to long jail terms because of their cooperation. After the war, both were eventually deported and freed in the American Zone in Berlin.

69. AMERICAN PASTOR—GERMAN SPY

MAP 8 ➤ **Carl Krepper residence:** 1906 East Allegheny Avenue

The four Nazi saboteurs landing on Long Island in 1942 as part of OPERATION PASTORIUS were counting on operational support from Carl Krepper, a naturalized German American and Lutheran pastor in Philadelphia. Krepper was well placed for the task. He arrived in New York City as a theology student in 1909, was ordained in 1910, and spent the next 25 years serving congregations in Philadelphia and New Jersey. During his first decade in Philadelphia, Krepper resided in the Friedens Lutheran Church parsonage, 3087 Emerald Street. In 1920 he was listed as residing at 1906 East Allegheny Avenue with his wife and son. Krepper and his family traveled to Germany between 1935 and 1941, and on one of those trips the pastor was recruited as a spy for the Abwehr (German military intelligence).

Carl Krepper

Lutheran pastor Carl Krepper, who cooperated with Nazi intelligence, once lived in the parsonage of Friedens Lutheran Church on Emerald Street.

Although Krepper was initially recruited for propaganda work to keep the United States out of the European conflict, his mission expanded with America's entry into the war. In December 1941 Krepper returned from Germany and secretly prepared a series of safe houses for the PASTORIUS saboteurs' use during their planned two-year mission. When the operation was compromised and the FBI made arrests in the PASTORIUS case, Krepper's name and address was found written in invisible ink on a handkerchief carried by one of the New York saboteurs. Once the secret message—"Pas Krepper, Route 2, Rahway, N.J."—was deciphered, the saboteurs were apprehended before they could take advantage of Krepper's operational support. Krepper was arrested, tried, and found guilty in 1945. He served six years of a 10-year sentence before dying in obscurity in Massachusetts in 1972.

70. THE NAZI SPY WHO LOVED AMERICA

MAP 11 ➤ **William Colepaugh residence:** 245 Holstein Road, King of Prussia, Pennsylvania

William Colepaugh spent more than a decade in prison following his conviction for spying for Germany. Once released, he moved to King of Prussia and became a model citizen.

A German U-boat quietly put two Abwehr spies ashore in Maine in November 1944. Erich Gimpel, a German national with a background in radio work, and William Colepaugh, a Connecticut-born dropout of MIT, worked their way undetected from the shoreline through Boston and on to New York City. Their mission was to collect intelligence and transmit it to Germany by ciphered radio messages.

In New York, the pair spent two weeks subletting an apartment, buying and modifying a shortwave radio, and living well on the German government's $60,000 cash and stash of diamonds. They bought new clothes and enjoyed the city's famous nightlife. The money was quickly spent, and just as quickly Colepaugh decided he wasn't cut out for espionage. After confessing the nature of the mission to a friend, he told the story to the FBI. His partner, Gimpel, was arrested.

William Colepaugh

The mission, code name MAGPIE, lasted barely a month. On Governors Island, New York, the two spies were tried before a military court, found guilty, and sentenced to death. Fortunately for the pair, the war ended two months after their convictions, and President Truman reduced the sentences to life. Gimpel served 10 years in Alcatraz, was paroled, returned to Germany, and in 1957 wrote a book, *A Spy for Germany*, that described his experiences.

Colepaugh served his sentence in Leavenworth Prison, was paroled in 1960, married, and moved to 245 Holstein Road, King of Prussia, Pennsylvania, where he used metalworking skills learned in prison to build a successful business career. He was an avid fisherman, volunteered to work with the Boy Scouts, and joined the Rotary Club. Few of his friends and neighbors could have guessed he had once been a German spy.

71. BREACHING PHILADELPHIA SECURITY

MAP 4 ➤ ***Philadelphia Record***: 317–319 North Broad Street

In February 1942, two months after the United States entered World War II, a pair of Philadelphia newspapermen decided to test security around the city. Frank Toughill and William B. Mellor Jr. of the *Philadelphia Record*—then located at 317–321 North Broad Street in the Packard Motor Car Corporation Building—dressed themselves in uniforms of U-boat commanders, complete with emblems and swastika armbands, and walked the city streets. Affecting theatrical German accents, the reporters asked directions of policemen and other citizens. "We prowled the waterfront, with its costly vital defense shipping," they reported, "and nobody thought we were a menace." The stunt made news across the country.

What the newspapermen did not know was that a similar, albeit subtler, infiltration of Philadelphia's defense facilities was part of the training program for OSS recruits. In one instance, a wily OSS recruit used paperwork identifying himself as an employee of the movie studio 20th Century Fox. While in the city, his cover was working as a producer of a film about the war effort. He checked into a luxury hotel and wined and dined the managing director of a local steel mill. Eventually gaining access to the mill, he collected from the trash sheets of carbon paper that had been used to make copies of sensitive procurement documents, thereby demonstrating how the facility's inattention to security could be exploited by a spy.

72. HITLER'S FEMME FATALE

MAP 13 ➤ **Immigration Detention Center:** 101 South King Street, Gloucester City, New Jersey

Born in Hungary in 1891, Stephany Julienne Richter became Princess Stephanie von Hohenlohe through marriage in 1914 to the Austrian prince Friedrich Franz von Hohenlohe-Waldenburg-Schillingsfürst. They divorced in 1920, but she retained the title of princess, left Germany, and relocated to London. There she began relationships with a number of prominent men, including Harold

German adventuress Stephanie von Hohenlohe was held in the Gloucester City Immigration Detention Center of New Jersey following her arrest.

Harmsworth, First Viscount Rothermere. Harmsworth, cofounder of England's *Daily Mail* and *Daily Mirror* newspapers, was an ardent Nazi supporter and promoter of the British Union of Fascists. One of Rothermere's notable editorials, which appeared in January 1934 in the *Daily Mail*, carried the headline "Hurrah for the Black Shirts!" Although from a Jewish background, the princess was designated an "honorary Aryan" by Heinrich Himmler.

When suspected of spying for Germany and ordered out of the United Kingdom in 1939, von Hohenlohe moved to San Francisco. There she renewed her affair with Fritz Wiedemann, a Hitler aide then serving as Germany's consul general. As a result, the princess fell under surveillance by the FBI. Agents compiled an extensive file, with one report concluding, "She is known to have very close connections with high officials of the Third Reich, is described as being extremely intelligent, dangerous and clever, as an espionage agent to be 'worse than ten thousand men,' reputedly [to] be immoral, and capable of resorting to any means, even to bribery, to gain her ends."

Von Hohenlohe displayed multiple skills of espionage: dispensing propaganda, acting as an agent of influence, and serving as a courier. At one point in 1940, she arranged a clandestine meeting between British spy William Wiseman and Wiedemann in suite 1024–1026 at the Mark Hopkins Hotel in San Francisco.

However, her personal life was far from that of a disciplined spy. Newspapers in the United States and Europe reported her antics as a celebrity "international adventuress," while she left a trail of lawsuits, unpaid bills, and high-profile lovers in virtually every city she inhabited.

After von Hohenlohe was arrested and threatened with deportation from the United States in 1941, she began a series of legal maneuvers that moved her court battle to Washington, DC, where she was detained by immigration authorities at the Raleigh Hotel. Once ensconced in the hotel, she began an affair with US commissioner of immigration and naturalization Lemuel Schofield, who was also a resident of the Raleigh. Scholfield, who had faced down Al Capone and had drawn headlines in Philadelphia as a hard-liner for Prohibition, was no match for the charms of the princess.

Von Hohenlohe was arrested again in Wilmington, Delaware, by the FBI the day after Pearl Harbor was attacked and held at the Immigration Detention Center, 101 South King Street, Gloucester City, New Jersey. After being moved to a facility in Texas, she apparently cooperated with OSS interrogators seeking information on the psychological makeup of Nazi officials, including Hitler.

Released in 1945, von Hohenlohe reunited with the still-smitten Schofield, who left his wife and four children, and the two settled in New York. The couple made the rounds of fashionable nightspots and parties, ingratiating themselves into high society. She was dressed "like a duchess, on hand for some of the better lorgnette-and-liquor parties, and sponsored by one of the oldest names in the social register," syndicated columnist Robert C. Ruark wrote in March 26, 1947. "Unless she's moved since I called last, the Princess is holed up in the Hotel Gotham, which evidently has a stronger stomach than the 42 countries who denied Steffi the right to enter."

The couple eventually moved to Schofield's country home, Anderson Place, in Charleston Township near Phoenixville, Pennsylvania. Schofield died in 1955, leaving little of his once-sizable estate for the princess, in part because he failed to pay taxes the previous six years. Still looking for her prince, von Hohenlohe moved in with Albert H. Greenfield—a founder of Bankers Trust, a Philadelphia real estate mogul, and a philanthropist—at his estate, Cobble Close Farm, 310 Cooper Road, Red Bank, New Jersey. The arrangement lasted only a few years. Hohenlohe returned to Europe in 1959 and died in Geneva, Switzerland, on June 13, 1972.

73. CONSTANCE DREXEL: THE PHILADELPHIA HEIRESS WHO WASN'T

MAP I ➤ ***Public Ledger***: South Sixth and Chestnut Streets, southwest corner (building demolished)

During World War I, newspaper correspondent Constance Drexel made headlines by volunteering as a Red Cross nurse in France. Papers praised the courage and selflessness of the newspaperwoman who had written for the *Boston Globe* and worked as a European correspondent for various news services.

Constance Drexel

Adding flavor to the story were unconfirmed reports the adventuresome newspaperwoman was a member of the notable Drexel family of Philadelphia. The dispatches she sent from Europe were picked up by multiple newspapers, and a job at Philadelphia's *Public Ledger*, southwest corner of South Sixth and Chestnut Streets, followed. A jet-setter at a time before jets, Drexel's international travel was reported as that of a "society girl" and "socialite," befitting an heiress descended from the famous banking family. In Philadelphia, she maintained a modest apartment at 26 South 21st Street (today a parking lot).

In reality, Drexel was not related to the family of the same name. She had been born in Germany to an upper-class family, immigrated to the United States as a child just after her father gained citizenship, and grew up in Roslindale, Massachusetts. As the clouds of World War II began to form, she moved back to Germany and, at the start of the war, was employed briefly by an American broadcaster. In 1940 she began a series of Sunday night propaganda broadcasts for the Nazi regime in which she was introduced over the airwaves as a member of the "Drexel family of Philadelphia."

William Shirer referenced Drexel in his book *Berlin Diary*. "The Nazis hired her, so far as I can find out, principally because she's the only woman in town who will sell her American accent to them," he wrote. Then, in a February 14, 1943, newspaper column, Shirer expanded his recollections, calling her "a mixed-up and ailing woman of about fifty who always had a bad cold. . . . She was the worst broadcaster I ever heard."

Drexel acquired the label "radio traitor" as one of a handful of Americans who made propaganda broadcasts for the Nazi regime. Paid $32 a week, she reported primarily on cultural issues and rarely ventured into topics centering on politics or the war, topics that characterized

Onetime European correspondent for Philadelphia's *Public Ledger*, Constance Drexel made propaganda radio broadcasts for Nazi Germany.

broadcasts of another American-born Nazi radio personality, Mildred Gillars (also known as Axis Sally).

Following the war, Drexel surrendered to a *Stars and Stripes* reporter in Vienna in August 1945, giving her name as Constance Louise Katherine Drexel. When she returned to the United States in 1946, she was detained and investigated by the Department of Justice for treason. Pleading necessity to earn a living, the case was dismissed in 1948 when the Justice Department failed to provide sufficient evidence to support treason charges.

Drexel died on August 28, 1956, at the home of a relative in Waterbury, Connecticut.

74. BRITISH OPERATIVE, PHILADELPHIA

MAP 8 ➤ Port of Philadelphia

American supplies were a lifeline to Great Britain during the early years of World War II. The United States, although officially neutral, shipped hundreds of millions of dollars in armaments and other supplies across the Atlantic to England. Protecting the shipments from sabotage was one mission of the secretive intelligence organization British Security Coordination headquartered in New York City. Headed by William Stephenson, the BSC established a security division led by English baronet Sir Connop Guthrie. From his command post in the Cunard offices in lower Manhattan, Guthrie deployed consular security officers (CSOs) to major US ports, including Philadelphia.

In Philadelphia, the CSO was New Zealander Douglas Gordon Braik, who served in World War I before relocating to study architecture at the University of Pennsylvania School of Fine Arts. In his role as CSO, Braik worked closely with American authorities, including the FBI, the Office of Naval Intelligence, and the US Coast Guard Temporary Reserves' Volunteer Port Security Force.

For the BSC, the consular program proved effective in combating sabotage. By the end of the war, the BSC had more than 30 CSOs and staff stationed throughout the United States and at least 40 in South America. In total, CSO officials conducted more than 30,000 inspections a year aboard merchant ships, and according to official accounts, the inspections were instrumental in ensuring not a single British vessel was lost or delayed due to sabotage during the war.

CSO duties also extended beyond counterintelligence. The CSOs collected intelligence and arranged with local authorities to return seamen arrested for drunkenness to their ships and addressed other dockside problems so vessels sailed on schedule. They also sought to quiet disputes with unions and set up their own saloons, hostels, and social clubs to offer a safe environment for the seamen.

Although the CSOs worked closely with the FBI, local authorities, and military intelligence, their efforts did not always run smoothly. In one instance, the Baltimore CSO barely avoided a diplomatic flap when the crews of several Danish vessels chartered by the British did not report back to their ships in Maryland. The CSO, anxious to see the ships and cargo depart, hired trucks and, along with his staff, went from waterfront bar to waterfront bar in search of the Danish crews. Local authorities, outraged, filed an official protest with the US State Department.

Following the war, Braik became chief of design at the Philadelphia Housing Authority and collaborated on projects with famed architect Louis Kahn. His home was at 99 East Stewart Avenue, Lansdowne, Pennsylvania.

75. FRANCE FOREVER, OLD CHAP!

MAP 9 ➤ **Eugène Jules Houdry residence:** Righters Mill and Mill Creek Roads, Ardmore, Pennsylvania

On September 28, 1940, several high-profile citizens held a charter meeting of the France Forever (France Quand-Même) organization at Independence Hall, 520 Chestnut Street, a location that was rich in historical significance. France, which had fallen to Germany in June, was now an occupied country. France was America's oldest ally, supporting its bid for freedom from the first days of the republic. Now under the control of Germany, France was calling for assistance from America.

Eugène Jules Houdry, 1919

Eugène Jules Houdry presided over the well-publicized event. A chemist by training, Houdry had made a fortune in a new method of oil refining and lived on an estate at Righters Mill and Mill Creek Roads in Ardmore, Pennsylvania. Members of the association included French expatriates and Americans of French descent. The purpose, according to press reports, was to "aid Britain in every lawful means." France, in the association's view, was not irrevocably lost, nor was the Vichy government legitimate.

It all seemed very French except that it was not begun by the French at all. Houdry was a French patriot, as were many of its members and officers, but the organization was a creation of British intelligence. Nominally headquartered

The British-backed France Forever organization used posters to build public support for the Allied forces during World War II.

in Philadelphia and incorporated in Pennsylvania, France Forever's executive offices, originally located at 8 West 40th Street in New York City, were moved to 30 Rockefeller Plaza in New York, a few steps from the BSC run by William Stephenson. The France Forever operation provided credible cover for British messages, obscuring their true source.

"We are convinced that France and all enslaved European democracies can be freed only by British victory and that a German victory over Britain will be the signal for an attack on all of the Americas," said Dr. Albert Simard, a popular France Forever representative.

With the British in the background, France Forever collected donations—sent to the address at Rockefeller Center—and organized lectures, rallies, and speeches around the country. One lecture held in Carnegie Hall on December 20, 1940, was headlined by a long list of Free France officials and notable American supporters. Meetings at the Bellevue-Stratford Hotel, 200 South Broad Street, Philadelphia, made news for their high-profile guest lists, while smaller events, such as one held at the Bundles for Britain in Cincinnati, featured films and lectures. France Forever broadcast on the British-controlled, 50,000-watt shortwave radio station WRUL in Boston.

New York businessman Sanford "Sandy" Griffith, using his company, Market Analysts Incorporated, managed the effort. It shared its address, West 40th Street, with the original address of France Forever and another BSC front organization, the American Irish Defense Association. Documents released after World War II suggest that American officials were aware of the BSC and France Forever connection. In one early letter dated August 3, 1940, written to FDR's adviser and British liaison Ernest Cuneo, Griffith wrote, "I have been asked to head up a committee of Americans who are in sympathy with the best of old French ideals and want no traffic with the Vichy France. Have you any candidates?"

Perhaps Cuneo did make some suggestions. Possibilities include playwright Robert E. Sherwood, who lectured for the France Forever effort and later joined William J. Donovan's Office of the Coordinator of Information (later the OSS), and literary scholar Conyers Read, another France Forever supporter.

WHAT'S IN A CODE NAME?

Code names, an essential component of espionage, could not escape British wit. When choosing code names, British intelligence officers during World War II seemingly could not resist a bit of dry humor. Duško Popov, the double agent who posed as an Abwehr spy, was code-named TRICYCLE, presumably for his proclivity of entertaining two women at once. Juan Pujol García, another double agent, was reputed to have been code-named GARBO for his acting skills in relaying false intelligence reports to the Germans. An operation to turn captured German spies into double agents was code-named the TWENTY COMMITTEE with the Roman numeral XX also indicating a double cross.

In an example of darker humor, an operation code-named MINCEMEAT was said to have been first imagined in 1939 by British intelligence officers including Ian Fleming, creator of the fictional James Bond. The deception operation involved obtaining the body of a homeless man, dressing him in the uniform of the Royal Marines, and putting the body, along with a cache of fraudulent but official-appearing documents, out to sea off the Spanish coast, where German intelligence would certainly discover it. Although initially rejected, the plan was later refined by British intelligence officers Charles Cholmondeley and Ewen Montagu and enacted in April 1943. Based on the MINCEMEAT deception, German intelligence misread the location of the Allied invasion of Sicily.

5

THE FIRST ERA OF SOVIET ESPIONAGE

(1919–1947)

The United States did not officially recognize the Soviet government for fifteen years following the Bolshevik Revolution. Diplomatic relations between the two countries were in their infancy, and a Philadelphian served as the first US ambassador to the USSR. Soviet intelligence, meanwhile, was rapidly expanding its presence in the United States by staffing the embassy and affiliated trade organizations with spies operating under the cover of government officials or commercial representatives. They aggressively recruited other spies, with ideologically sympathetic socialists, American communist sympathizers, and labor unions among the most attractive targets.

The social and political environment was fertile for the Soviet intelligence service. Then in the grip of the Great Depression, economic hardship in the United States lured many to radical politics. For instance, the Communist Party of the United States (CPUSA) was a home for true believers in the communist cause or for those who could be convinced of its eventual triumph. One Philadelphia labor man became a feared Soviet assassin. Some Americans recruited as spies for the USSR in the 1930s penetrated senior levels of the US government during World War II. Once defectors and investigations revealed these penetrations, a wave of suspicions and arrests fueled a postwar Red Scare that ensnared both the guilty and the innocent.

When the United States entered World War II, the navy expanded its counterintelligence operations around Philadelphia's ports. On the offensive front, the Office of Strategic Services recruited officers and staff from the city's university, research, and business communities.

76. A PHILADELPHIAN IN MOSCOW

MAP 6 ➤ **William C. Bullitt Jr. grave site:** Woodlands Cemetery, 4000 Woodland Avenue

William C. Bullitt Jr., America's first ambassador to Soviet Russia, grew up at 222 West Rittenhouse Square, Philadelphia, and at the family's estate Oxmoor (today called Rosedon), 500 Waterloo Road, Devon, Pennsylvania. A standout student at Yale—voted "Most Brilliant"—he graduated in 1913, then dropped out of Harvard Law School after one year and joined the staff of the *Philadelphia Ledger* as a reporter until becoming special assistant to the secretary of state in 1917. Bullitt attended the Paris Peace Conference, assigned to the Division of Current Intelligence Summaries in President Wilson's delegation; then he made a trip in 1919 to Russia, ostensibly to study conditions in the newly formed Soviet state. His secret mission, however, was to broker an agreement with the Bolshevik government to end the civil war that would lift the blockade and allow the Allies to withdraw the troops who had been sent to Russia in 1918.

Bullitt met with Lenin, but the Soviet conditions were not acceptable to the United States. The mission failed. The 28-year-old Bullitt, who either resigned

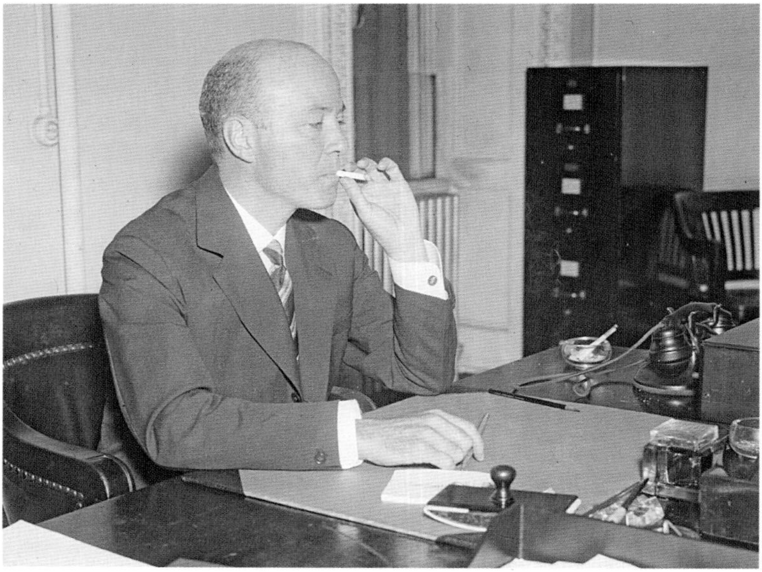

William C. Bullitt Jr., America's first ambassador to Soviet Russia, saw the US Embassy in Moscow overrun with Soviet spies. Bullitt's public service included ambassadorships in Moscow and Paris and working as an assistant to the secretary of the navy and as a personal envoy of President Roosevelt.

in protest or was fired by President Wilson, wrote a scathing letter to the president and publicized his resignation. When asked what he planned to do next, he answered, "I am going to lie in the sands of the French Riviera, and watch the world go to hell."

Rather than travel to the Riviera, however, Bullitt joined the new moving pictures industry and Famous Players-Lasky Corporation. He married Louise Bryant, widow of firebrand journalist John Reed, who died in Russia in 1920. He continued to court controversy and wrote *It's Not Done*, a scandalous novel of Philadelphia high society.

Following the election of Franklin Roosevelt as president, Bullitt returned to government service in 1933 as the ambassador to the Soviet Union. In this post he initially maintained what could very generously be called an idealistic view of the Soviet Union and diplomacy. "We should never send a spy to the Soviet Union," he wrote to the State Department. "There is no weapon at once so disarming and effective in relations with the Communists as sheer honesty." Bullitt demonstrated this philosophy as ambassador, heading an embassy that did not include the standard use of safes, couriers, or codes. Papers were left unattended, and communications went out over open telegraph lines.

As a result, the embassy was overrun with Soviet spies, and American diplomats were under constant surveillance. Spaso House, the ambassador's residence, was also a target, and its phone lines were tapped. The caretaker of the ambassador's residence, known as Sergei, kept his basement apartment locked and off-limits to diplomatic staff. When the situation became intolerable, even for Bullitt, a contingent of US Marine guards—the first to be dispatched to a US Embassy—was assigned to Moscow. The Narodnyy Komissariat Vnutrennikh Del (NKVD), predecessor to the Komitet Gosudarstvennoy Bezopasnosti (KGB), responded by deploying a counterforce of attractive women tasked to seduce the Marines.

During this period, Tyler Kent, an American code clerk who had a Russian girlfriend at the time, was likely recruited to spy for the Soviets and later spied for Germany when posted at the US Embassy in London. Bullitt himself was linked to a Russian woman, Olga Lepeshinskaya, a dancer with the Bolshoi Theatre. Said to be a favorite of Joseph Stalin's, she later married twice, both times to Soviet intelligence officers. The Bullitt-Lepeshinskaya affair, according to contemporary gossip detailed in Doris Kearns Goodwin's *No Ordinary Time: Franklin and Eleanor Roosevelt*, was responsible for ending Bullitt's quasi-engagement to FDR's personal secretary, Marguerite "Missy" LeHand. Leaving Moscow in 1936, Bullitt was appointed US ambassador to France. By then, disillusioned with the Soviet system, he became a vocal critic of the USSR.

Unable to secure a senior diplomatic post in Roosevelt's third-term cabinet, he left the State Department in 1941. Still in the public spotlight, he gave lectures and wrote articles advocating intervention in the war against Germany. "There is no easy way by which we can escape from war with Hitler," he wrote

HOW DOES THAT MAKE YOU FEEL?

William C. Bullitt Jr., who worked as a journalist and author between and after his diplomatic postings, undertook a curious project in the 1930s. In a meeting in Vienna with Sigmund Freud, the father of psychoanalysis, the two agreed to collaborate on a book—an in-depth psychoanalysis of President Woodrow Wilson. Freud and Bullitt completed the manuscript, *Thomas Woodrow Wilson, Twenty-Eighth President of the United States: A Psychological Study*, in the 1930s, but it was not published until 1966 by Houghton Mifflin Company.

in *Life* magazine, April 21, 1941. "We cannot get off this planet."

A fact-finding mission he undertook to the Near East and Africa provided critical intelligence for OPERATION TORCH and Roosevelt's decision to invade North Africa. Appointed special assistant to the secretary of the navy in June 1942, Bullitt acted as the personal envoy of the president, meeting with foreign leaders, including Charles de Gaulle and Winston Churchill.

A year later Bullitt made an unsuccessful run for mayor of Philadelphia in 1943, a candidacy which was said to have been prompted by the president. After the failed campaign, Bullitt continued to write and became increasingly hawkish in his anti-communist views. The August 24, 1954, issue of *Look* featured his article, "Should We Support an Attack on Red China?"

Bullitt died February 15, 1967, at Neuilly-sur-Seine, a suburb of Paris, France, and is buried at Woodlands Cemetery, 4000 Woodland Avenue, Philadelphia.

77. POLO WITH THE RED ARMY

MAP I ➤ **Charles W. Thayer residence:** 116 Pine Street

Fellow Philadelphian Charles W. Thayer joined William Bullitt in Moscow, as the ambassador's secretary, to open the first US Embassy in the USSR in 1933. Thayer, born on the Kyneton estate in Villanova, Pennsylvania, was a West Point graduate who resigned his commission in favor of joining the US Foreign Service. "The Army's just finished educating you and now you want to quit—to become a damned cookie-pushing diplomat—and in Russia of all places," Col. George Patton lambasted him, as quoted in Thayer's memoir, *Bears in the Caviar*.

Charles W. Thayer, a native of this Philadelphia Society Hill neighborhood, promoted polo and American baseball to his Soviet host.

Charles W. Thayer

As it turned out, Thayer did little cookie pushing. He cut a dashing figure, riding through Moscow on a Harley-Davidson motorcycle with a sidecar. In an effort to establish better relationships between the two countries, he taught a group from a Russian cavalry regiment to play polo, ordering a complete set of mallets and balls from London. He also attempted to introduce baseball to Moscovites and organized a Christmas party featuring three trained circus seals—Lyuba, Misha, and Shura—which caused havoc during the diplomatic function. As Thayer would later recall, cultural differences between the two countries became apparent when he was asked to consult on a local production of Ben Hecht and Charles MacArthur's 1928 play, *The Front Page*, and was surprised when the character of the editor appeared in a top hat and tails. The Russian theater company assumed that was how capitalist bosses in America dressed, even hard-bitten Chicago newspapermen.

Thayer, whose Philadelphia residence was 116 Pine Street in Society Hill, enjoyed a colorful career in and out of diplomacy following his Moscow posting. He served as a diplomat in Afghanistan prior to enlisting in 1944 in the army, where he was recruited into the OSS. Sent to Yugoslavia during the war and to the occupation command in Austria following the war, Thayer assisted in organizing the State Department's secret Office of Policy Coordination, which later merged into the CIA. From 1947 to 1948, he headed the State Department's International Broadcasting Division, which oversaw Voice of America.

The author of eight books—including *Bears in the Caviar* (1951), *Hands across the Caviar* (1953), and *Unquiet Germans* (1957)—Thayer died in 1969 and is buried at the Church of the Redeemer Cemetery, 230 Pennswood Road, Bryn Mawr, Pennsylvania.

78. CHEMIST, INVENTOR, AND SPY

MAP 2 ➤ **Ben Franklin Hotel (now the Franklin Residences):** 834 Chestnut Street

In the decade prior to World War II, Soviet intelligence focused on the United States. Though America was not yet considered the USSR's main enemy (*glavniy protivnik*), Stalin wanted its advanced technology. One target for Soviet spies was the University of Pennsylvania's world-class biological research faculty. Among the scientists targeted was Earl W. Flosdorf, who pioneered a method to freeze-dry blood plasma in the 1930s. The process not only represented a significant advance in battlefield medicine but could also be turned to military or darker purposes by Soviet scientists.

Flosdorf, a collector of expensive antique cars, was recruited and paid secretly by the Soviets from 1936 through 1938. Assigned the code name OUTPOST, he met with his handler at the Benjamin Franklin Hotel (now the Franklin Residences), 834 Chestnut Street. Over time he may have received as much as $25,000 for providing the Soviets with a device that could freeze-dry materials for biological attack. Another potential biological warfare application was Flosdorf's research into a rare parrot disease called psittacosis that had a 100 percent fatality rate among owners who contracted it from their pets.

Deactivated in 1938, Flosdorf was approached again by the Soviets following World War II, though it is uncertain what, if any, scientific secrets he provided. Flosdorf's story came to a horrific end on April 29, 1958, in his Creamery Road farmhouse in Forest Grove near Doylestown. Given to fits of rage, the noted scientist killed his wife with a shotgun blast in front of their 12-year-old son; then he turned the gun on himself.

The Benjamin Franklin Hotel (now the Franklin Residences) has been the site of numerous intelligence operations over the years, including clandestine meetings between Soviet handlers and the University of Pennsylvania biologist Earl W. Flosdorf.

79. CODE NAME BLACK

MAP 4 ➤ **Charles W. Berg Laboratories:** 1827–1829 North Fifth Street

Thomas Lessing Black was recruited to spy in the 1930s by Soviet intelligence officer Gaik Ovakimian, working under the cover of a representative for AMTORG, the Soviet-American trading company. The American chemist was assigned the code names BLACK and PETER as he conducted industrial espionage and handled fellow Philadelphian spy Harry Gold, a member of the Soviet's atomic spy ring. By first providing his handler with chemical industrial processes for oils, leather, and other mundane items, he gained sufficient trust to be recruited as an agent spotter and handler. Black, in turn, recruited Harry Gold, who worked at a sugar processing firm but later became one of the Soviets' most important agents in the penetration of the US Manhattan Project.

An explosion and chemical fire in 1954 at the Charles W. Berg Laboratories killed eleven first responders. Investigators suspected, but could not prove, sabotage.

Eccentric chemist and spy Thomas Lessing Black was a prime suspect in the fire and explosion that destroyed Charles W. Berg Laboratories, though his guilt was never definitively established.

During World War II, Black worked at the US Bureau of Standards and is referenced in seven secret messages deciphered by American cryptographers in the VENONA communications intercept project but not made public until 1995. After the war ended, Black, then a chemist at the Charles W. Berg Laboratories, 1827–1829 North Fifth Street, became a suspect when a chemical storage tank exploded on October 28, 1954, killing ten firemen.

Black, who was seen as eccentric, came under suspicion and, when questioned, admitted to having been the Soviet agent who recruited and handled Harry Gold. A search of Black's residence at 1929 North Sixth Street uncovered a substantial cache of communist and socialist reading material and secret papers kept from his days as a Soviet spy. However, as nothing implicating him in sabotaging the facility was discovered, he was released.

■ 80. AN ASSASSIN CALLED THE MINK

MAP 5 ➤ **Yellow Cab Company:** 1206 North 31st Street

George Mink

Born in czarist Russia at the turn of the century, George Mink came to the United States on August 2, 1913, at age 17. His father had died, and the teenager was sent to live with an uncle in Philadelphia. He enlisted in the navy in June 1917, compiled a seven-month service record of being disruptive and a loafer, and was discharged in January 1918. Later, he claimed he was born in Scranton, and investigators were further misled by a paper trail that led them to believe Mink had been born in Philadelphia. At some point in the early 1920s, Mink, now a committed communist, was recruited by Soviet intelligence. His daytime job from 1928 until 1933 was driving a taxi for the Yellow Cab Company located at 1206 North 31st Street.

"'The Mink' was a Red, all right!" a fellow cabbie told a reporter years later. "He was always startin' arguments, and they were so silly you'd get all burned up and lose your head." Mink was also active in Philadelphia and on the West Coast in the Seamen's Union, where he proved himself a tough, reliable, and feared enforcer.

Mink's intelligence connections were finally revealed in 1935. When traveling with two companions on a mission for the Glavnoye Razvedyvatel'noye Upravleniye (GRU, Soviet military intelligence), he attempted to rape a maid in a Copenhagen hotel. An investigation by Danish police uncovered false passports, and the clandestine trio was arrested on charges of espionage. With his legal fees paid by Moscow through an intermediary, Mink was deported to the Soviet Union. He eventually resurfaced as an assassin during the Spanish Civil War. Operating under the direction of the NKVD's Alexander Orlov, Mink was linked to multiple murders throughout Europe, including that of secret police defector Ignace Reiss in Switzerland and anti-Stalinist Italian professor Camillo Berneri in Barcelona, Spain.

After returning to the United States, Mink was widely rumored to have murdered Juliet Poyntz in New York City. Accounts of the murder vary, though in one version the disillusioned communist was lured to Central Park, pushed into a waiting car, and hastily buried in a shallow grave outside the city. In another version, Mink took Poyntz aboard a Soviet ship docked in New York, where she was murdered and her body dumped in the Atlantic. Walter Krivitsky, who defected to the West in 1937, reported having been strong-armed by three men, one of whom he said he recognized as Mink. Krivitsky escaped into a New York City subway.

Mink also may have been recruited to take part in the NKVD operation to murder Leon Trotsky. In 1938 Trotsky, then living near Mexico City, publicly announced Mink was in Mexico to assassinate him. Two years later, just before the failed NKVD attack on Trotsky's compound on May 23, 1940, Mink was reportedly captured by Trotsky's bodyguards. Joseph Hansen, Trotsky's chief secretary, later told the FBI that in 1940 Mink's captors threw him into a crater 30 miles outside the city. In its February 1941 edition, the Soviet publication *Novoye Russkoye Slovo* (New Russian Word) reported, "According to the latest confirmed information Mink was liquidated in December [1940]." Whatever Mink's fate, these references are the last reports of the assassin's sudden disappearance.

81. JOURNALIST-SPY TURNED SKEPTIC

MAP 3 ➤ **I. F. Stone birthplace:** 636 South Wharton Street

Rumors swirled around the loyalties of journalist I. F. Stone for years. Was the radical left-wing journalist a little too radical? And was he more than just a journalist? Born Isidor Feinstein Stone in 1907 in his parents' house on 636 South Wharton Street, Stone dropped out of the University of Pennsylvania to begin his career in journalism, eventually becoming an editorial writer at the *Philadelphia Inquirer*, 400 North Broad Street. He then moved to the *New York Post* and by 1933 abandoned the paper's pro-Roosevelt position for increasingly radical views that included advocacy for a "Soviet America."

Firebrand journalist I. F. Stone was born into modest circumstances in this South Wharton Street home (now with a black door).

For decades Stone moved from one liberal publication to another and started his own newsletter, *I.F. Stone's Weekly*, as rumors of his communist sympathies periodically emerged. Not until a few years after his death in 1989, when his reputation as a journalist with a courageous conscience was firmly enshrined, did the extent of his deception become known. Previously top-secret VENONA decrypts of Soviet communications, released in the mid-1990s, surfaced Stone's name.

Recruited by Soviet intelligence in 1936 and given the code name PANCAKE, Stone regularly provided intelligence information to his Soviet handlers. "Relations with PANCAKE have entered the channel of normal operational work," his Soviet handler in New York City reported in May 1936. Whether Stone's spy work, which is reported to have included "talent spotting" and acting as courier, lasted into the 1940s, as some claim, remains in dispute. The VENONA materials reveal a Russian intelligence officer referencing the code name BLIN, which is Russian for "pancake," following World War II. However, it seems unlikely Stone was still on good terms with the Soviets into the 1950s. Following a visit to the Soviet Union in 1956, he publicly expressed his disillusionment. He wrote, "Whatever the consequences, I have to say what I really feel after seeing the Soviet Union and carefully studying the statements of its leading officials, this is not a good society and it is not led by honest men."

I. F. Stone, 1972

82. GOLDEN ATOMIC SECRETS

MAP 8 ➤ **Harry Gold residence:** 6823 Kindred Street

Harry Gold, a critical link in the Soviet atomic spy network, was nobody's idea of a spy or secret agent. An FBI file paints Gold unflatteringly as "short and fat . . . [with a] round full face, prominent protrusion of eyes." The son of an immigrant woodworker, Gold grew up in Depression-era Philadelphia at 6823

Harry Gold

A trusted courier for Soviet intelligence, Harry Gold spent most of his non-prison life living in this house on Kindred Street.

The Earle Theatre and Fox Theatre were clandestine meeting sites for Harry Gold and his Soviet handler. Both have long since been torn down.

Kindred Street and graduated from South Philadelphia High School for Boys (now known as South Philadelphia High School). He was employed by the now-defunct Pennsylvania Sugar Company, 1037 Delaware Avenue (renamed Columbus Boulevard), site of today's Rivers Casino. Fellow employees would

Harry Gold worked at the Heart Station of Philadelphia General Hospital while leading a double life as a Soviet spy.

later describe Gold as diffident, quiet, and always willing to lend a hand. Classmates at the University of Pennsylvania, Drexel Institute of Technology, and St. Joseph's University, where he received his college education, also remember Gold as helpful, if inconspicuous.

What none of his colleagues, friends, or family suspected was that from 1934 until 1945, Gold was deeply involved in Soviet intelligence operations, including the infamous Rosenberg atomic spy case. By appealing to his emotional antipathy to Nazi anti-Semitism, the Soviets recruited Gold to spy by first asking him for proprietary data on processes at the sugar refinery and, when he positively responded, then grooming him to work clandestinely.

Variously code-named GOOSE, ARNO, and MAD, Gold was seen by

Before his death during heart surgery, convicted spy Harry Gold earned patents for medical devices he developed while in prison.

the Soviets as a valued asset, even if others found him unremarkable. In Philadelphia Gold met his Russian handler at the Earle Theatre, 1046 Market Street, or at the Fox Theatre, 1600 Market Street, while he served as a courier for secret messages delivered to Soviet scientist-spy Klaus Fuchs (code name REST and CHARLES). Because Soviet intelligence officers could not travel in the United States without drawing the FBI's attention, the nerdy, technically adept Gold was an ideal messenger to carry messages across the country. In one instance, he traveled from Philadelphia to Santa Fe, New Mexico, to meet with Fuchs and then to Albuquerque to meet with the brother of Ethel Greenglass Rosenberg, David Greenglass (code name CALIBER or KALIBR), who was a machinist on the Manhattan Project.

In the eyes of his masters, Gold's espionage merited special recognition, and in 1943 he was awarded one of the Soviet Union's highest honors, the Order of the Red Star. Few foreigners received the honor, which was typically reserved for Soviet soldiers and spies for courage, bravery, and outstanding service during peace and wartime.

Life turned sour for Gold in the late 1940s. After losing his job at the sugar refinery, he approached one of his Soviet contacts for a legitimate job. It was a profound breach of operational security because his new employer, an engineering firm specializing in chemical processes, was already under suspicion for industrial espionage. Now Gold was in the FBI's sights, rendering him too high a risk to continue his spy work.

Gold left the engineering firm and landed a job at the Heart Station of Philadelphia General Hospital (closed in the 1970s), 34th Street and Curie Avenue, but his spying had been exposed. In the spring of 1950, the FBI closed in. During an interview at the FBI field office in the Widener Building, 1 South Penn Square, Gold agreed to a search of his home. There, agents found the trappings of a quiet life, including a bedroom cluttered with technical journals and paperback mysteries. But when a street map for Santa Fe was discovered, the always helpful Gold confessed almost immediately to his clandestine courier work. In subsequent questioning at the Benjamin Franklin Hotel (now the Franklin Residences), 834 Chestnut Street, he implicated Greenglass, a lead that eventually led the FBI to Julius and Ethel Rosenberg.

PATENTED SPY

The man who began his career in industrial espionage before becoming one of the atomic spies eventually took out several patents while in a federal prison. Best known of these was US Patent number 2,963,350, which was awarded in 1960 for a low-cost, rapid blood sugar test. The filing for the patent lists the US Penitentiary at Lewisburg, Pennsylvania, as Gold's address.

Gold was tried, convicted, and received a 30-year sentence but served less than 15 years in the US Penitentiary at Lewisburg, Pennsylvania, prior to parole.

Strangely enough, prison life seemed to agree with Gold. He worked in the prison's medical unit, conducted research, and even obtained patents for medical devices. Paroled in 1965, he returned to his Kindred Street home and job as chemist at the John F. Kennedy Hospital on Roosevelt Boulevard. He died in 1972 while undergoing heart surgery and was buried at nearby Har Nebo Cemetery, 6061 Oxford Avenue.

PAPER PAROLE

David Greenglass testified that Soviet handler Anatoli Yakovlev provided Harry Gold with half of an irregularly cut side panel of a Jell-O box to use as identification when he met with David and Ruth Greenglass in Albuquerque. The spies could confirm Gold's identity by matching it with their half of the box. The flavor, though not confirmed, has been identified as raspberry. The Greenglass testimony has been disputed, but the type of recognition parole described is classic spy tradecraft.

Anatoli Yakovlev stamp

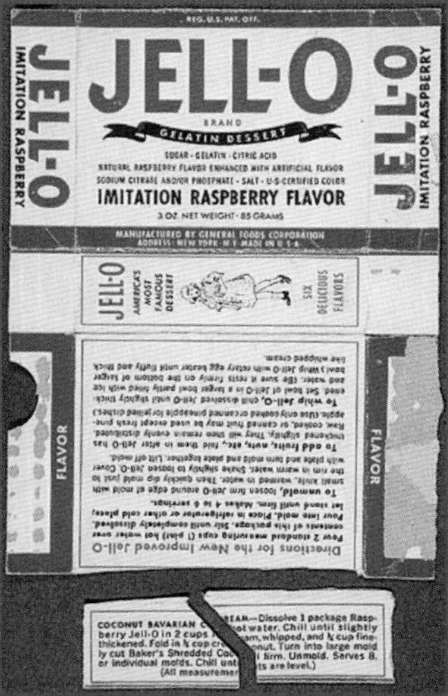

When meeting, Soviet spies sometimes used two halves of a torn Jell-O box to verify identities.

83. THE TRUE BELIEVER FROM BRYN MAWR

MAP 9 ➤ **Henry Collins childhood home:** 151 North Merion Avenue, Bryn Mawr, Pennsylvania

Henry Hill Collins Jr. grew up in Bryn Mawr, 151 North Merion Avenue (today part of Bryn Mawr College), on the Welsh-named Bettws-Y-Coed estate. The family fortune made in the specialty paper business with A. M. Collins Manufacturing Company, 226 West Columbia Avenue, Philadelphia, enabled Collins to attend Princeton and acquire a master's degree in business administration from Harvard. He seemed destined for great things. The child of privilege with two Ivy League degrees was also an avid birder who authored texts on ornithology while waging campaigns to save hawks. "Henry Collins was all that Princeton

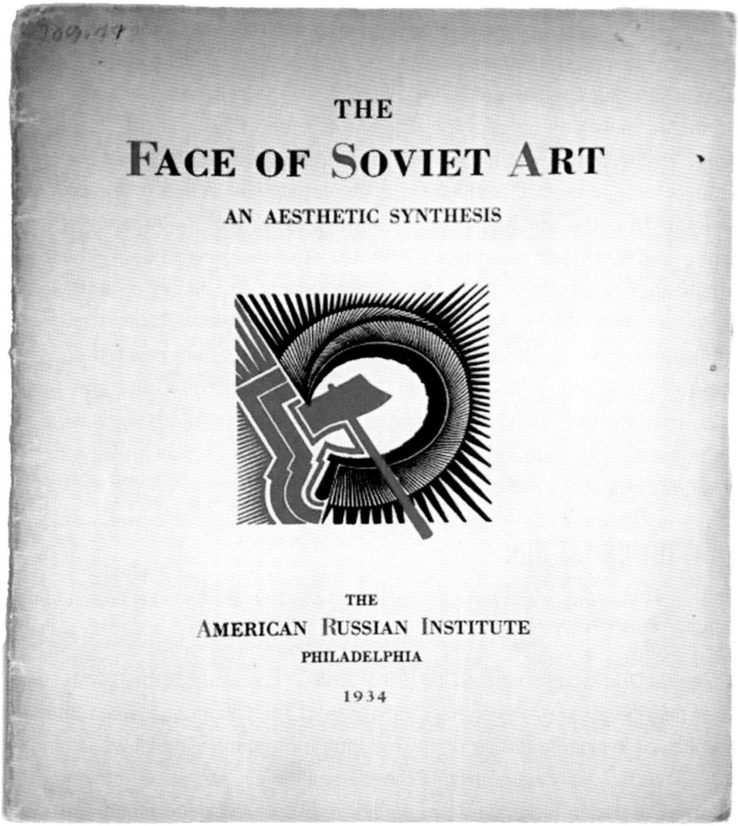

Publications of Philadelphia's now-defunct American Russian Institute painted a positive image of the Soviet government.

and Harvard can do for a personable and intelligent young American of good family," Whittaker Chambers later wrote in his book *Witness*.

Collins, however, joined a Marxist study group in prewar Washington, DC, that served as cover for the espionage ring known as the Ware Group. Headed by Harold Ware, the group was primarily a network of Soviet agents including well-known and alleged spies such as Whittaker Chambers, Alger Hiss, and Harry Dexter White. Several Ware Group members were employed in government positions, where they aggressively sought secrets and calculated ways to advance the careers and access of others in the network.

Employed at the New Deal National Recovery Administration and then the Agricultural Adjustment Administration, Collins acted as the Ware Group's treasurer, talent spotter, and recruiter while volunteering his St. Matthews Court apartment in Washington for meetings. His multiple attempts to secure employment in the State Department were unsuccessful, though he did eventually work for congressional committees, including the House Committee on Interstate Migration, the Senate's US Small Business Committee, and the House Military Affairs Subcommittee. During World War II, he served as a commissioned officer, earned five European campaign stars, and fought in the Battle of the Bulge. Following the war, he acted as a district officer of displaced persons.

Collins remained a true believer in the communist cause to the end. After returning from the war, he became executive director of the American Russian Institute in New York, identified by the US attorney general as a Soviet front organization. As a result, the institute lost funding and closed in 1948.

When called before the House Un-American Activities Committee (HUAC) in 1948 and again in 1953, Collins refused both to answer pointed questions about his activities on behalf of the Soviets and to identify others as agents. Aside from the testimony of his alleged coconspirators, there was insufficient proof against him to bring charges of espionage. Collins died on May 20, 1961, of injuries sustained in a car crash.

84. SPY ON THE RUN

MAP 2 ➤ **War Library and Museum of the Military Order of the Loyal Legion of the United States:** 1805 Pine Street

Alexander Orlov (code name SCHWED or SWEDE) was one of the Soviet Union's most daring spies. He helped recruit three of the Cambridge spies in Britain. In Spain, he trained guerrilla fighters during that country's civil war in the late 1930s, hosted American author Ernest Hemingway, and pulled off one of the greatest thefts in history by persuading the Spanish government to entrust the Soviet Union with its gold reserves, some 510 tons of the precious metal, for "safe keeping."

However, despite his remarkable successes, Orlov fell under suspicion during Stalin's purges. Given notice of his recall to Moscow in 1938, he fled

Alexander Orlov

rather than risk a show trial and execution. He sold his impressive art collection and absconded with between $22,000 and $60,000 (approximately $400,000 to $1 million in today's dollars). He then had two letters hand carried from Canada to Paris. One letter was addressed to NKVD chief Nikolai Yezhov (known as the Poison Dwarf) and another to Stalin, threatening to reveal everything he knew about Soviet intelligence if either he or his family remaining in the USSR were pursued.

It was a bold strategy, but as Orlov may have expected, the deal was not accepted. The equivalent of an all-points bulletin on the defector was sent throughout Soviet intelligence channels immediately after his departure. Nevertheless, he transited Canada and slipped across the US border with his wife, Maria, and his terminally ill child, Vera. The family arrived in New York, where he was previously posted as a Soviet intelligence officer; then they moved to Philadelphia.

Orlov adopted the name Leon Koornick, borrowed from a cousin, and moved his family to a series of hotels including Benjamin Franklin Hotel (today the Franklin Residences), 834 Chestnut Street; the Bellevue-Stratford Hotel (today the Hyatt at the Bellevue), 200 South Broad Street; and the Walnut Park Plaza Hotel (today the Walnut Park Plaza), 6250 Walnut Street. He frequented the War Library and Museum of the Military Order of the Loyal Legion of the United States, 1805 Pine Street, for writing and research.

While in Philadelphia, Orlov broke his silence only once, writing an anonymous letter to warn exiled revolutionary Leon Trotsky of an assassination plot. The letter offered a detailed description of the assassin, but Orlov did not know the name of the assassin. Two identical letters were sent—one to Trotsky and a duplicate to Natalia Sedov, Trotsky's wife. Orlov

Museum of the Military Order of the Loyal Legion of the United States

gambled that if one was intercepted, then perhaps the other would get through. Apparently, one did reach Trotsky, though the details of the imminent assassination attempt were not enough to convince the exiled communist. Assuming the letter was the work of NKVD agent provocateurs, he ignored the well-intentioned warning.

Although the Orlov family initially planned to make Philadelphia a permanent home, the Orlovs eventually moved to California. There, Vera died from a heart weakened by rheumatic fever on July 14, 1940. The Orlovs relocated to a suburb of Cleveland, Ohio, under the alias Berg. For a decade, the couple led a spartan lifestyle, reportedly subsisting on corn flakes while both eluding Soviet intelligence and escaping the FBI's attention.

Following Stalin's death, Orlov revealed himself in April 6, 1953, by authoring an article in *Life* magazine titled "The Ghastly Secrets of Stalin's Power." The first in a series, Orlov's piece methodically outlined Stalin's corrupt and bloody regime. The articles were followed a year later by his first book, *The Secret History of Stalin's Crimes*. His sudden appearance surprised American spy catchers as much as the Soviets. Eventually Orlov moved briefly to Michigan, where he obtained a teaching position at the University of Michigan and wrote *Handbook of Intelligence and Guerrilla Warfare*. The defector died in Cleveland in 1973.

85. THE SPIES OF LONG BEACH ISLAND

MAP 13 ➤ **Loveladies Harbor:** Long Beach Island, New Jersey

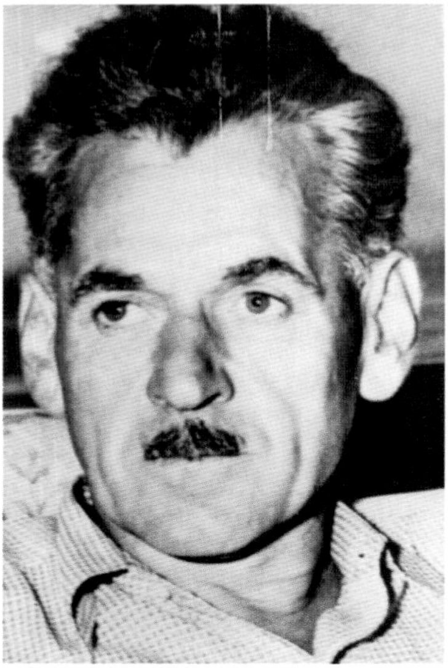
Nathan Silvermaster

Nathan Silvermaster (code name PAL and ROBERT), a respected government economist at the US Department of Agriculture and US Department of the Treasury, secretly ran an expansive Soviet spy ring during World War II. From early 1940 to the mid-1940s, Silvermaster's network reached into the White House and the OSS. When onetime Soviet spy Elizabeth Bentley described what she knew of the spy ring's penetration of Washington power centers to the FBI, the communists' reach seemed nearly unbelievable.

Not only did members of the Silvermaster spy ring conduct traditional espionage but they also assisted each other in acquiring government jobs in sensitive positions. For example, a secretary was placed in the Treasury Department to help Harry Dexter White, one of the ring's most valuable agents.

The operation was run by Silvermaster; his wife, Helen (code name DORA); and William Ludwig Ullmann (code name POLO and PILOT). Ullmann, who worked as a Treasury Department economist, served as the spy ring's photographer, copying secret documents in a darkroom set up in the Silvermasters' basement.

Following Bentley's confession, the Silvermasters and Ullmann were placed under surveillance but not arrested, since Kim Philby of the British foreign intelligence service (MI6) had previously warned the Soviets of Bentley's defection. Eventually questioned publicly before the HUAC in 1948, members of the spy ring adamantly denied the charges. In fact, the government did have conclusive evidence of spying, collected through the top-secret VENONA communications intercept project, but presenting the evidence would have revealed its source. When weighed against the likely convictions of the Silvermasters and Ullmann, maintaining the VENONA secrets was judged to be of more value, and the Soviet spies escaped justice.

The trio moved north and bought 235 acres of bayside property on Long Beach Island, New Jersey. The three then undertook to build a development that became known as Loveladies Harbor, approximately 80

THE ARRANGEMENT

Helen Silvermaster, with the consent of her husband, began a long-term affair with William Ludwig Ullmann, who lived in the Silvermasters' home. The arrangement left the Soviet handlers dismayed. "Surely these unhealthy relations between them cannot help but influence their behavior and work with us negatively," their cautious Soviet handler complained to Moscow. Surprisingly, the Ullmann-Silvermaster trio outlived the spy ring by decades.

BARONESS OF THE JERSEY SHORE

Helen Silvermaster was a White Russian baroness by birth. Born Elena Witte in 1899, her father was Baron Peter Witte, an adviser to Czar Nicholai II. Her granduncle count Sergei Witte had served as his prime minister.

Baron Witte, arrested during the Bolshevik Revolution of 1917, was later released, and the family immigrated first to China and then to San Francisco. Along the way Helen accumulated a failed marriage and a child, Anatole, before she met and married Nathan Silvermaster, another Russian. She relinquished her title when she became a US citizen and did not advertise her royal lineage during her time in Washington, DC. However, later in her life, following her successful entrance into the New Jersey real estate field, newspaper stories inevitably referred to her as a baroness.

miles from Philadelphia. Today, an "Ullmann design" property commands a premium price.

Nathan Silvermaster died in 1964 at age 65 at the Jefferson Medical College Hospital in Philadelphia. Helen Silvermaster died in 1991 and Ullmann in 1993.

86. THE MAN WHO FOUGHT HOLLYWOOD, NAZIS, AND COMMUNISTS

MAP 11 ➤ **Schulberg residence:** US-202 and Lower York Road, New Hope, Pennsylvania

Seymour "Budd" Schulberg, the son of a Hollywood film mogul, courted controversy with his book *What Makes Sammy Run?* (1941). The dark, rags-to-riches portrayal of his protagonist, Sammy Glick, as a backstabbing and deceptive screenwriter earned Schulberg the enmity of Hollywood. An unconfirmed story circulated that Samuel Goldwyn offered to pay Schulberg not to publish the book because he felt it perpetuated anti-Semitism.

Budd Schulberg was an American screenwriter, television producer, novelist, and sports writer.

During World War II, Schulberg joined the navy and was assigned to the OSS and director John Ford's film unit. Serving with the Field Photographic Branch, Schulberg documented the D-Day operations and the liberation of concentration camps. He later worked for the Office of Military Government–United States in Germany, collecting film footage to be used in the Nuremberg trials, and arrested German movie actress and Hitler's propagandist filmmaker, Leni Riefenstahl, at her chalet in Kitzbühel, Tyrol.

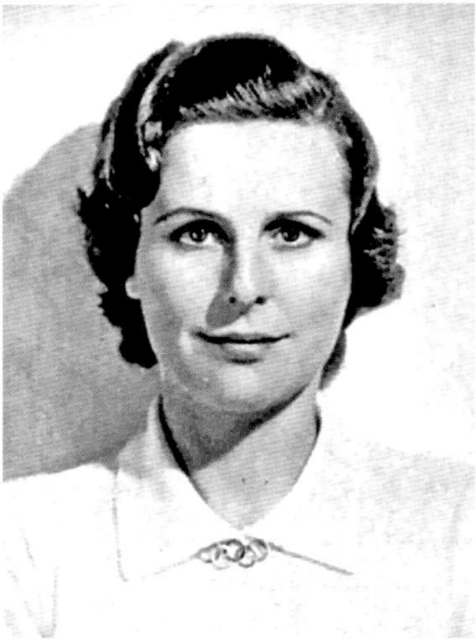

Leni Riefenstahl ca. 1936

"She gave me the usual song and dance," Schulberg recalled in a taped interview. "She said, 'Of course, you know, I'm really so misunderstood. I'm not political.'" Schulberg then drove Riefenstahl to Nuremberg in an open vehicle, where she identified war criminals in film footage.

Schulberg's brother, Stuart, was also in the OSS. Their team worked through some 10 million feet of Nazi film to create a four-hour documentary used at the Nuremberg trials.

Following the war, Seymour returned to Philadelphia and a house in Upper Makefield Township, before purchasing a home in 1947 on US-202 and Lower York Road, New Hope, Pennsylvania. He lived there with his wife, Victoria Anderson, and their three children until 1954. During this period Schulberg published his second novel, *The Harder They Fall* (1947), which was later made into a 1956 movie with Humphrey Bogart.

In 1951 Schulberg was called to testify by the House Committee on Un-American Activities as a friendly witness. He had joined the CPUSA in 1934 at the age of 20 but severed ties six years later when pressured to conform his writing to communist doctrine and after Stalin agreed to a pact with Hitler.

"They say that you testified against your friends, but once they supported the party against me, even though I did have some personal attachments, they were really no longer my friends," he said years later in an interview. "And I felt that if they cared about real freedom of speech, they should have stood up for me when I was fighting the party." Years later, he claimed the Red Scare of the senator Joseph McCarthy era represented a greater threat than the communists did to the United States, though the party represented a threat to freedom of speech.

Schulberg's greatest success came in 1954 with the release of *On the Waterfront*, which exposed corruption in the world of longshoremen. The film won eight Academy Awards, including one for best screenplay.

87. THE FAVORITE SON WAS A SOVIET SPY

MAP 10 ➤ **Laird Lichtenwalner recruitment:** Swarthmore College, 500 College Avenue, Swarthmore, Pennsylvania

Born into a prominent family living at 25 South Fourth Street, Emmaus, Pennsylvania, Laird Lichtenwalner became a standout student and athlete,

Once a football star at Swarthmore College (pictured here), Laird Lichtenwalner, also known as Stephen Laird, became a respected reporter for national publications such as *Time* magazine. He was likely recruited by Soviet intelligence while a student at Swarthmore, but his secret was not revealed until after his death.

graduating from Swarthmore in 1936 with a degree in political science and varsity letters in football, basketball, and lacrosse. Said to be inspired by Vincent Sheean's popular book *Personal History*, which his dentist father gave to him, Laird set his sights on a career in journalism.

SWARTHMORE'S FRESHMAN SPY

Oleg Troyanovsky, who was likely involved in Swarthmore classmate Stephen Laird's recruitment as a Soviet spy, would have had connections to Soviet intelligence. He attended the American School in Japan, where his father was posted, and then the Sidwell Friends School in Washington, DC, while his father became the USSR's ambassador to the United States. After a freshman year at Swarthmore in the 1930s, Oleg completed his education at the Moscow Institute for Foreign Languages and Moscow University. At the start of World War II, the younger Troyanovsky was working for TASS, the Soviet news service, which provided a traditional cover for Soviet spies, and eventually became a high-profile diplomat. Troyanovsky's public résumé includes a reference to two years spent in intelligence prior to entering the Soviet diplomatic corps in 1944.

After a number of foreign postings, including in Japan, he was named to the USSR's top spot at the United Nations in 1977. Troyanovsky developed a reputation at the UN as a genial, smiling diplomat, given to commenting on American stereotypes of Soviets as dour apparatchiks. Speaking lightly accented English, he exuded a suave, unflappable demeanor. When Maoists, posing as photographers, splashed him with red paint, he was reported to have quipped, "Better red than dead."

Oleg Troyanovsky (center) attended multiple American schools while his diplomat father was posted in the United States. He later held Soviet government positions that involved intelligence responsibilities

After taking a job as a reporter for the local *Chester (PA) Times*, Lichtenwalner changed his name to the more pronounceable Stephen Laird. He moved to New York to work for *Fortune* magazine in 1937 and *Time* magazine in 1940, and was reputed to be Washington's youngest correspondent.

The press in Chester recorded each step of the hometown son's meteoric rise in journalism, enthusiastically announcing his selection as *Time*'s foreign correspondent in Berlin and then London. During a brief stint as a Hollywood producer for RKO from 1944 to 1945, he was reported to be developing a film titled *A Palace on Main Street* set in Emmaus that apparently was never produced. A job at the United Nations (UN) followed, then a short stay at *Newsweek*, before he joined CBS at the invitation of Edward R. Murrow. That job saw him assigned to a variety of foreign postings, including Poland, London, and Geneva, between 1946 and 1951.

What none of his friends or coworkers could have guessed was that Laird was a Soviet spy code-named YUN. Possibly he was recruited while still at Swarthmore, where the football coach had assigned him to tutor fellow player Oleg Troyanovsky, the son of Aleksandr A. Troyanovsky, the first Soviet ambassador to the United States. Decades later, Laird's pupil served as the Soviets' representative to the UN from 1977 to 1986.

By whatever means he became a clandestine agent, Laird was no doubt seen as a prize for Soviet intelligence. His job at *Time* magazine, whose founder, Henry Luce, was an ardent anti-communist, would have put him in the center of American politics with regular access to policy makers. The CBS assignments also enabled his access to overseas intelligence.

Laird returned briefly to Pennsylvania at the end of his career, settling near Swarthmore; then he returned to Europe, where he died in Chartes, France, in 1990. Five years later he was identified by the VENONA intercepts as having been a Soviet spy.

88. THE YORKSHIREMAN WHO BROUGHT BRITAIN'S FIGHT TO AMERICA

MAP 11 ➤ **Springhouse Farm:** 2184 Springhouse Lane, Quakertown, Pennsylvania

Eric Knight remained proud of his British and Yorkshire roots throughout an eventful life. Born in 1897, he went to work at age 10; then, barely a teen, he immigrated to Canada before moving to the United States. He was a laborer in a Philadelphia lumberyard prior to winning a scholarship to the prestigious Boston Latin School in Massachusetts.

During World War I, Knight served in the Canadian Light Infantry, fighting in numerous battles, including the Second Battle of the Somme. After the war, he returned to Philadelphia, rented an apartment at 222 Spruce Street, and worked at Philadelphia's *Public Ledger*. There he became one of the nation's first movie reviewers. After working briefly as a Hollywood screenwriter,

Knight produced a string of successful novels. They included *Song on Your Bugles* (1936), which depicted Northern England's working class, and, writing under the pseudonym Richard Hallas, the 1940 hard-boiled detective classic, *You Play the Black and the Red Comes Up.*

When World War II began, Knight was living comfortably at Springhouse Farm, 2184 Springhouse Lane, Quakertown, Pennsylvania. At Springhouse he adopted Toots, the runt of a litter of cross-collie pups that would inspire him to write *Lassie Come-Home*. The book, published in 1940, became an instant best seller. As a celebrity author, Knight then produced a series of books and lectures promoting the British fight against Germany to combat the isolationist mood in the United States. His novel *This Above All* (1941) was made into a movie with Tyrone Power and Joan Fontaine a year later. The internationally acclaimed motion picture director Frank Capra recruited Knight as one of the primary screenwriters for seven US government films in the series called *Why We Fight*. The films were produced for the Office of War Information, a component of the Office of Strategic Services.

The degree to which Knight was involved with either British or American intelligence activity remains unclear, though Greg Christie, author of *Knight: Yorkshireman, Storyteller, Spy* (2018), concluded there may have been contact during a 1938 trip to England. Thereafter, Knight became a well-known face among Washington's senior government officials, often attending meetings at President Roosevelt's home in Hyde Park, New York. His personal interest in spying is evident in a film treatment he proposed to Fox Film in the mid-1930s. The never-produced treatment would have depicted a young Belgian girl, played by the famous child actress Shirley Temple, operating as a courageous courier for secret Allied intelligence during World War I.

Knight's last published work was a handbook for American servicemen heading to Britain. Called *A Short Guide to Britain*, the pamphlet offered advice to American soldiers on how to understand and cooperate with their British counterparts. Its 38 pages included many tips, such as, "The British Are Tough. Don't be misled by the British tendency to be soft-spoken and polite. If they need

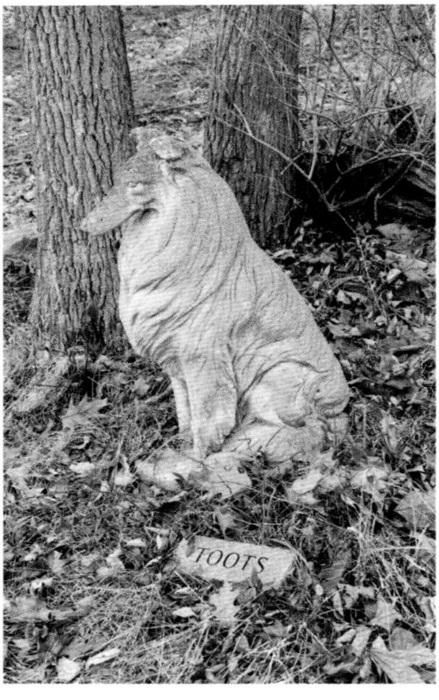

The international classic *Lassie Come Home* written by Eric Knight is based on the author's beloved collie, Toots. A memorial remembering Toots stands in the woods at Springhouse Farm.

THE WRITER WAS A SPY

John L. Spivak developed the reputation of a crusading socialist journalist in the post–World War I decades while working at a variety of American newspapers including the *New York Sun*, *New York Call*, International News Service, and far-left periodicals such as *New Masses*. He wrote exposés on the Ku Klux Klan, corrupt unions, robber barons, and Nazis, and his books, which covered much of the same ground, reported on the living conditions for African American prisoners in the south, the corruption of politicians, and the threat of anti-Semitism.

Spivak was also a Soviet agent code-named GRIN. Identified as a spy in decrypted intercepts of Soviet intelligence communications during World War II, he spied on the Trotskyites in the 1930s and apparently worked with Soviet spymaster Jacob Golos in New York. Spivak provided the Soviets with information he collected as a reporter, recruited other agents, and acted as a courier. In one operation, Spivak was said to have involved labor lawyer Leon Josephson in the burglary of the New York law offices of O. John Rogge, the attorney for Manhattan Project spy David Greenglass. The pair photographed confidential documents and passed the material to Rosenberg sympathizers in France for publication and replay in the United States.

Crusading journalist and spy John L. Spivak aligned with the Trotsky wing of the Communist Party so he could spy on them for his Moscow controllers.

During the 1950s, while living on Church Road, Perkasie, Pennsylvania, and using pen names, Spivak authored articles for numerous magazines. A June 1953 article in *Esquire*, "The Three Last Wide-Open Towns," and an April 1958 *Better Homes & Gardens* feature, "A Town Where the Teacher Is the Apple of All Eyes!," were written under the name Monroe Fry. "Sex Orgies in Philadelphia High Society" appeared in the October 1957 issue of *Fury* under the name William Blaise.

In 1967 Spivak published his autobiography, *A Man in His Time*. He briefly retired to Florida but returned to south Philadelphia following the death of his wife, Mabel, in 1980 and died at age 84 the following year at Temple University Hospital.

to be, they can be plenty tough. The English language didn't spread across the oceans and over the mountains and jungles and swamps of the world because these people were panty-waists." There were sections on cultural and culinary differences such as beverages. "The British don't know how to make a good cup of coffee. You [Americans] don't know how to make a good cup of tea. It's an even swap."

Knight, then an army major headed to the Middle East, died on January 21, 1943, in the crash of a C-54 military transport in Dutch Guiana (now Suriname). Thirty-five military and civilian personnel were killed, including FBI special agent P. E. Foxworth. Knight's mission was to establish a branch of the Armed Forces Radio in Cairo.

89. BED AND BREAKFAST SPY

MAP 11 ➤ **Hede Massing residence:** 1767 Country Lane, Quakertown, Pennsylvania

Onetime Soviet spy Hede Massing operated a country bed and breakfast business in this house north of Philadelphia.

Hede Massing (also known as Hede Tune, Hede Eisler, and Hede Gumperz) was a redheaded Viennese actress with a dramatic flair that extended to espionage. Trained by Soviet master spy Ignace Reiss in the 1920s, Massing was a keen judge of human frailty and an apt student of tradecraft, a combination that made her an effective recruiter. Code-named REDHEAD, she operated in New York and multiple cities in Europe throughout the 1920s and early 1930s. Along the way she crossed paths with a virtual who's who of Soviet spies, including Vassili Zarubin, Boris Bazarov, Joszef Peter, Earl Browder, Richard Sorge, Gerhart Eisler, Paul Massing, Noel Field, and Alger Hiss.

By 1938, at the height of Stalin's purges, Massing was a US citizen. She had quit spying, a risky move that she somehow survived, and moved to the quiet of Haycock Township with her husband, Paul. The couple rented a 120-acre farm near the marina in Lake Nockamixon and then purchased a smaller property with a large stone house at 1767 Country Lane, Quakertown, Pennsylvania. They converted the latter to a bed and breakfast business.

Following questioning by the FBI in the late 1940s, Massing became a confidential informant for the US government. Among her notable contributions was testimony corroborating Whittaker Chambers's accusations that named Alger Hiss as a Soviet spy. She also testified against Hiss in his second perjury trial, which ended with his conviction and five-year prison sentence.

After the Hiss trial, she returned to New York to write her memoirs, which she titled *This Deception*. The *Philadelphia Inquirer* reported the book was scrapped by its original publisher, Farrar, Straus and Young, because Massing refused to delete a chapter on former State Department official and suspected spy Laurence Duggan, who either jumped or was pushed from his midtown New York office window in 1948. The publisher, citing concerns for Duggan's widow and children, could not persuade Massing to relent in her assertion of Duggan's espionage. The now-defunct publisher Duell, Sloan and Pearce, bought the rights to the manuscript in March 1951 and published the book with the chapter intact. Massing died in 1981 in her home on Washington Square in New York.

90. SHE FOOLED EVERYONE

MAP 10 ➤ **Josephine Truslow Adams:** Swarthmore College, 500 College Avenue, Swarthmore, Pennsylvania

A strange episode of American-Soviet espionage began in 1940 at Swarthmore College, 500 College Avenue, Swarthmore, Pennsylvania. There, Josephine Truslow Adams, an art teacher and descendant of America's second and sixth presidents, was approached by Esther Lape, a friend of Eleanor Roosevelt's, to paint a portrait of the First Lady as a gift. Roosevelt briefly visited the college in 1941, during which time she met Adams. Although reputed to be a member of the Daughters of the American Revolution (DAR), Adams was a longtime supporter of radical causes and headed the Philadelphia chapter of the Descendants of the American Revolution, a Soviet front organization.

Earl Browder

Adams testified before a House judiciary subcommittee on February

10, 1941, in opposition to wiretapping by law enforcement and was fired by the college a month later only to become a local cause célèbre. A 1941 letter to Eleanor Roosevelt received a personal reply from the First Lady, but subsequent letters either went unanswered or were shunted off to others. Adams also lobbied against the imprisonment of CPUSA head Earl Browder on passport fraud charges, and the two met at a Fourth of July communist celebration following his release from prison in 1942.

Whether Adams's efforts contributed to Browder's eventual release or not is unknown. His cause was a popular one among the far left, and his supporters included several well-known people. However, her claims seemed to have convinced Browder as well as the Soviet intelligence apparatus that she was close to the Roosevelts. A secret cable to Moscow sent in July 1943 by the GRU *rezident* (chief of station) in New York City, Pavel Mikhailov, references a woman (almost certainly Adams) "from an aristocratic family who has known the President and his wife for a long time, evidently a secret member of the communist party." A year later, another secret cable to Moscow reported that Browder asked Adams to meet with FDR at Hyde Park and the White House.

Adams somehow convinced Browder of her nearly unlimited access to the president and assured him that his letters went directly to FDR. She also relayed to Browder what she claimed were FDR's responses. The deception was fantasy, not espionage, as there is no record she ever visited with the president or the First Lady. Adams's letters, retained by the Franklin D. Roosevelt Library's archives, are rambling and nearly incoherent, with text extending up and down the margins.

In the 1950s Adams volunteered to provide evidence of a communist conspiracy to the FBI. The agents who interviewed her in the New York City office found her unreliable and dropped the matter. When she wrote to the Senate's Subcommittee on Internal Security in 1957 and offered to reveal her role in the Roosevelt-Soviet conspiracy, she was invited to testify. Only portions of her testimony were released, but those were enough to push her back into the spotlight as someone who could reveal FDR as a secret Soviet agent. This landed her a publishing deal with David McKay, the onetime comic book publisher, for a book titled *I was Roosevelt's Secret Emissary*. However, the prospective ghostwriter, Isaac Don Levine, who had written for the Soviet defector Walter Krivitsky, backed out of the project following his review of what Adams claimed was correspondence with FDR. The book never appeared.

Growing increasingly unstable, Adams was institutionalized first in New York and then at the Norristown Asylum for the Insane (today Norristown State Hospital), 1001 Sterigere Street, Norristown, Pennsylvania. She there died in 1969.

TARGETING ANCESTRY

Although its name seemed to denote a respectable organization composed of respectable people, the Descendants of the American Revolution was one of dozens of front organizations that the Soviet Union established in the United States prior to World War II. Founded in 1937, descendants sought to attract members from the established Daughters of the American Revolution and the Sons of the American Revolution. Branches of the descendants' organization were established in New York, Philadelphia, and Boston.

"This move is symptomatic of the growing dissension in the D.A.R. ranks," said Mrs. Edward Sohier Welch, a member of the Boston branch of descendants. "There is a feeling that the D.A.R. has become too hide-bound and reactionary, and has forgotten the principles of democracy for which their ancestors fought." As was the case of most Soviet front groups, many of the members were likely unaware of organization's purpose or its source of funding.

During her time as an active member of descendants, Josephine Adams was a vocal critic of US government legislation and policies that were opposed to Soviet interests. One example was her objection to the military draft after the Soviet Union and Nazi Germany signed a nonaggression pact.

91. SPIES IN THE "VILLAGE"

MAP 8 ➤ **Frankford Arsenal:** Tacony and Bridge Streets

For nearly three years beginning in 1993, Alexander Vassiliev—a former officer in the KGB and now a journalist—was given controlled access to the organization's closed intelligence archive as he researched a book on Soviet spying operations in the United States. He eventually compiled some 1,115 pages of densely written notes in eight notebooks covering the 1930s and

Alexander Vassiliev

The sprawling Frankford Arsenal complex, with a history beginning in the early 1800s, was a target of Cold War Soviet spies. The arsenal closed in the late 1970s.

FOR THE MONEY

The Soviets were not the first to have seen Frankford Arsenal as an attractive target. On December 4, 1917, at the height of World War I, William Lebwoski, a pro-German employee at the facility, was apprehended for "spoiling shells." Lebwoski was quoted as telling the arresting officer, "Why should I wrap paper around fuses when I get more money for not doing it?" Thousands of defective shells had been shipped to Gen. John J. Pershing's army in France as a result of Lebwoski's actions.

1940s, resulting in a collection of many previously unrevealed names and details of Soviet operations and recruited agents in America. His research produced tantalizing clues about espionage in Philadelphia (code name VILLAGE) and some of its resident spies who escaped discovery by US counterintelligence.

Included in the Russian notebooks is the name Lester Hutm, who is described as a former employee of the Frankford Arsenal at Tacony and Bridge Streets. During World War II, Frankford was a major munitions supplier to the US war effort and naturally a high-value target for Soviet intelligence. Hutm was given the code name 115TH and would have been in a position to supply information of great value for the USSR's ongoing and possible future war preparations.

The notebooks also mention Alexander Portnov (code name ALI), identified as a Russian sculptor whose home is referred to as BASE (*BAZA*). This is likely Philadelphia sculptor Alexander Portnoff, whose work was widely exhibited and now appears in the collections of numerous museums, including the Philadelphia Museum of Art, 26th Street and Benjamin Franklin Parkway. Portnoff, whose home was at 908 Clinton Street, became a naturalized US citizen in 1915 and died in 1949 at age 62.

A third Philadelphian, code-named 113TH, was Harry Rosenthal, an employee of an unidentified insurance company. Also included in one World War II–era Soviet intelligence cable is an inquiry about the potential for recruiting Marion Schultz (code name LAVA), identified as a Russian-born mechanic working in the Philadelphia Naval Shipyard who was active in Russian War Relief and Slavic organizations. The mystery of what these spies accomplished remains.

92. TWO SPY LEGENDS MEET IN PHILADELPHIA

MAP 2 ➤ **Hyatt at the Bellevue:** 200 South Broad Street

One the most significant "recruitments" for US intelligence occurred at the end of the 1940 Republican National Convention held at the Philadelphia Municipal Auditorium and Convention Hall. Wendell Willkie, a former Democrat with more business than political experience, won the nomination on the sixth ballot. Allen Dulles, a delegate from New York, supported Thomas Dewey, a more traditional Republican candidate and seasoned politician.

Dulles was moving through a crowded hotel lobby, likely the Bellevue-Stratford Hotel (today the Hyatt at The Bellevue) at 200 South Broad Street, when he was approached by William "Wild Bill" Donovan. The two had known each other in New York, and at Donovan's suggestion, the pair moved their conversation to the hotel's bar. There, Donovan revealed his plans for an intelligence organization in anticipation of when America inevitably would enter World War II. Donovan had already made fact-finding trips to Europe at President Roosevelt's request and was certain an intelligence organization was needed. Dulles, who had gained international experience after World War I as a diplomat and later with his Wall Street law firm, Sullivan and Cromwell, seemed suited to the work. According to Stephen Kinzer in *The Brothers: John Foster Dulles, Allen Dulles, and Their Secret World War*, Dulles responded, "When do you want me to start?"

Allen Dulles

William J. Donovan

"As soon as the election's over," Donovan was said to have answered. "I'll call you."

By July 1941 Donovan was heading a new intelligence organization, the Office of the Coordinator of Information (COI), which he would restructure the following year as the Office of Strategic Services. The call to Dulles came soon after the attack on Pearl Harbor from a mutual friend, David K. E. Bruce. Dulles agreed and initially worked out of New York before being posted to Bern, Switzerland, as Agent 110.

Following the war, Dulles returned to New York to practice law and participated as a consultant to study the new Central Intelligence Agency before joining it on January 4, 1951, as the deputy director of plans. He subsequently became the longest-serving director of central intelligence (DCI), holding that position from 1953 to 1961.

LOST IN TRANSLATION

As a young diplomat in Constantinople (today Istanbul) in the 1920s, Allen Dulles exhibited an early affinity for espionage. There, he monitored Soviet radio traffic and sent to Washington detailed reports of the Bolsheviks' intentions beyond Moscow. At the time the United States, lacking a national intelligence organization, relied primarily on diplomats for such reporting, but Dulles's operation was canceled because of the cost of translators.

The future DCI also became embroiled in the *Protocols of the Learned Elders of Zion* controversy. The tract had been circulating for a few years, inflaming anti-Semitism in Europe and the United States. Philip Graves, a reporter for *The Times* of London, uncovered a French text that bore a striking resemblance to the *Protocols*, though it made no reference to Jews. The text's publication date, confirmed as 1856, proved the *Protocols* was a plagiarized fraud. Dulles sent a dispatch to Washington on August 31, 1921, along with Graves's account that had appeared in *The Times* on August 16–18, 1921. Dulles's message, which reached Washington on September 22, was circulated, but no action was taken.

93. THE WAITER WHO BECAME CHAIRMAN

MAP 4 ➤ **John Jay McCloy residence:** 2136 North 19th Street

As a child, John Jay McCloy lived at 2136 North 19th Street and then 874 North 20th Street. After the death of her husband, McCloy's mother worked as a hairdresser, a job that enabled her to provide a solid education for the children. McCloy, a brilliant student, was accepted at Amherst College, where he worked as a waiter to pay expenses, and then attended Harvard Law School. His studies were interrupted by World War I and service as a captain in field artillery. After the war, McCloy returned to Harvard Law, graduating in 1921.

John J. McCloy, although born into humble beginnings, became president of the World Bank and served in official capacities under seven presidents. His first exposure to espionage was as an investigator of the Black Tom Island explosions. Later he was instrumental in the formation of the OSS.

From there he moved to New York and practiced law in a number of Wall Street firms, including Cravath, de Gersdoff, Swaine, and Wood (today

Cravath, Swaine, and Moore LLP). He likely experienced a taste of secret operations by representing one client, Bethlehem Steel, in the 1920s while litigating the 1916 Black Tom Island sabotage explosion. The case ran for nearly a decade as McCloy accumulated evidence to prove the explosion was an act of sabotage. In a trial before the German-American Mixed Claims Commission in the Hague, McCloy prevailed when the court found Germany responsible for the devastating blast and issued a $50 million judgment.

John J. McCloy

Brought to Washington as a consultant in 1940 by Secretary of War Henry Stimson, McCloy was later appointed assistant secretary of war. He successfully advocated for legislation supporting the Allies in initiatives such as the Lend-Lease Act and later headed the program that led to the internment of 120,000 Japanese Americans during World War II.

During his time in Washington, McCloy became convinced of the need for an intelligence organization in the lead-up to America's entrance into the war. "I am somewhat obsessed with the necessity of establishing a propaganda or information bureau for our defense. . . . It is more essential than artillery," he wrote New York City mayor Fiorella La Guardia in 1941. McCloy had powerful allies in his efforts. William Donovan, a World War I Medal of Honor recipient and Wall Street lawyer, was also lobbying the president for a centralized civilian intelligence component, and British intelligence officer Ian Fleming was advising Donovan to take on McCloy as his "chief of staff" for such an endeavor.

Donovan and McCloy met in the spring of 1941, according to the latter's biographer. Although no notes of the meeting were made, McCloy is credited with proposing the new intelligence entity be named the Office of the Coordinator of Information rather than Donovan's suggested Coordinator of Defense Information. McCloy then drafted the orders that formed the COI, which later became the OSS. Buried within the document was an expansionist phrase that enabled the new organization to carry out any "supplementary activities" requested by the president.

The concept received formal backing from FDR in July 1941. Among the duties assigned to the COI were to "collect and analyze all information and data, which may bear upon national security: to correlate such information and data, and to make such information and data available to the President and to such departments and officials of the Government as the President may determine; and to carry out, when requested by the President, such supplementary activities as may facilitate the securing of information important for national security not now available to the Government."

Almost a year later, in June 1942, the COI was transformed into the OSS. That organization laid the groundwork for the postwar CIA.

McCloy was appointed president of the World Bank in 1947 and served as the military governor and high commissioner for Germany in 1949. In that post, he oversaw a budget of some $1 billion to rebuild Germany's government and industry. The *New York Times* quoted McCloy in his March 12, 1989, obituary as saying, "I had the powers of a dictator as High Commissioner of Allied Forces in West Germany, but I think I was a benevolent dictator. I think the rebuilding came off very well, with no significant problems. It wasn't a matter of ordering things done so much as using orderly persuasion with the Germans."

He later held office as the chairman of the Chase National Bank (today JP Morgan Chase), the chairman of the Ford Foundation, a disarmament adviser and negotiator to President John F. Kennedy, and the chairman of the General Advisory Committee on Disarmament of the US Arms Control and Disarmament Agency.

Over the years of a long career, McCloy served seven presidents, both Democrat and Republican. "I saw my public service in terms of getting things done," McCloy was quoted as saying in a 1989 *New York Times* article. "I never considered myself a politician, but rather a lawyer, so the question I asked myself in the various jobs I had was, 'What should we do to solve the problem at hand?' Then I tried to proceed accordingly."

McCloy died March 11, 1989, at age 93.

94. THE BEST, BRIGHTEST, AND UNORTHODOX FOR THE OSS

MAP 9 ➤ **William P. Davis III residence:** 111 Ringwood Road, Bryn Mawr, Pennsylvania

When William "Wild Bill" Donovan recruited officers for the Office of Strategic Services, he cast a wide net among the nation's intelligentsia and business communities. The United States was new to the international spy game, and Donovan knew he needed unorthodox thinking from the brightest minds. To this end, Donovan sought out leading American businessmen and scholars for the OSS.

William P. Davis III, an officer of the OSS, worked closely with the British Special Operations Executive during World War II. Following the war, like most others, Davis returned to his previous profession as a Philadelphia banker.

Donovan came under early criticism for hiring what many considered too many bankers and lawyers for his new intelligence organization. He responded, "You know, these bankers and corporation lawyers make wonderful

second-story men." Donovan understood that businessmen of the day who were involved with international trade came with valuable established skills such as a proficiency in foreign languages, a knowledge of other cultures, and many contacts across the globe. They also possessed organizational skills that were vital to assembling a wartime intelligence organization as quickly as possible.

One business recruit was Philadelphia banker William P. Davis III, who attended Chestnut Hill Academy and William Penn Charter School before graduating from Princeton. He then became a banker with a junior-level job at the First Pennsylvania Banking and Trust Company and resided at 111 Ringwood Road, Bryn Mawr, Pennsylvania.

Davis was selected to head special operations for the OSS and coordinated with the British Special Operations Executive in Algiers to create a Special Operations Center that worked with the French Free Forces. Subsequently he became involved with guerrilla forces in Italy and China, and by the end of the war he held the rank of colonel. For his actions, he received the Legion of Merit with oak leaf cluster and the Order of the British Empire. Davis then returned to his job at First Pennsylvania Banking and Trust Company, eventually rising to become vice-chairman of the board before retiring in 1974.

Only at the disbanding of the OSS did Donovan publicly acknowledge the true makeup of his organization, which also included car mechanics, bartenders, career criminals, artists, and actors. Among the notables were film star Sterling Hayden, African American future Nobel laureate Ralph Bunche, and college gridiron-star-turned-professional-wrestler Joseph "Jumping Joe" Savoldi.

Author Corey Ford in *Donovan of the OSS* described the scene as Donovan addressed the assembled OSS veterans at the Riverside Stadium Skating Rink in Washington, DC, on September 28, 1945. "We have come to the end of an unusual experiment. This experiment was to determine whether a group of Americans constituting a cross-section of racial origins, of abilities, temperaments and talents, could risk an encounter with the long-established and well-trained enemy organizations. How well that experiment has succeeded is measured by your accomplishments and by the recognition of your achievements." The significance of those accomplishments was affirmed two years later in the creation of the Central Intelligence Agency.

95. WHEN HISTORIANS MAKE HISTORY

MAP 9 ➤ **Conyers Read home:** Wistar Road, Villanova, Pennsylvania

Among the first members of the new COI staff chosen by William Donovan was Conyers Read, a historian of the Elizabethan era from Philadelphia. His merchant father, William F. Read, sold women's clothing under the name Lansdowne through his retail outlet, William F. Read and Sons, 211 Chestnut Street, and in larger department stores.

After graduating from Central High School, 1700 West Olney Avenue, the younger Read attended Harvard, where he described himself as being "in danger of falling between a college chair and an office stool." He then went to Balliol College at Oxford, returned to Harvard for a doctorate, and eventually became an instructor at the University of Chicago. Following service with the Red Cross during World War I, he helped run the family business for several years before returning to academia.

Conyers Read

Once World War II began in Europe, Read became active in the interventionist movement, heading the Pennsylvania branch of the Committee to Defend America by Aiding the Allies as well as the Fight for Freedom Committee. Whether he was aware of the connection these organizations had to British intelligence is unknown. Supported financially or directed by British intelligence, the organizations were formed to counter the popular America First Committee, which was partially funded and directed by Germany.

From the COI, Read headed the British Empire Section of the OSS. Despite his lack of espionage experience, he possessed a remarkable understanding of British intelligence history. His three-volume work, *Mr. Secretary Walsingham and the Policy of Queen Elizabeth* (1925), was said to represent the definitive biography of Sir Francis Walsingham, Queen Elizabeth's spymaster. Donovan proposed that Read should write an official history of the OSS, but he never undertook the project.

Read also recruited other academics for the COI and OSS, some of whom became national and international figures. Among them was William L. Langer, a Bostonian Harvard professor with a specialty in the history of diplomacy. After the war, Langer joined the Central Intelligence Agency and formed the Office of National Estimates. Another Read recruit for the OSS was Ralph Bunche, then teaching at Howard University. When the war ended, Bunche joined the US Department of State and was one of the drafters of the United Nations Charter. In 1949 he headed successful negotiations between Israelis and Arabs to accept an armistice agreement for which he was awarded the 1950 Nobel Peace Prize.

Following the war, Read returned to academia, teaching English history at the University of Pennsylvania. He died in 1959 at his home on Wistar Road, Villanova, Pennsylvania, at the age of 78.

96. DESPERATE TECH MISSION

MAP I ➤ **American Philosophical Society:** 105 South Fifth Street

The Tizard mission, named for its lead scientist, Henry Tizard, was among the most secretive operations of World War II. A delegation of Britain's leading scientists was assembled to visit the United States in 1940 to solicit cooperation in developing new military technology. Radar, jet propulsion, gunsights, plastic explosives, and the atomic bomb were part of the agenda, but since America was still officially neutral, secrecy was essential.

In 1940 the American Philosophical Society hosted a lecture by Archibald V. Hill, a British scientist whose visit to the United States set the stage for wartime US-UK scientific collaboration.

In advance of the Tizard delegation, Archibald V. Hill (known as A. V. Hill), a Nobel laureate traveling under the auspices of the Royal Society, arrived in the States in March 1940 with a list of scientists, politicians, academics, and military personnel to contact. In addition to laying the groundwork for the Tizard mission, Hill was to ascertain the attitudes of military, scientific, and political leaders toward the war; to evaluate American technology as to its usefulness to the British cause; and to determine what Americans knew, if anything, about Britain's secret technologies.

Archibald V. Hill

Little information is available regarding Hill's trip. However, his lecture at the American Philosophical Society, 105 South Fifth Street, on April 20, 1940, may hold some clues as to his success. Attending the lecture at America's oldest scientific institution were scientists from RCA, demonstrating a new, high-powered microscope; Philip C. Jessup, professor of international law at Columbia University; Thomas Gates, president of the University of Pennsylvania; and Earle Radcliffe Caley, an assistant professor of chemistry at Princeton. Hill must have been pleased with the reception.

The Tizard mission, which took place in August 1940, was deemed a success. Tizard met with the newly formed National Defense Research Committee headed by Vannevar Bush to initiate a level of cooperation between Britain and the United States that would later be seen as unprecedented.

97. PROSECUTOR OF SPIES

MAP I ➤ **Law Firm of Biddle, Paul, and Jayne:** 505 Chestnut Street

Francis Biddle was raised at 2017 Pine Street in a family of privilege, attending the elite prep school the Haverford School outside of Philadelphia and the Groton School before entering Harvard and Harvard Law School. He became the private secretary to US Supreme Court justice Oliver Wendell Homes Jr. and then practiced law at the family firm of Biddle, Paul, and Jayne, 505 Chestnut Street.

Francis Biddle

Appointed US attorney general in 1941, an office he held until 1945, Biddle tracked pro-Soviet organizations and created what became known as the Biddle List, which included what he viewed as subversive groups, such as the CPUSA, the American Youth Congress, and the League of American Writers. Originally comprising 11 organizations, the list would eventually grow over the years to include some 90 groups.

Eight would-be Nazi saboteurs involved in OPERATION PASTORIUS were tried by a military tribunal in 1942. Six were executed; two received prison terms and were later deported.

In the 1942 case against eight German saboteurs, President Roosevelt directed the trial be conducted by a military tribunal, not a civilian court, and appointed Biddle as the prosecutor. According to Joseph E. Persico's *Roosevelt's Secret War: FDR and World War II Espionage*, the president was firm in his resolve, saying, "I want one thing clearly understood, Francis: I won't give them up. . . . I won't hand them over to any United States Marshal

THE BIDDLE AFFAIR

Francis Biddle's stiff manners during the Nuremberg trials were found off-putting by some Europeans. "Isn't it curious that the only aristocrat on the bench is an American?" British author Rebecca West told a colleague. West, assigned to cover the postwar criminal proceedings for the *New Yorker* magazine, knew Biddle from the time she had spent in Washington. Now in Germany, the pair began an affair, touring the countryside together, and West occasionally worked at Biddle's rented villa. Evidence of her affection at the time was a piece titled "Extraordinary Exile," which West wrote for the September 7, 1946, issue of the *New Yorker*. "Francis Biddle looks like a highly intelligent swan, occasionally flexing down to commune with a smaller waterfowl, for Sir Geoffrey Lawrence, English president of the court, who sits beside him, is much smaller, though of a dignity that keeps the German lawyers scuttling." Later the affair ended acrimoniously, with Biddle and West eventually returning home to their respective spouses.

armed with a writ of *habeas corpus*. Understand!" When the implementation of the tribunal was challenged, the US Supreme Court ruled in Biddle's favor. Six of the eight would-be saboteurs were eventually hanged, while the other two were imprisoned until the end of the war and deported to Germany.

After assuming the presidency upon Roosevelt's death, President Truman wanted to select his own cabinet members and asked for Biddle's resignation as attorney general in 1945. In *Truman*, David McCullough described an uncomfortable president making the request. When Biddle graciously acceded, he put his arm around the president and commented, "You see, it's not so hard." A short time later, Truman appointed Biddle a judge at the International Military Tribunal at Nuremberg.

Biddle died in 1968 and is buried in the St. Thomas Episcopal Church Cemetery, Bethlehem Pike and Camp Hill Road, Whitemarsh, Montgomery County, Pennsylvania.

98. VOLUNTEER PROTECTION

MAP 4 ➤ **Packard Motor Car Company Building:** 317–321 North Broad Street

During World War II Philadelphia was the home of the Volunteer Port Security Force (VPSF) of the US Coast Guard Temporary Reserve. The idea of the VPSF came to Philadelphians Donald Jenks, the assistant director of the Division of Railway Transport, Office of Defense Transportation, and Dimitri F. White, a former Russian army officer who served as the manager of the Philadelphia office of the Cunard White Star and as the chairman of an organization named the British Ministry of War Transport, Philadelphia Committee.

The Volunteer Port Security Force, established to prevent acts of wartime sabotage, was initially located in the Packard Motor Car Company Building on North Broad Street.

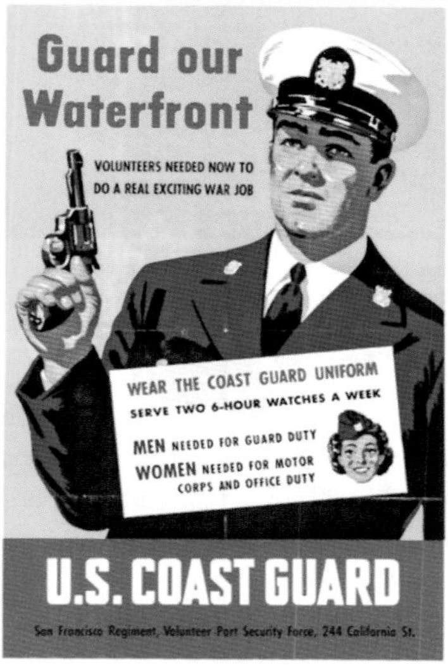

Initially called the Philadelphia Plan, the civilian security concept envisioned a group of trained volunteers guarding key wartime facilities in the United States. The first enrollees entered VPSF in September 1942 with a temporary headquarters at the Land Title Building, 100 Broad Street. By the end of the war, the headquarters had moved to the 16th floor of the Packard Motor Car Company Building (also known as the Press Building), 317–321 North Broad Street, and the VPSF had a presence at more than 20 US ports.

99. THE PHILADELPHIA EXPERIMENT

MAP 3 ➤ **Philadelphia Naval Shipyard:** 4701 Intrepid Avenue

The Philadelphia Naval Shipyard was a target of spies and saboteurs in every American war from 1776 through the Cold War.

Persistent conspiracy theories of government cover-ups center on what has been called the Philadelphia Experiment. Allegedly in 1943, "the government" applied principles advanced by Albert Einstein to render the USS *Eldridge* invisible in the Philadelphia Naval Shipyard. The tale may have originated in the mid-1950s from UFO enthusiast Morris K. Jessup's correspondence with a mysterious man known as Carlos

One enduring myth of World War II asserts that the US government had a project to make the destroyer USS *Eldridge* invisible.

Miguel Allende—also known as Carl M. Allen—who claimed to have witnessed the experiment.

Over the years, the story expanded from simply making the 306-foot destroyer invisible to include teleportation, time travel, parallel dimensions, and space aliens. In one telling, the ship was transported to New York harbor and, in another version, was said to suddenly appear in Norfolk, Virginia. Although neither the science nor the time line noted in the ship's log substantiate any of the claims, the fanciful tales persists, and a movie *The Philadelphia Experiment* (1984) was based on the fiction.

100. THE GOVERNOR SPY

MAP 9 ➤ **George H. Earle III residence:** Gray's Lane, Haverford, Pennsylvania

George H. Earle III, born in Haverford, Pennsylvania, in 1890, could trace his family lineage to the *Mayflower* and America's founders. Earle's more immediate family made its fortune in the sugar business, and he seemed destined to become one of Philadelphia's business titans.

George H. Earle III, 1937

Instead, Earle dropped out of Harvard in 1916 and joined General Pershing in his pursuit of Mexican general Francisco "Pancho" Villa. During World War I, as part of the US Navy, Earle commanded his family's yacht, the *Victor*, which served as a submarine hunter. Following the war, he headed Philadelphia's Flamingo Sugar Mills and sat on the boards of multiple companies. Living on the fashionable Gray's Lane in Haverford, he acquired a reputation as a polo-playing sportsman who flew his own airplane and raised prize-winning Doberman pinschers.

Earle joined Roosevelt's 1932 presidential campaign and served a short stint as a diplomat in Vienna in 1933. He is remembered for saying to the president of Austria, as he presented his diplomatic credentials, "I loathe the Nazis." Returning to Philadelphia in 1934, he ran for governor of Pennsylvania, won the election, and became the first Democrat to hold that office in more

During World War I, George H. Earle III commanded the family yacht, donating its service as the USS *Victor* and patrolling the East Coast in search of enemy vessels.

than 40 years. Governor Earle instituted policies that he called the Little New Deal, while detractors ridiculed him as "Sugar Boy." Throughout his four years in office, he acquired a reputation for literally tearing up copies of legislation he opposed.

Earle returned to diplomacy in 1940, this time in Bulgaria. As an outspoken opponent of Nazism, he created a diplomatic flap when he allegedly beat a confession out of a suspected German spy found in the American Embassy. On another occasion, he initiated a nightclub brawl when German officials requested the band play "Horst Wessel Lied" (Host Wessel song). Earle, according to reports, then requested "It's a Long Way to Tipperary," a popular song among Allied troops during World War I. A bottle was thrown, then another, followed by full-scale brawl. Roosevelt reportedly dubbed it the Battle of the Bottles in the Balkans and delighted in telling the story.

State Department officials requested Earle be prohibited from other postings, but Roosevelt commissioned him a lieutenant commander in the US Navy Reserve and sent him to Turkey as assistant naval attaché. Earle was to report what he learned directly to the president. In particular, he was to confirm or discredit rumors that key officers in the German army were ready to surrender given the right incentives. Before reaching Turkey, Earle sent word to a former acquaintance, Hungarian nightclub dancer Adrienne Molnar, to meet him in Istanbul. With Molnar playing the role of femme fatale, Earle was able to make contact with German intelligence officers.

His dispatches were filled with rumors, fictions, and some valuable information. A 1943 report asserted, "Turkish source of my last four telegrams gives me following just received. Devastating robot land torpedo plane attack on England will surely take place this month from Northern France and Belgium." What he was describing, apparently, was the first of the German rockets, the V-1, although his timetable was off, since the first of the so-called buzz bombs did not land in England until 1944. Another piece of information spoke of a threat of a "stratospheric" attack on America. This proved real when wartime decrypts detailed the potential of the Messerschmitt Me-264 long-range strategic bomber to reach the United States.

MUSIC TO SPY EARS

When President Roosevelt's personal spy George Earle arrived in Istanbul during World War II, espionage was so common in the city that as diplomats or suspected intelligence officers entered a nightclub, they might have been serenaded by the house band with the popular song "Boo Boo, Baby, I'm a Spy." One verse has these lyrics:

I'm so cocky I could swagger,
The things I know would make you stagger,
I'm ten percent cloak and ninety percent dagger,
Boo, boo, baby, I'm a spy!

101. KATYN MASSACRE

MAP 11 ➤ **Memorial site:** The National Shrine of Our Lady of Czestochowa Cemetery, 654 Ferry Road, Doylestown, Pennsylvania

Lavrentiy Beria

In 1944 President Roosevelt assigned Ambassador George Earle, the former governor of Pennsylvania, to investigate reports of the Katyn forest massacre during which thousands of Polish citizens—including military officers, intelligentsia, and members of the press—were found buried in mass graves. Polish prisoners from internment camps were transported to three sites and, on orders from Lavrentiy Beria, were executed in the spring of 1940 by the NKVD. The most notable site was the Katyn Forest outside Smolensk, Russia. The 22,000 victims included police officers, military personnel, and intelligentsia.

When the Germans discovered the mass graves in 1943, the Soviets blamed the German army, but Earle, through his intelligence contacts, soon became convinced the Soviets, not the Germans, were behind the mass murder. Roosevelt, seeking to keep the alliance with the Soviets on course for the duration of the war, ordered Earle's final report suppressed. He followed up with a desist order when Earle asked permission to publish it independently.

The president's refusal to release the damning report about a wartime ally created a breach between the two, resulting in Earle's posting to American Samoa, where he remained for the remainder of the war. Afterward he served as the assistant governor of the territory.

Earle, who died in 1974, did not live to see the evidence of Soviet guilt that mounted over the years. Not until 1992 was the Soviets' role officially acknowledged when Russian president Boris Yeltsin presented a copy of the execution order along with 41 other documents to the Polish president Lech Walesa.

At the National Shrine of Our Lady of Czestochowa Cemetery, 654 Ferry Road, Doylestown, Pennsylvania, a plaque commemorates and honors the victims of the massacre.

102. NAVAL INTELLIGENCE IN PHILADELPHIA

MAP 2 ➤ **Bankers' Security Building:** 1313–1317 Walnut Street

To strengthen the counterintelligence and investigative capabilities of the Office of Naval Intelligence (ONI) for matters involving merchant and military ships in 1919, then acting secretary of the navy Franklin Roosevelt created a structure called the District System. The ONI's district office in Philadelphia, officially known as DIO-4ND, was established in 1932 and headquartered in

The US Navy Yard, Philadelphia

Building 1 in the Philadelphia Naval Shipyard. Initially comprising a single officer, the staff doubled in 1937 with the addition of a civilian employee. When the war in Europe began, the District Office expanded, and ONI's District System emerged as an important national counterintelligence organization.

On November 1, 1940, Director of Naval Intelligence Rear Admiral Walter S. Anderson expanded the scope of the system's authority with a message to all DIO offices: "You are not restricted to any particular field of investigative effort by the delimitation agreement with the FBI." With exceptions, such as bank robbery and kidnapping, which continued to be investigated by the FBI, the DIO system now had authority to investigate a wide range of known or suspected criminal activities within its jurisdiction.

DIO-4ND's regional jurisdiction included Philadelphia's Naval Base and Shipyard and the US Naval Supply Depot, Air Station, and Air Test Center in Willow Grove, Pennsylvania. Additional agents were stationed in Pittsburgh and Harrisburg, as well as in Camden, New Jersey, and in Cleveland, Columbus, and Cincinnati, Ohio.

By 1941 and America's entrance into the war, DIO-4ND moved to the 14th floor of the Bankers' Security Building, 1313–1317 Walnut Street, and employed a staff of 202 officers and 118 enlisted men. The move, according to naval records, was necessary "to facilitate the acquisition of intelligence information from all sources and to locate DIO-4ND near other government agencies." After the end of the war, DIO-4ND was downsized and relocated to the Naval Shipyard, Building 734, where it remained until the component was abolished and replaced by the US Naval Investigative Service in March 1966.

103. SPIES ON THE WATERFRONT

MAP 8 ➤ Port of Philadelphia

US military ships embarking from New York ports during World War II forced the rerouting of foreign merchant ships to Philadelphia; thus, new security measures were needed at the Philadelphia port. Sailors on the incoming ships, even those from neutral countries, became a focus of counterintelligence operations. In 1943 the Office of Strategic Services received a tip from British Security Coordination that an Abwehr spy, José Laradogoitia, was aboard the Spanish freighter *Manuel Calvo*.

A Basque by birth, Laradogoitia would have appeared to be an ideal agent to send to America. As a teenager he had jumped ship and spent an extended period in the United States, primarily living with his brother in Idaho, until being deported for writing bad checks. Now, set to return to the States, he would come armed with training by German intelligence and outfitted with secret writing materials, three ciphers, and a Spanish accommodation address—Serafina Elorriaga, Hero 26, Bilbao, Spain.

Upon arrival, Laradogoitia was detained by the ONI officers and turned over to the FBI. He then agreed to become a double agent and, under direction of the FBI, began sending letters to the mail drop in Spain. Laradogoitia's efforts identified other German spies who were sent to resupply him with money or to steal military technology secrets.

104. SPY, FARMER, PITCHMAN

MAP 12 ➤ **David Ogilvy home:** 420 West King Street, Lancaster, Pennsylvania

David Olgivy

David Ogilvy, the legendary Madison Avenue ad man, was also a spy and Pennsylvania farmer. Based on training received from pollster George Gallup, the British-born Ogilvy first freelanced for the British Security Coordination, providing the British with US polling data on people's attitudes toward the war and Great Britain. He was then recruited as a full-time staffer to conduct confidential polls that proved vital for British intelligence to create anti-fascist messaging for American audiences.

Following the war, Ogilvy turned down a job with MI6 and resided at 420 West King Street, Lancaster, Pennsylvania, before purchasing a 100-acre farm in Salisbury Township, Pennsylvania, for $23,500. Ogilvy used a third party to bid on the property in the heart of the close-knit Amish community and dreamed of becoming a gentleman tobacco farmer.

As a farmer, Ogilvy met the same fate as his unsuccessful grandfather. "The years spent in Lancaster County were the richest of my life. But it became apparent that I could never earn my living as a farmer," he wrote in his memoir, *Blood, Brains & Beer*. "I worried too much. I worried about the price of tobacco and cabbage and wheat. . . . I was not physically strong enough to do the work. I found hoeing weeds and topping tobacco unbearably tedious. I was not sufficiently mechanical to keep the farm machinery in repair. I was ignorant of animal husbandry, which cannot be learned out of books."

At 38 years old and with $6,000 in the bank, Ogilvy moved to New York, where he established one of Madison Avenue's most prominent advertising firms, Ogilvy & Mather. Internationally famous campaigns created by agency include the "The Man in the Hathaway Shirt" and "Only Dove Is One Quarter Moisturizing Cream."

105. THE OSS EXPLORER

MAP 9 ➤ **Brooke Dolan II residence:** 417 Fishers Road, Bryn Mawr, Pennsylvania

Brooke Dolan II

Adventure-driven OSS officer Brooke Dolan II lived in this Philadelphia home.

Descended from one of Philadelphia's most notable families, Brooke Dolan II exhibited a taste for adventure early in life. While still in his twenties, he led two expeditions to Tibet and China to collect animal and plant specimens for the Philadelphia Academy of Natural Sciences (today the Academy of Natural Sciences of Drexel University). He returned from one trip with a Tibetan mastiff as a personal pet.

Dolan was recruited into the Office of Strategic Services in 1942 and returned with OSS officer Ilya Tolstoy, the grandson of the Russian author, to Tibet to establish contact with its government. During the successful discussions with Tibetan officials, the two became the first Americans to meet with the 14th Dalai Lama, Tenzin Gyatso. President Roosevelt's OSS emissaries

SCIENCE OR NONSENSE?

One of the men accompanying Dolan on his early expedition to Asia was Ernst Schäfer, a German national and ornithologist. In 1938 Schäfer led a separate German expedition into Tibet at the behest of Heinrich Himmler, head of the Schutzstaffel (Protection Squadron, or SS). While the expedition may have been cover for intelligence gathering, some have speculated that Schäfer's mission was related to occultism, which the Nazi elites were obsessed with at the time.

brought gifts when they visited the young Dalai Lama in Lhasa: a personal letter from the president, an autographed photo, and a gold Patek Philippe chronograph pocket watch (known as Reference 658) that also displayed the phases of the moon and the days of the week. In return, the Dalai Lama presented gifts for the president: a personal photograph, a scarf of honor, three Tibetan gold coins, and three hand-sewn *thangas* (religious tapestries or paintings). For their work, both Tolstoy and Dolan received the Legion of Merit.

Dolan subsequently transferred to the US Army Air Forces and was posted to Chungking (Chongqing), China, with the rank of captain. He died on August 19, 1945, and is buried in the National Memorial Cemetery of the Pacific, Honolulu, Hawaii.

When the Dalai Lama visited Washington, DC, in June 2016, he unexpectedly displayed the watch Dolan had delivered to him. The revelation resolved the mystery of the watch's whereabouts, a question whose answer had eluded timepiece historians for more than seven decades.

HELLO, DALAI!

In November 1979 the Dalai Lama was a guest at the Union Club in New York, where he watched a screening of the OSS film shot during Dolan and Tolstoy's 1942 Tibetan expedition. Described as a travelogue, the film was given to the Dalai Lama as a gesture of goodwill and friendship. The *New Yorker* reported on November 19, 1979, the Dalai Lama seemed to appreciate the movie. "Thank you very much," the holy man said through an interpreter. "It was an excellent film."

OSS officers Brooke Dolan (far left) and Ilya Tolstoy (third from left) traveled to Tibet to meet with the young Dalai Lama and gave him gifts from President Franklin Roosevelt.

■ 106. THE DEATH AND LIFE OF LOUIS KAHN

MAP 2 ➤ **Louis Kahn office:** 1501 Walnut Street

When renowned architect Louis Kahn died suddenly in a restroom of New York's Pennsylvania Station in 1974, authorities found notifying his family difficult. The Philadelphia address on his passport, 1501 Walnut Street, was a cluttered office above a cigar store. As it turned out, Kahn had not one but three families at separate addresses, and, at the time of his death, each family apparently assumed he was with one of the others.

Following his service in the OSS, Louis Kahn returned to Philadelphia to become a nationally honored architect.

The architect designed the Yale University Art Gallery; the Salk Institute; the Kimbell Art Museum in Fort Worth, Texas; the Jatiyo Sangsad Bhaban (National Assembly Building) in Dhaka, Bangladesh; and a business school in India, as well as multiple private homes; but he led a secretive private life. He grew up in poverty in Philadelphia's Northern Liberties neighborhood and was reported to have walked across the city to attend art school at the University of Pennsylvania. He eventually taught architecture there as well as at Yale, MIT, and Princeton.

Louis Kahn

During World War II, Kahn served in the Office of Strategic Services in its Visual Presentation Branch. Comprised of officers with creative minds in design and visual arts, the branch also included Buckminster Fuller, Walt Disney, Eero Saarinen, and Lewis Mumford. The work began as part of the OSS's short-lived predecessor organization, the Office of the Coordinator of Information, to create techniques for visual presentations of reports for the president and senior policy makers. By the end of the war,

"The sun never knew how great it was until it hit the side of a building."

—Louis Kahn

more than 100 designers, artists, editors, illustrators, engineers, and filmmakers made up the branch.

Following the disbanding of the OSS in September 1945, the Visual Presentation Branch was moved to the State Department, and most of its better-known civilians returned to private practice.

107. THE REAL INDIANA JONES?

MAP 6 ➤ **University of Pennsylvania Museum of Archaeology and Anthropology:** 3260 South Street

Indiana Jones, a swashbuckling academic and archaeologist who battled Nazis, thrilled moviegoers with daring deeds and narrow escapes. But was there a real-life Indiana Jones? The adventures of Rodney S. Young and his fellow archaeologists come close to those of Harrison Ford's character. Young joined the spy world with an Ivy League education from Princeton and Columbia University along with a specialty in Near Eastern archaeology. Born in 1907 into a wealthy New Jersey family, and as a scion of the Ballantine Ale fortune, he spent years at excavations in Greece uncovering the mysteries of the ancient world. At the start of World War II, he was the first American volunteer ambulance driver in Greece, driving an ambulance that he raised funds to buy. After being wounded during an air raid, he returned home to work for the Office of Strategic Services, America's fledgling intelligence operation; then he went to Cairo to oversee operations from 1944 to 1945 as head of the OSS Greek Desk.

Rodney S. Young may have been the "real Indiana Jones." The adventurous archaeologist commanded clandestine spy operations during World War II.

According to Susan Allen's *Classical Spies: American Archaeologists with the OSS in World War II Greece*, Young participated in nearly 60 missions throughout the region that involved intelligence gathering, sabotage, exfiltration, and support of guerrilla fighters. His agents were varied, but several were American archaeologists, including John Franklin Daniel III from the University of Pennsylvania.

After the war, Young took a position at the Mediterranean Section of the University of Pennsylvania Museum of Archaeology and Anthropology, and he rarely spoke of his wartime exploits. His more than two decades overseeing the museum's excavation at Gordium (sometimes called Gordion), not far from Ankara in Turkey, and as a professor and chairman of classical archaeology at the University of Pennsylvania earned him a place in archaeology history, not his work as a secret agent.

Carleton Stevens Coon

Rodney S. Young, archaeologist and spy, was the curator of the Mediterranean Section of the University of Pennsylvania Museum of Archaeology and Anthropology.

Young was not the only Indiana Jones type from Philadelphia. To his students at the University of Pennsylvania, Carleton Stevens Coon was a mild-mannered anthropologist with a background that stretched back to Harvard and fieldwork throughout North Africa. While still a teen, Coon had taught himself hieroglyphics, which eventually led him to the new field of anthropology. Recruited by the OSS during World War II, Coon collected tactical intelligence on enemy communications and transportation and recruited resistance fighters to wage guerrilla warfare in North Africa. To this end, Coon designed a plastic explosive molded in the shape of mule dung that he and his fighters scattered along desert roads to disable German vehicles.

What made archaeologists particularly attractive candidates as spies was their knowledge of local languages, customs, and terrain. In contrast to most American tourists, whose interests were primarily in visiting foreign capitals, archaeologists possessed detailed, hard-earned knowledge of remote outlying areas that often proved vital to war planning.

108. PRACTICING DECEPTION

MAP 4 ➤ **ITE Circuit Breaker Company:** North 19th and Hamilton Streets (site redeveloped)

Roger W. Hall must surely rank among the most colorful OSS officers. Along with his friend and fellow OSS officer William Colby, as the commanding officer of the Second Section, Norwegian Special Operations Group, he accepted the surrender of 10,000 German troops in Norway in 1945.

Earlier in his OSS service, as part of his operational training, Hall was directed to infiltrate the facility of a Philadelphia defense industry. He targeted a circuit breaker manufacturer, likely the ITE Circuit Breaker Company, North 19th and Hamilton Streets. According to Hall's 1957 memoir, *You're Stepping on My Cloak and Dagger*, he posed as Capt. Robert Hawthorne, a Purple Heart recipient with a noticeable limp. Recently returned from the front lines, Hawthorne was looking for a job. So convincing was his legend that the wounded veteran was invited to give an impromptu speech in the company cafeteria for the firm's war bond rally.

"My previous dramatic experience had been limited to one performance as The Dormouse in *Alice in Wonderland*, as rendered by Miss Mowery's Kindergarten, but it stood me in good stead," Hall wrote. According to his recollection of the five-minute speech, there wasn't a dry eye in the house, and he received a standing ovation along with a date with the daughter of one of the company's vice presidents. Although he was able to successfully infiltrate the plant, Hall's commanding officer was less than pleased when a glowing news report of his speech appeared in the next day's newspaper as well as the announcement that he had been hired by the firm's public relations department.

In contrast to Colby, who would rise to become the DCI, Hall left the intelligence field following the war. Despite Colby's invitations, the irascible Hall turned down repeated offers to join the CIA because he felt the agency was "too bureaucratic."

Spending much of his postwar career as a freelance writer and editor, Hall published dozens of stories and two novels—*All My Pretty Ones* (1959) about the fashion industry and the espionage thriller *19* (1969). He also did stints as a radio host and a sports announcer. However, he remains best known for his OSS memoir. Hall died on September 20, 2008, at his home at Brandywine Hundred, Wilmington, Delaware, at age 89.

109. THE "FATHER OF COMBAT SWIMMING"

MAP 6 ➤ **University of Pennsylvania Perelman School of Medicine:** 3400 Civic Center Boulevard

Christian J. Lambertsen

In 1939 a medical student from the University of Pennsylvania demonstrated a new type of compact underwater breathing apparatus for US Navy officials. The officers who witnessed the demonstration were unimpressed and dismissed the device. They already had approved underwater gear used for salvage work that included large brass helmets and hoses tethered to shipboard air compressors. What the student, Christian J. Lambertsen, created was radically different: it featured an oxygen supply that the diver wore on his back along with a lightweight and compact breathing device that covered his mouth and nose. He called it the Lambertsen Amphibious Respiratory Unit but later changed the name to the Self-Contained Underwater Breathing Apparatus (SCUBA).

The navy might not have cared for the invention, but the Office of Strategic Services was keenly interested. The rebreather component featured a

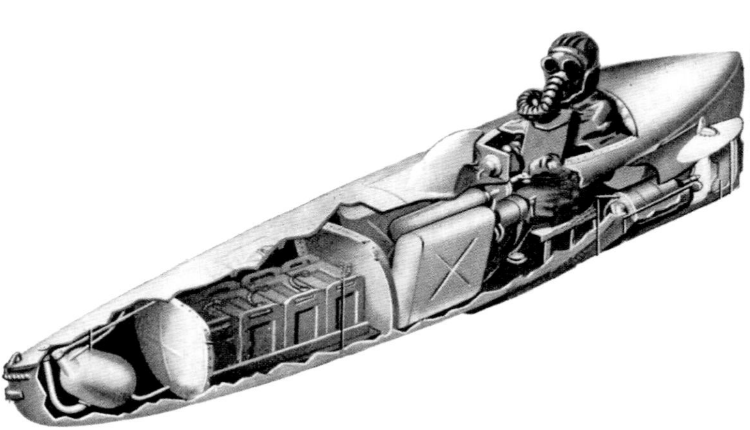

The Sleeping Beauty submarine technology anticipated the adventures of James Bond. The two-man submersible enabled clandestine underwater infiltration of protected waterways and harbors.

scrubber that eliminated carbon dioxide in an exhaled breath and returned it as oxygen to the diver. Thus, the system did not emit telltale bubbles on the water's surface to betray the presence of a diver.

The OSS recruited Lambertsen to train divers for secret missions. He saw action in Burma, where he accompanied commando teams using the new gear in clandestine dives to attach explosives to Japanese vessels. Lambertsen's rebreather was also used with one of the Allies' innovative secret devices, the Motorized Submersible Canoe, or "Sleeping Beauty" submarine, an early version of today's recreational diver propulsion vehicle.

Following the war, Dr. Lambertsen settled in Newtown Square, a suburb of Philadelphia; held a professorship at University of Pennsylvania's Perelman School of Medicine, 3400 Civic Center Boulevard; and continued to develop better SCUBA gear for navy special operations units through the 1980s. The "Father of Combat Swimming," as Lambertsen was called, died in 2011 and was buried at sea not far from the US Army Special Forces Underwater Operations School in Key West, Florida.

6

A COLD WAR AND BEYOND

(1948–Present)

The city that led the struggle to win America's freedom in the 18th century became a battleground of a new type of geopolitical conflict in the second half of the 20th century. Philadelphia's scientific and manufacturing companies played critical roles in projects essential to the Cold War and became targets of espionage. Intelligence organizations turned to technology for comparative advantage, tested the limits of engineering, redefined what was possible, and reshaped clandestine collection.

From the Quaker City came technology vital for the first reconnaissance satellite images, which opened a window into Soviet weapons systems and military capabilities otherwise shielded behind an iron curtain of secrecy. When Soviet submarines carrying nuclear missiles threatened to change the international balance of power, a Philadelphia shipyard produced critical equipment for what has been called America's "greatest covert action"—the clandestine recovery of a sunken Soviet sub with a payload of nuclear-tipped missiles lying three miles below the Pacific Ocean's surface.

Philadelphia also remained a center of more traditional espionage activities. Soviet intelligence officers used the city's public places—hotels, theaters, and historical landmarks—for clandestine meetings. The city's universities and companies producing military systems became targets for countries seeking to steal US industrial and scientific secrets. Harry Gold, who played a central role in the Soviet penetration of the US nuclear program,

was a native Philadelphian. Jack Barsky, who entered the United States in 1978 with forged identification and an assumed name with forged documents in service of the KGB, eventually settled inconspicuously in the area in an attempt to hide his past life from authorities.

By 1990 countering terrorism was a national priority for the FBI. The terrorist attack on the United States on September 11, 2001 (9/11), directed by Islamic extremists intensified worldwide anti-terrorism efforts. Philadelphia's homegrown terrorists, Americans who became radical jihadists and joined international terrorist organizations, were discovered among the city's residents. Their apprehension by the Philadelphia field office honored the defiant United Flight 93 passengers' call to action—"Let's roll!"—heard on 9/11 before their plane crashed near Shanksville, Pennsylvania, only 40 minutes from its target in Washington, DC. "Never again" became the rallying call for the coordinated actions of US intelligence and law enforcement officers, who have since prevented hundreds of terrorist attacks.

110. SPY FRIENDS OF PRESIDENTIAL CANDIDATE

MAP 6 ➤ **1948 Progressive National Convention:** The Municipal Auditorium and Convention Hall (demolished in 2007), 3400 Civic Center Boulevard

During the summer of 1948, the Philadelphia Municipal Auditorium and Convention Hall, with seating for 14,000 people, hosted three national political conventions: Republicans in June, Democrats in early July, and the Progressive Party in late July. The Progressives' 3,420 delegates nominated Henry Wallace, an established liberal, for president. Wallace had been Roosevelt's vice president during his third term and served as secretary of commerce under President Truman.

In these early months of the Cold War, the Progressives stood for peace with the USSR, no military draft, and ending the Marshall Plan to rebuild Europe. The party's positions were so well aligned with Soviet interests that the Communist Party USA decided to support the Progressive ticket rather than field its own candidate. The FBI was alarmed that members of Wallace's inner circle were confirmed Soviet agents, all with code names assigned by their handlers: Martha Dodd Stern (code name LIZA), Alfred Stern (code name LOUIS), and John Abt (code name BAT). Other Wallace advisers associated with Soviet intelligence were Harry Magdoff (code name KANT), Victor Perlo (code name RAIDER), and Charles Kramer (code name PLUMB). Wallace himself had been

The Philadelphia Municipal Auditorium and Convention Hall hosted Soviet spies, some of whom were delegates, at the Progressive Party's 1948 national convention. Former vice president Henry Wallace was selected the party's nominee for president.

assigned a code name of LOTSAN or BOATSWAIN.

Dodd, the daughter of a former American ambassador and the wife of a wealthy Wall Street stockbroker, was best known for her affairs with both high-ranking Nazi officers and Soviet intelligence operatives prior to America's entrance into World War II. Although the Soviets expressed disdain for her numerous and often less than discreet sexual escapades, they continued to use her and her husband for their high-society contacts and as a reliable source of funds. John Abt, an American lawyer and politician, spent most of his career as the chief counsel to the CPUSA. In 1944 Abt, along with Magdoff, Perlo, and Kramer, were all part of the Soviet intelligence network that also included Elizabeth Bentley (code name CLEVER GIRL).

Martha Dodd Stern and Alfred Stern were among the influential Soviet agents within Wallace's inner circle.

Wallace, not unreasonably, was branded a communist by political foes, yet the candidate refused to retreat from his party's pro-Soviet positions. As a result, early supporters fled the Progressive Party en masse and returned to the Democratic Party, giving President Truman sufficient support to win the general election. In the end, Wallace garnered less than 2 percent of the national vote.

111. DELMAR: THE SPY WHO GOT AWAY

MAP 3 ➤ **Soviet target:** Building 638, Philadelphia Naval Shipyard

Building 638, a Manhattan Project facility in Philadelphia's Naval Yard, was infiltrated by Soviet spy George Koval.

George Koval may have done more to contribute to the surprise 1949 Soviet atomic test than any of the USSR's other "atomic spies" except for Klaus Fuchs. Less well known than the NKVD and its efforts to steal America's atomic secrets are the activities of the GRU (Soviet military intelligence), which had the same objective. In his 2002 book, *GRU and the Atom Bomb*, Russian historian Vladimir Lota provided details of a mysterious spy code-named DELMAR.

DELMAR's identity and significance may never have come to the public's attention had Russian president Vladimir Putin not posthumously awarded Koval a gold star with the highest honor of "Hero of the Russian Federation"

Klaus Fuchs (left) and George Koval (right) reported America's Manhattan Project atomic secrets to the USSR. Koval's espionage was publicly acknowledged by Russian president Vladimir Putin in 2007, but the full extent of his spy activities has never been disclosed.

in November 2007. In the ceremony Putin publicly named Koval as the previously unidentified DELMAR.

Born in Sioux City, Iowa, to Russian immigrant parents, Koval went to Moscow after high school in the early 1930s to attend college. While there, the young man, who spoke un-accented American English and was a product of American culture, received tradecraft training from Soviet intelligence officers. Returning to the United States in 1940, Koval was the all-American boy. "He played baseball and played it well," a former friend remembered. Koval was drafted in 1943, and military testing, having established his exceptionally high IQ, led to an assignment to America's most secretive wartime effort, the Manhattan Project.

DENIED SOCIAL SECURITY

George Koval, who lived to see the demise of the Soviet Union, was living on a modest Russian government pension during the last years of his life. In an attempt to improve his income, he applied for Social Security benefits at the American Embassy in Moscow. His application was denied.

Koval worked for two years with a top-secret clearance at nuclear laboratories in Oak Ridge, Tennessee, and Dayton, Ohio, and at the secret thermal-diffusion pilot plant inside Building 638 of the Philadelphia Naval Shipyard that housed the Boiler and Turbine Testing Facility. While inside the project, Koval learned about a new method of nuclear initiation using polonium 210 and passed the information to Moscow via a still unidentified courier known only as CLYDE. The information would later prove critically important to the Soviets' successful nuclear detonation in 1949.

At the end of the war, Koval mustered out of the military and entered the City College of New York, where he received a bachelor's degree (cum laude) in electrical engineering in 1948. He then quietly returned to the Soviet Union under the guise of a vacation to Poland. He died in 2006 at the age of 92 (some sources state his age as 93 or 94) in Moscow.

112. WITNESS TO TREASON

MAP 4 ➤ **Whittaker Chambers birthplace:** 2232 West Diamond Street (vacant lot)

Jay Vivian Chambers, at one time a senior writer-editor for *Time* magazine, is better known as Whittaker Chambers, the Soviet spy who turned against the USSR. Recruited as an agent by the Soviets in the early 1930s, he later recanted and

A once grand home where Whittaker Chambers, a Soviet agent turned anti-communist informer, was born in 1901 is now an abandoned lot.

Whittaker Chambers

THE BAMBI CONNECTION

Before Whittaker Chambers gained fame in the Alger Hiss spy case, he was best known for his translation of the German classic *Bambi: A Life in the Woods* by Austrian author Felix Salten. Chambers's English-language edition, published by Simon and Schuster in 1928, captured the hearts of Americans and was later used as the basis for the Walt Disney animated film in 1942.

became one of the most controversial Americans of the Cold War.

Chambers's 1901 birth certificate recorded his Philadelphia address as 2232 West Diamond Street. Like many young people of his generation, he became infatuated with communism. Chambers secretly spied for the Soviets for six or seven years in the 1930s until becoming disillusioned and breaking the relationship in 1937. He came to public attention in 1948 during a congressional hearing by identifying Alger Hiss—the president of the Carnegie Endowment for International Peace and a highly regarded former State Department officer—as a member of a Soviet spy ring. Hiss denied the allegation, and a decades-long dispute over which of the two men was truthful followed.

Chambers died in 1961 with Hiss continuing to insist he was innocent of the charges of espionage. However, 34 years later, Chambers's account that Hiss collaborated with the Soviets was corroborated by the 1995 release of the once top-secret VENONA intercepts of World War II–era secret Soviet communications. Hiss died a year later.

113. THE MYSTERY OF REINO HÄYHÄNEN

MAP 12 ➤ **Defector's grave site:** Greenmount Cemetery and Cremation Garden, 721 Carlisle Avenue, York, Pennsylvania

The key witness against Soviet master spy and *illegal* Rudolf Abel in 1957 was his onetime assistant Reino Häyhänen. A hard-drinking, undisciplined spy, Häyhänen was a marked contrast to Abel, the security-conscious professional. When Häyhänen was recalled to Moscow following a series of operational blunders, he defected in May 1957 while in transit in France. A month later Abel, who had lived virtually invisibly as a painter in the New York bohemian community of artists and writers, was arrested thanks to Häyhänen's information.

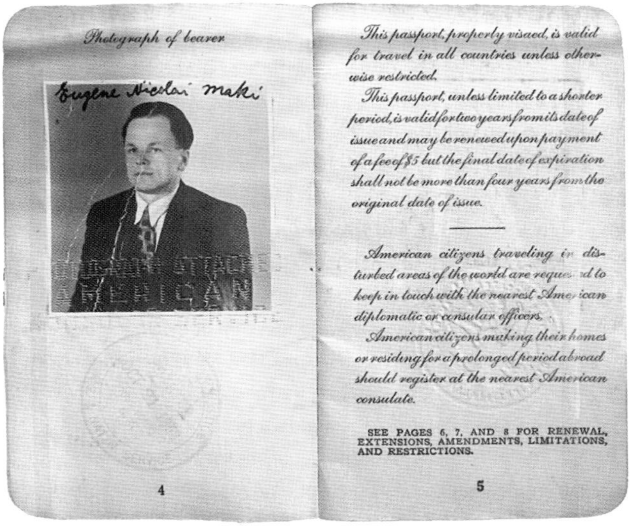

Reino Häyhänen, whose careless tradecraft was responsible for the apprehension of Soviet *illegal* Rudolf Abel, lived in York County during the last years of his life.

Abel's trial created a media sensation. He was convicted, imprisoned, and returned to the USSR in 1962 in exchange for downed U-2 pilot Francis Gary Powers. Following defection, Häyhänen and his wife entered something akin to the Witness Protection Program. They first lived in Peekskill, New York, under the aliases Eugene Maki and Hanna (sometimes Hannah) Maki; then they moved to Keene, New Hampshire, where they became John Eugene Linden and Anita H. Linden before moving again to Delroy in York County, Pennsylvania. The two-acre farm they purchased was reportedly on East Prospect Road.

According to local news articles, neighbors thought the couple odd. Häyhänen was once seen watering his lawn during a rain storm. Another neighbor noticed him dumping camera equipment in a nearby water-filled ore hole. A local farmer was said to have complained when his cows began turning up with lacerations on their legs, apparently from cuts caused by broken vodka bottles thrown into a neighboring stream. Strangers driving cars with out-of-state license plates seemed to regularly visit the couple.

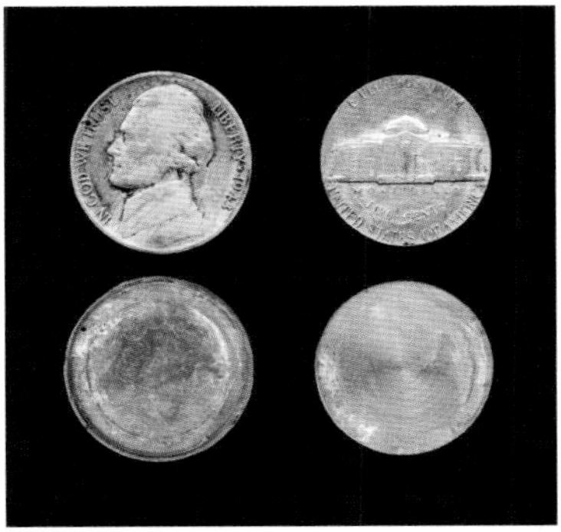

Soviet spy Reino Häyhänen inadvertently gave a "hollow" nickel containing microfilm to a newspaper boy. The mystery of its contents was not solved until the spy's defection several years later.

In August 1961 Häyhänen was arrested for drunk driving in York County. As local officials remembered it, he was represented by two lawyers from Washington, DC. The case moved quickly, and within 24 hours he was released after the lawyers paid a small fine on his behalf. A few weeks later, on August 24 (or 22), 1961, Häyhänen died in York Hospital, likely from cirrhosis of the liver. Funeral arrangements were made by a lawyer based in Keene, and Häyhänen was buried in Greenmount Cemetery, 721 Carlisle Avenue, York, Pennsylvania. The widow, Hanna, was reported to have moved to Philadelphia shortly after his death. Whether she kept the name Linden is not known.

However, the mystery surrounding Häyhänen lingered. In 1964 James Donovan, who had defended Abel in court, released his book *Strangers on a Bridge: The Case of Colonel Abel and Francis Gary Powers*. Later made into the film *Bridge of Spies*, the book details Donovan's role as Abel's court-appointed defense attorney. However, it also includes a note on Häyhänen's 1961 death. "Hayhanen left the witness stand; four years later he would be dead, killed in a mysterious automobile crash on the Pennsylvania Turnpike," Donovan wrote.

A few weeks following the book's publication, the *New York Times* ran a short piece noting Donovan's announcement of Häyhänen's death in the book. Why Donovan placed the date and state correctly but attributed the death to an automobile fatality remains a mystery.

114. JAMES BOND FROM PHILLY

MAP 2 ➤ **Academy of Natural Sciences (today the Academy of Natural Sciences of Drexel University):** 1900 Benjamin Franklin Parkway

Ian Fleming named his agent 007 after a Philadelphia ornithologist. The real James Bond was born in Philadelphia and lived in the United Kingdom as a child before returning to the United States. Fleming said he was in Jamaica when he read the author's name on Bond's 1936 book, *Birds of the West Indies*. "It struck me that this brief, unromantic, Anglo-Saxon and yet very masculine name was just what I needed, and so a second James Bond was born," he later wrote.

Ornithologist James Bond of Philadelphia, seen in 1974 at the Academy of Natural Sciences

The ornithologist James Bond shared a taste for travel with his fictional namesake. He participated in a number of research expeditions to collect data on birds from which he published more than a hundred books and scholarly papers. As the curator at the Academy of Natural Sciences in Philadelphia (today the Academy of Natural Sciences of Drexel University),

The Academy of Natural Sciences was the professional home of ornithologist James Bond, the man whose name was appropriated by Ian Fleming for his spy novels.

1900 Benjamin Franklin Parkway, Bond earned a host of awards and professional honors.

In a letter to Bond's wife, poet and novelist Mary Fanning Wickham Bond, Fleming gratefully acknowledged the value of the name that dominated his writing career. "In return, I can only offer you or James Bond unlimited use of the name Ian Fleming for any purposes you may think fit," Fleming wrote. "Perhaps one day your husband will discover a particularly horrible species of bird which he would like to christen in an insulting fashion by calling it Ian Fleming."

James Bond died in 1989 and is buried at the Church of the Messiah Cemetery, Gwynedd, Montgomery County, Pennsylvania.

115. WHAT GOES UP . . .

MAP 6 ➤ **General Electric Re-entry Systems Building:** 3198 Chestnut Street

The General Electric (GE) Re-entry Systems Building, 3198 Chestnut Street, originally built as the Pennsylvania Railroad Freight Building in 1929, housed a small army of scientists, engineers, and technicians. Within the six-story, 650,000-square-foot structure, some of the most difficult problems of designing reentry space vehicles were addressed.

GE received a new space reconnaissance challenge in the 1950s. In a shared effort with Lockheed Aircraft Corporation (today Lockheed Martin), the US Air Force, and the CIA, engineers began designing a container for a payload of 70-millimeter film canisters for the world's first reconnaissance satellite. As designed, the satellite would make its overflights across the Soviet Union and drop the container, called the bucket, at a precisely designated time and location for midair retrieval. To prevent the container's incineration as it

The Pennsylvania Railroad Freight Building housed a team of General Electric scientists and engineers whose work was critical to America's first space reconnaissance program.

reentered the earth's atmosphere, an advanced technology heat shield protected the container; then parachutes deployed to slow its decent, and a specially equipped aircraft snatched the falling bucket in midair.

Cover for the classified satellite program, Discoverer, included the story that the United States was developing a scientific satellite system to study atmospheric conditions and weather patterns. In reality, the advanced reconnaissance system was the CIA-directed Corona satellite program.

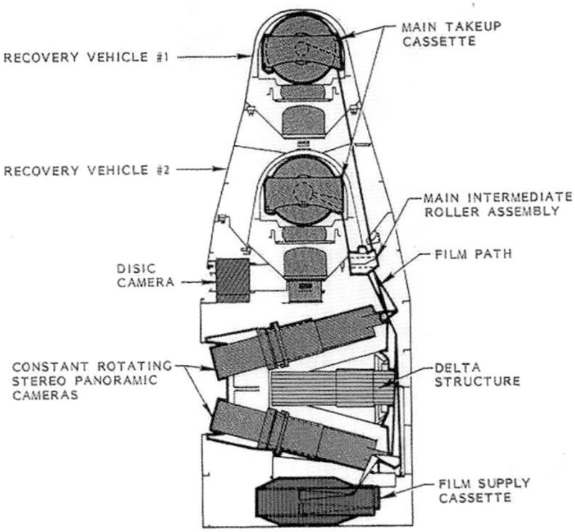

The Corona satellite carried a camera that produced high-quality images of Soviet missile sites, never before identified.

Multiple technical problems plagued the program at the start. However, after 12 failures, on August 10, 1960, a launch succeeded when frogmen at sea successfully retrieved a bucket without a camera and film. Representing an engineering milestone, it was the first time a man-made object was recovered from space. However, not everyone was happy. "Congratulations on random success," read the cable the CIA's Richard Bissell Jr. sent to the team leaders.

The next launch, Mission 9009 on August 18, 1960, included a camera and film. It was a success. An air force C-119 Flying Boxcar retrieved a capsule with 20 pounds—more than half a mile—of Kodak film on August 19, ushering in a new field of space reconnaissance. Corona's first successful mission, which included 17 orbits of Earth and seven passes over the Soviet Union, produced more images than all the previous 24 U-2 flights over the USSR combined.

The GE facility closed in 1993, though the building is on the National Register of Historic Places and is considered a historic aerospace site by the American Institute of Aeronautics and Astronautics. The structure has been converted to residences, and its primary entrance is located on Walnut Street.

116. CLANDESTINE PHILANTHROPY

MAP 9 ➤ **Catherwood Foundation:** 807 Lancaster Avenue, Bryn Mawr, Pennsylvania

Journalists and private historians have reported that during the early years of the Cold War, the CIA countered aggressive Soviet attempts to subvert European democracies by working clandestinely with US-based private foundations such as the Catherwood Foundation, then located at 807 Lancaster Avenue, Bryn Mawr, Pennsylvania. Other Philadelphia entities that provided funds unattributed to the US government for these operations included the Fund for International Social and Economic Education, the Borden Trust, and the Andrew Hamilton Fund.

According to a story in the *Philadelphia Inquirer*, Cummins Catherwood, who headed the Catherwood Foundation, took particular pride in the fund's ability to move quickly with disbursements, though not mentioning its clandestine activities. "You might say we're the venture capital of the foundation field," he told the paper in a May 4, 1954, interview.

Catherwood's foundation may have unknowingly brushed against espionage in funding a 1948 scientific expedition to the West Indies. Composed of scientists representing a number of wildlife specialties, the expedition team included ornithologist James Bond from Philadelphia's Academy of Natural Sciences (today the Academy of Natural Sciences of Drexel University). While the expedition was conducted several years prior to Ian Fleming's first James Bond adventure, Fleming later explained that he borrowed the name for 007 after reading Bond's book *Birds of the West Indies*.

■ 117. THREE MILES UNDERSEA

MAP 10 ➤ **Sun Shipbuilding and Drydock Company (today the site of Harrah's Philadelphia Casino and Racetrack):** 777 Harrah's Boulevard, Chester, Pennsylvania

Among the most ambitious of the CIA's 20th-century covert operations was the attempted recovery of the Soviet G-II class submarine *K-129*. The diesel-electric-powered sub, which carried nuclear missiles, sank 1,500 miles northwest of the Hawaiian Islands on August 20, 1968. Its recovery would provide an intelligence treasure trove. However, the sub's weight and position at an extreme depth of 16,500 feet presented unprecedented engineering obstacles.

In addition to the technical and engineering challenge, the operation would become impossible if the Soviets learned of the effort. Howard Hughes and the Hughes Tool Company agreed to provide a commercial cover by creating the USNS *Hughes Glomar Explorer* (T-AG-193), a 619-foot ship for a deep-sea mineral exploration and mining project. The vessel was constructed at the Sun Shipbuilding and Drydock Company in Chester, Pennsylvania (today the site of Harrah's Philadelphia Casino and Racetrack, 777 Harrah's Boulevard, Chester, Pennsylvania). The shipyard, founded in the early 20th century, had a history of constructing oil tankers and was part of the Emergency Shipbuilding Program for troop and supply ships in World War II.

Hughes's Global Marine Development Incorporated constructed the *Glomar* under a cover story that the ship would conduct deepwater manganese mining. At the CIA the operation, code-named Project Azorian, presented new

The USNS *Hughes Glomar Explorer* cost an estimated $350 million to build, and the mission it conducted is recognized as one of the largest and most successful clandestine operations in CIA history.

technological challenges for intelligence that were as audacious as those associated with the earlier Corona satellite program. At the time, the record depth for recovering a ship from the ocean floor was 245 feet. While other deepwater recoveries had taken place, the heaviest object ever brought to the surface weighed only a few hundred pounds. By contrast, the *K-129* was more than three miles beneath the surface and weighed 2,000 tons.

Completed in 1974 at a cost estimated at $350 million, the *Glomar* arrived at the recovery site on July 4, 1974. A few days into the operation, the *Glomar* was approached by two Soviet ships—the *SB-10* ocean tug and the *Chazhma.* Queried by the Soviet ships' crews, the *Glomar*'s crew maintained its cover story of mining operations. As surveillance by the *Chazhma* continued and a Soviet helicopter circled overhead, *Glomar* crewmen donned disguises, and the ship radioed a stream of messages detailing the progress of its purported mining operations. After *Chazhma* departed, the *SB-10* observed the *Glomar* for almost two weeks but left the area without confrontation.

The *Glomar* operation eventually recovered a portion of the Soviet sub with an intelligence value that remains classified. Engineering advances made in designing the *Glomar Explorer* pioneered major progress in deepwater mining and nautical heavy lift technology.

The secrecy around the project was originally breached by the *Los Angeles Times* in February 1975, though the story contained numerous factual errors. A more accurate and sensational version of the story appeared a month later from the syndicated columnist Jack Anderson on his television and radio show. The disclosures precluded the CIA and the *Glomar* from undertaking attempts to recover the other parts of the submarine.

Twenty years after the operation, the government sold the *Glomar* to private interests, and in 2015 the remarkable vessel was scrapped.

118. DIRECTOR OF CENTRAL INTELLIGENCE

MAP 9 ➤ **Richard Helms birthplace:** Cambria Court, St Davids (Wayne), Pennsylvania

Richard Helms, born March 30, 1913, on Cambria Court in St. Davids, an affluent Philadelphia suburb, became one of the CIA's longest-serving directors. His family eventually moved to South Orange, New Jersey, and Helms later prepped at the Swiss boarding school Institut Le Rosey before graduating from Williams College and beginning his career as a reporter for the United

Richard Helms

Press wire service. He was assigned to Berlin, where he witnessed the rise of fascism and Hitler. When the United States entered the war, Helms was an early recruit to the Office of Strategic Services and, after the war, the Central Intelligence Agency.

Helms became the CIA's head of operations (deputy director of plans) in 1962 and was named the director of central intelligence in 1966 by President Lyndon Johnson. While the DCI prized accurate agent reporting, he had a keen interest in advancing the use of technology for collection and operational security. As America's top spy, Helms was suave, good looking, and quotable, a regular presence in the Washington social scene. Incredible by today's security standards, his telephone number and address were listed in the phone book.

For Helms and the CIA, the late 1960s and early 1970s were turbulent years that included the Vietnam War, the exposure of controversial covert action programs, and the Watergate political storm. The CIA could have been drawn more deeply into the political crisis save for Helms's refusal to cooperate with Richard Nixon and the White House's plans. "Not only would I have gone to jail if I had gone along with what the White House wanted us to do, but the agency's credibility would have been ruined forever," he later recalled, according to Tim Weiner in *Legacy of Ashes: The History of the CIA*.

Helms's tenure as the DCI ended following Nixon's reelection in 1972. Replaced in early 1973 by James Schlesinger, Helms was appointed ambassador to Iran later that year and served until 1976. In 1977 Helms was charged with a crime of lying under oath during the 1973 congressional hearings about the CIA's role in supporting the opposition to the government of Chilean president

CLOSE SHAVES FOR SPIES

The future head of the CIA Richard Helms married Julia Bretzman Shields, the daughter of Frank Shields—an MIT professor and inventor of Barbasol shaving cream—in 1939. Given Helms's intelligence career, there is some irony that Barbasol's iconic and ubiquitous red, white, and blue can has been used as a concealment device for decades by real and amateur spies to hide secrets and valuables. No Barbasol concealment is more distinctive than the one deployed in the blockbuster movie *Jurassic Park* to smuggle dinosaur embryos off the island.

Salvador Allende. "I had found myself in a position of conflict," he told a federal judge in defending his testimony. "I had sworn my oath to protect certain secrets. I didn't want to lie. I didn't want to mislead the Senate. I was simply trying to find my way through a difficult situation in which I found myself."

For his actions, Helms received a two-year prison sentence and a $2,000 fine. The jail time was later suspended, and according to the *New York Times*, retired agency officers showed their support by making contributions to pay the fine. Of the matter of the conviction, the man who served US intelligence for three decades and six presidents from Roosevelt to Nixon said, "I don't feel disgraced at all. I think if I had done anything else I would have been disgraced." Helms died in 2002 at age 89 and is buried at Arlington National Cemetery.

119. WORKING-CLASS HERO

MAP 7 ➤ **Robert Ames childhood residence:** 4624 Pechin Street

CIA officer Robert Ames, no relation to the traitorous Aldrich Ames, took on some of the agency's most challenging assignments during rising terrorism in the Middle East. Born in 1934, the son of a steelworker, Ames was raised in the working-class Philadelphia neighborhood of Roxborough, 4624 Pechin Street, and attended nearby Roxborough High School, 6498 Ridge Avenue (today known as the Academies at Roxborough High School). He graduated from La Salle University, 1900 West Olney Avenue, and played on the school's basketball team, which won the National Collegiate Athletic Association championship in 1954 and placed as runner-up in 1955.

Robert Ames, one of the CIA's top officers on the Middle East, grew up in a Philadelphia middle-class neighborhood.

Ames's service in the US Army was followed by a CIA career beginning in 1960 and his specialization in the Middle East. Given to wearing cowboy boots, Ames presented the folksy personality of a trustworthy professional. A colleague described Ames as "anonymous, perceptive, knowledgeable, highly motivated, critical, discreet—with a priest's and cop's understanding of the complexity of human nature in action." Ames's skill eventually led to his becoming a trusted interlocutor with the Palestine Liberation Organization's leadership, including Ali Hassan Salameh.

While visiting the US Embassy in Beirut, Lebanon, on April 18, 1983, Ames was killed in a terrorist bombing of the embassy that took the lives of 63 people, including the chief of station and six other CIA officers. He is buried in Arlington National Cemetery.

■ 120. SPIES' NIGHT OUT

MAP 2 ➤ **Favored meeting site:** Sylvania Hotel, 1324 Locust Street

At the end of the Cold War, KGB major Vasili Mitrokhin's defection to the West in 1992 is recognized as one of the most significant exposures of Soviet espionage operations in the history of the Soviet Union. While serving for decades as a senior archivist for its intelligence service, Mitrokhin kept detailed notes on the service, its personnel, and its worldwide operations. The meticulous notes became the basis of a series of books, including *The Sword and the Shield*, written with British intelligence historian Christopher Andrew. That text has a small appendix titled "Some Favorite KGB *Yavkas* (Meeting Places) in the 1960's" that lists dozens of specific meeting locations in America's largest cities, including Philadelphia.

Soviet spies seemed fond of Philadelphia landmarks as meeting places. According to Soviet records, three favorite operational *yavkas* during the 1960s were in or near two major theaters and a historic hotel. The 1902 Randolph Theatre, 1116 Chestnut Street, was a cinema jewel that once featured live performances by Fred Astaire, Charlie Chaplin, and the Marx Brothers. It closed its doors in the early 1970s and was eventually demolished.

The nearby Stanton Theatre (more popularly known as the Milgrim) at 1620 Market Street opened in 1914 with a distinctive interior decorated with plaster cupids. By the 1950s, mostly B movies, action thrillers, and horror films were being shown there. The Stanton ended its long run in the early 1980s and, along with other theaters on the block, was replaced by an office building.

The Randolph Theatre, Stanton Theatre, and Hotel Sylvania are some of the Philadelphia public spaces Soviet intelligence agents used for clandestine meetings.

The archives' reference to the "Silvanna Hotel" is almost certainly the Hotel Sylvania, 1324 Locust Street. Built in the 1920s, the stylish hostelry hosted an array of celebrities, including the notorious Philadelphia bootlegger Max "Boo Boo" Hoff, who ran his liquor and boxing promotion businesses out of a second-floor suite. The property, now the Arts Condominiums, is advertised as a "landmark community of true urban living."

It was not the architecture, the local history, or even the opportunity to enjoy a B movie that attracted Soviet spies to these theaters and the hotel. Located in the city's center with multiple entrances and exits, combined with crowds of people, the public locations offered intelligence officers an environment for having brief encounters with agents or evading surveillance. There, the spy could easily blend into the throngs of theatergoers, become "lost" among hundreds of other locals, and vanish, if necessary, unobserved through a convenient doorway.

121. RETIRED BUT NOT FORGOTTEN

MAP I ➤ **Robert Lipka trial site:** US Courthouse, 601 Market Street

As a 19-year-old soldier from Millersville, Pennsylvania, assigned to the National Security Agency (NSA), Robert Lipka became one of the youngest KGB agents inside the American intelligence community in the mid-1960s. Mercenary in his motives, Lipka volunteered to serve Soviet intelligence in 1965 and received between $500 and $1,000 for each package of NSA secrets he left in dead drops for his Soviet handlers. "He gave us whatever he got his hands on, often having little idea what he was turning over," wrote former KGB major general Oleg Kalugin, who detailed a case that is almost certainly Lipka's in his memoir, *The First Directorate* (later retitled *Spymaster: My Thirty-Two Years in Intelligence and Espionage against the West*).

Robert Lipka

What the teenage soldier (code name DAN or ROOK) handed over, according to Kalugin, were top-secret reports to the White House and classified information on US troop movements and communications of the North Atlantic Treaty Organization. Becoming unhappy with the amount of money he

Robert Lipka, recruited by the Soviets at age 19, was eventually arrested, tried, and convicted in a Philadelphia courtroom and sentenced to an 18-year prison term.

was receiving from the KGB, Lipka left the NSA in 1967 and went to college in Lancaster, Pennsylvania.

As the decades passed, it seemed as if he had gotten away with spying. However, information about the Soviet espionage operation published in the 1990s by Vasili Mitrokhin provided important clues for the FBI to identify Lipka. An FBI agent posing as a Russian intelligence officer contacted Lipka, then living quietly as a schoolteacher and coin dealer in Millersville, Pennsylvania, in 1996.

The former spy agreed to a meeting but refused to talk with the FBI undercover agent unless he could provide Lipka with his Soviet cover name, saying it began with the letter R. The well-briefed agent, knowing Lipka's fondness for chess, correctly guessed the cover name was ROOK. Relieved and believing the contact was from Russian intelligence, Lipka complained about having been shortchanged by his previous Soviet handlers, accepted additional money, and revealed his prior espionage.

With what amounted to a confession, the FBI arrested Lipka at his home in Millersville. Following a trial at the Philadelphia US Courthouse, 601 Market Street, the case ended with a plea bargain and an 18-year prison sentence. "I feel like Rip Van Spy," Lipka said when sentenced in September 1997. Released in December 2006, he died in 2013 at the age of 68. His total profit for betraying his country was less than $30,000.

122. A SPY ON THE USS *KITTY HAWK* (CV-63)

MAP 3 ➤ **Surveillance site:** Basin Street Bridge, Philadelphia Naval Shipyard

In May 1991 a sailor on the USS *Kitty Hawk* (CV-63) was approached by Seaman Matthew P. Braun and offered money in exchange for classified copies of the ship's damage control plan and information on anti-submarine warfare and tactics. The Naval Investigative Service (NIS) was promptly alerted, and the cooperative sailor was wired with a concealed Nagra recorder for his next meeting with Braun.

The meeting took place in a parking lot near the intersection of Langley Road and Basin Street. The location offered privacy but was exposed to long-range photo surveillance by an NIS technical team positioned 150 yards away in the north tower of the navy yard's Basin Street Bridge. An NIS officer and camera were also hidden behind a section of plywood near two hazardous

From a tower high above the Philadelphia Naval Shipyard's Basin Street Bridge, navy investigators captured the criminal transaction between Seamen Matthew P. Braun and an FBI informant.

The badge identifying officers of the US Naval Criminal Investigative Service, the successor to the Naval Investigative Service

waste storage tanks in the parking lot. Resulting images clearly showed a distinctive tattoo on Braun's right arm, confirming his identity.

Audio from the hidden recorder provided even more evidence. Thumbing through the documents, Braun was recorded muttering, "Bingo—this is exactly what they want." The would-be spy pleaded guilty at his court-martial, receiving a three-year jail sentence and a dishonorable discharge.

123. BOGUS BIRTHPLACE

When Russian spy and *illegal* Richard Murphy was arrested in New York in June 2010, a search of his safe deposit box produced birth certificate no. 545564

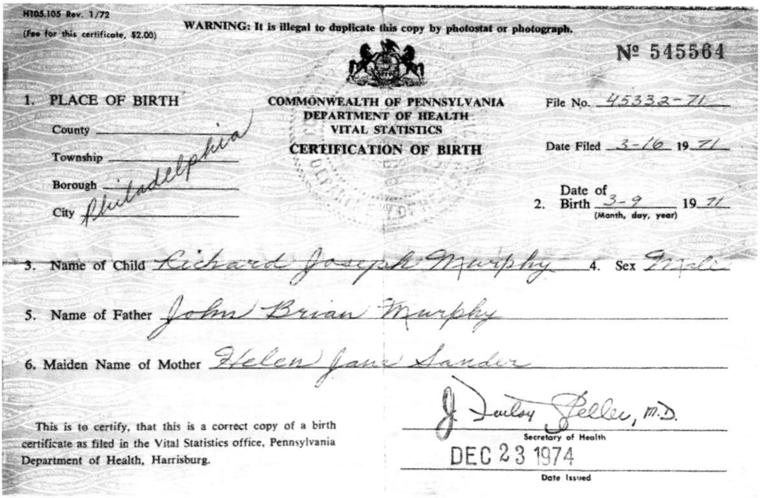

H105.105 Rev. 1/72
(Fee for this certificate, $2.00)

WARNING: It is illegal to duplicate this copy by photostat or photograph.

№ 545564

COMMONWEALTH OF PENNSYLVANIA
DEPARTMENT OF HEALTH
VITAL STATISTICS
CERTIFICATION OF BIRTH

1. PLACE OF BIRTH
County
Township
Borough
City Philadelphia

File No. 45332-71
Date Filed 3-16 19 71

2. Date of Birth 3-9 19 71 (Month, day, year)

3. Name of Child Richard Joseph Murphy 4. Sex Male

5. Name of Father John Brian Murphy

6. Maiden Name of Mother Helen Jane Sander

This is to certify, that this is a correct copy of a birth certificate as filed in the Vital Statistics office, Pennsylvania Department of Health, Harrisburg.

J. Finlay Feller, M.D.
Secretary of Health

DEC 23 1974
Date Issued

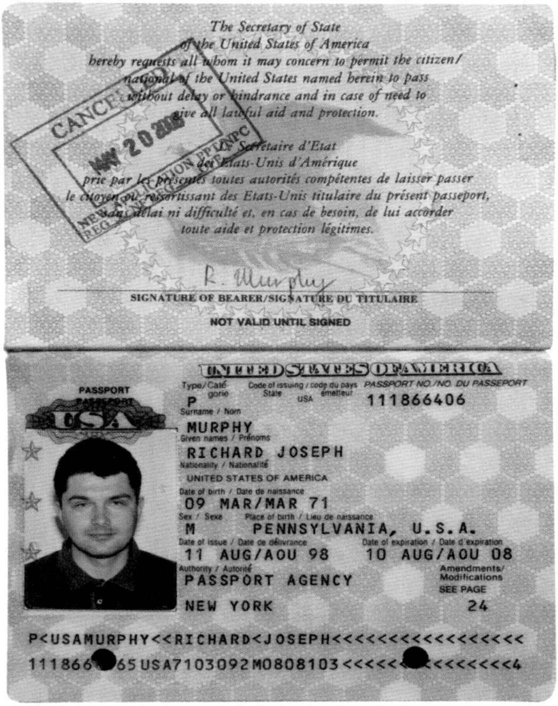

Soviet *illegal* Vladimir Guryev obtained a US passport in the name of Richard Murphy based on a forged Pennsylvania birth certificate.

for Richard Joseph Murphy, born March 9, 1971, in Philadelphia. Though appearing genuine, the birth certificate was actually a masterful forgery created by Russian intelligence on special security paper that duplicated the watermark of an original Pennsylvania birth certificate. Authorities were able to disprove its authenticity only by showing that no record of the birth certificate number ever existed in the municipal files. In fact, Richard Murphy's true name is Vladimir Guryev.

■ 124. A DANGEROUS MIND

MAP 7 ➤ **Chuck Barris hometown:** Bala Cynwyd, Pennsylvania

Former television personality Chuck Barris grew up in Bala Cynwyd, Pennsylvania, and attended Lower Merion High School and Drexel University (then known as Drexel Institute of Technology). Although he produced the popular television shows *The Dating Game* and *The Newlywed Show*, he is more widely recognized as the creator and host of *The Gong Show*. Billed as a talent competition, the prime-time show featured contestants whose performances were often outrageous or dreadful. If a member of the panel of judges had enough before the end of the act, he or she struck a large gong and summarily ended the act.

Publicity photo of Chuck Barris of *The Gong Show*, who claimed to be a CIA assassin

Barris's espionage fame came with his assertion that he moonlighted as a CIA assassin while hosting the show. The claim appeared in his book *Confessions of a Dangerous Mind: An Unauthorized Autobiography* (1982), and the bizarre tale garnered more publicity when George Clooney adapted the book for his 2002 film *Confessions of a Dangerous Mind*. "It sounds like he has been standing too close to the gong all those years," CIA spokesman Tom Crispell said when asked about the story. "Chuck Barris has never been employed by the CIA and the allegation that he was a hired assassin is absurd." Barris died March 21, 2017.

125. KGB PLANNING TERROR IN AMERICA

MAP 12 ➤ **Big Spring State Forest Picnic Area:** Blain, Pennsylvania

During the Cold War, the Sabotage and Intelligence Group (DRG), an arm of Soviet intelligence, cached weapons, explosives, and communications equipment across the United States. According to historian Christopher Andrew

Big Spring State Forest Picnic Area, Blain, Pennsylvania, was a secret cache site for the Soviet Sabotage and Intelligence Group, which was supposed to conduct acts of sabotage if a full-scale war erupted between the United States and the USSR.

in *The Sword and the Shield* and Stanislav Lunev, the highest-ranking GRU officer to defect to the United States, the DRG's objective was to create a clandestine capability that could be used to destroy key elements of America's critical infrastructure. Targets included dams, port facilities, and power grids. Each code-named target was described in detail with photographs, mapped locations, and getaway routes for those who would eventually be tasked with carrying out the sabotage operations.

One element of the DRG operated from a safe house in the Big Spring State Forest Picnic Area in Blain, near Harrisburg, Pennsylvania. Caches placed in New York, Minnesota, California, Montana, and Texas were similar to those the KGB secreted throughout Western Europe. These operations, which began in the 1960s, remain surrounded by mystery. The locations and contents of the caches, reportedly protected by *Molniya* [lightning] explosive booby traps, have never been revealed. One cache, believed similar to those used in the United States, was discovered in 1998 in Switzerland but exploded after authorities turned a fire hose on it.

126. CHEERFUL MERCHANT OF DEATH

MAP 9 ➤ **Samuel Cummings residence:** 639 Hazelwood Avenue, Ardmore, Pennsylvania

Born in 1927 to a well-to-do family from England, Samuel Cummings lived a life of high drama and low dealings. The family fortune, made in marketing mineral water, was lost in the stock market crash of 1929, and the death of his father soon afterward precipitated a family financial crisis. Having once lived comfortably at 639 Hazelwood Avenue, Ardmore, Pennsylvania, following the financial setbacks in 1930, the family reportedly moved from house to house, with Mrs. Cummings earning a living by what is today called house flipping. Samuel first attended the Episcopal Academy, then located at 376 North Latches Lane, Merion Station, Pennsylvania, before the family moved to Washington, DC, where he attended Sidwell Friends School and the old Central High School. Cummings enrolled at the George Washington University and studied briefly at the University of Oxford.

During his youth, Samuel Cummings, who became a notorious Cold War "gray" arms merchant, lived in this house before the family moved to Washington, DC.

By his own account, whose accuracy has been questioned, Cummings's love of weaponry began when he found an old Maxim machine gun in front of an American Legion Hall when he was just five years old. As Cummings told the story, he toted it home in his red wagon. The tale has some measure of credibility since the Leon Spencer Reid Post No. 547, 233 Simpson Road, Ardmore, founded in 1932, is less than a mile from the Cummings's Hazelwood Avenue address.

Whether the story of the Maxim is true or part of Cummings's self-invention, he eventually became one of the world's largest arms dealers. He served as weapons specialist during World War II but never saw combat. According to a 1988 *New York Times* article, he joined the fledgling CIA in 1950 and left in 1953 to establish the International Armament Corporation. The company, which specialized in small arms, opened an office and warehouses in Alexandria, Virginia.

By the mid-1960s, the company had stockpiled more than 700,000 rifles, pistols, shotguns, and other small arms—enough to outfit an army—all acquired prior to the Gun Control Act of 1968 that banned the importation of military firearms. "At that moment," Cummings bragged in an interview, "we could have instantly overwhelmed the American armed forces."

A high point for Cummings came when he obtained the US franchise from Carl Walther GmbH Sportwaffen to market the company's pistols. The deal included the Walther PPK, the sidearm used by the fictional spy James Bond in several of his adventures, and was highly profitable, but it triggered a US government investigation into the way Cummings marketed the handguns.

Over the years Cummings outfitted several armies, building Interarms into a major player in the international arms market. Along the way he maintained the persona of a genial merchant of death, selling guns to nations, rebel groups, and guerrilla fighters. His operation from a waterfront location on Prince Street in Alexandria, Virginia, did a brisk business under the name Potomac Arms, while two subsidiaries of Interarms, Ye Olde Hunter and Hunters Haven, operated from the same address. As the "go-to guy" for weaponry, Cummings's business strategy dictated that he not choose sides or favor a particular ideology. He sold weapons to Cuban dictator Fulgencio Batista and his communist successor, Fidel Castro, as well as to South Africa's apartheid regime. Reportedly, his weapons ended up on both sides of an attempted coup in Costa Rica. However, Cummings apparently did draw a line in refusing to supply arms to Muammar Gaddafi of Libya and Uganda's Idi Amin.

In the shadowy world of arms dealers, Cummings remained uncharacteristically open while quietly cultivating rumors about ties to the intelligence community. The acronym for one of his companies, Cummings Investment Associates, was not subtle. Unapologetic and sanguine about his profession, he often waxed philosophic in interviews. "The military market is based on human folly, not normal market precepts," he was quoted as saying by the *Washington Post* in December 1986. "Human folly goes up and down, but it always exists. Its depths have never been plumbed."

Eventually Cummings obtained British citizenship and settled in Monte Carlo, Monaco. He died there in 1998 at the age of 71.

MONACO'S ORIGINAL MYSTERY MAN

Samuel Cummings was not the only "merchant of death" with a history involving the Maxim machine gun or of calling Monaco home. In the late 19th century, Basil Zaharoff, known as the "Mystery Man of Europe," was famed for his allegedly shady international dealings and celebrity friendships. Stage actress Sarah Bernhardt was among his close circle of friends. Similar to Cummings, Zaharoff sold weapons, particularly the Maxim, to both sides in a conflict. His marketing strategy, known as *Système Zaharoff*, was to sell arms to one side and inform the adversary of the potential danger to sell it more of the same weapon. Working for the British armaments company Vickers, Zaharoff used spies, bribery, sexual entrapment, and sabotage to secure sales. He reportedly became one of the world's richest men and gained control of Monaco's famed casino. He died in 1936 at age 87.

Basil Zaharoff

127. TENNIS AND ESPIONAGE

MAP 7 ➤ **West Laurel Hill Cemetery:** 225 Belmont Avenue, Bala Cynwyd, Pennsylvania

William J. Clothier II, with his prominent Philadelphia name, was a tennis star, local celebrity, and CIA intelligence officer. His grandfather Isaac Clothier cofounded the (now defunct) Strawbridge & Clothier department store chain. The company's flagship store, built on the site of what was once Thomas Jefferson's office, 801 Market Street, was a Philadelphia landmark for decades. As a world-class tennis player, William paired with his father, William Clothier Sr., also a tennis champion, and won the national father-son tennis title two times.

The younger Clothier was recruited by the FBI in the 1940s and worked undercover as an archaeologist in Peru, Chile, and Cuba during the war years. He joined the CIA in 1952, and while much of his work there remains classified, among his known responsibilities was assisting in the resettlement of Cold War defectors. It was reported that in one instance he placed a Hungarian defector in a curator's job at a Philadelphia museum. A former colleague described Clothier as being "right out of FBI central casting—well pressed grey suit, white shirt, conservative tie, and often the accompanying hat."

Clothier retired from the agency in 1979. Maintaining a keen interest in tennis, he served as the director of the National Tennis Foundation and Hall of Fame and was a board member of the International Tennis Hall of Fame. Clothier died October 19, 2002, and is buried in the West Laurel Hill Cemetery, 225 Belmont Avenue, Bala Cynwyd, Pennsylvania.

SPIES ON THE CLAY COURT

William Clothier II was not the only American tennis-playing spy. Fred Kovaleski was already a well-established tennis pro when he was recruited by the CIA in 1951. Described in news reports as a "tall, dark-haired Defense Department worker," he competed in the National Tennis Championships in 1954. Although his life seemed to mirror that of the popular television show *I Spy*, which ran from 1965 to 1968, his son, Serge Kovaleski, a reporter for the *New York Times*, has said the similarities were simply coincidental.

Among the CIA's officers were world-class athletes such as tennis champion Fred Kovaleski.

As part of his CIA responsibilities, Fred Kovaleski played scores of matches with Yuri Rastvorov (code name DIPPER 19), a KGB lieutenant colonel who defected to the United States in August 1954 while posted in Japan. Kovaleski related in a 2006 *Washington Post Magazine* story written by his son that the two played several times a week during Rastvorov's 1954 debriefings. "I never hit a winner against him," Mr. Kovaleski said in the story. "The idea was to make him feel better about himself, to soothe his ego. And I think the tennis was real therapy for him."

Kovaleski left the agency in 1957 when his fiancée's family, which included Russian nationals, proved problematic for the agency. A business career followed with companies such as Revlon and Nabisco Brands. He died in 2018 at the age of 93.

A more shadowy spy story surrounds tennis legend Alice Marble. The winner of 18 Grand Slam championships between 1936 and 1940—seven in mixed doubles, five in singles, and six in women's doubles—Marble was said to have been recruited into US intelligence following the loss of her husband, Joe Crowley, during World War II. Marble related in her autobiography, *Courting Danger*, that she was instructed to reestablish contact with a Swiss banker who was a former lover. The goal was to gain access to Nazi finances. Revealed as a spy during the operation, she was shot while escaping pursuing German officers, but an American intelligence officer rescued her. The veracity of her account remains in question and has never been confirmed by official documentation although it ranks among the more colorful tales of World War II espionage.

128. NOT A ROUTINE TRAFFIC STOP

MAP 12 ➤ Portland–Columbia Toll Bridge connecting Portland, Pennsylvania, and Columbia, New Jersey

The end of a double life came for Russian *illegal* Jack Barsky just a few days before his 48th birthday in May 1997. Stopped by Pennsylvania State Troopers after crossing the Delaware River on the Portland–Columbia Toll Bridge, Barsky appeared to be involved in a routine traffic stop. After exiting his car, however, he was confronted by FBI special agents and taken into custody.

Barsky was driven to the Pocono Inn, 101 Broad St, Delaware Water Gap, Pennsylvania, and questioned for several hours before being released and allowed to return to his home at 438 Allegheny Road, Mount Bethel, Pennsylvania.

The apprehension was a cordial end to a spy drama that had begun years earlier at the height of the Cold War. Barsky, whose real name was Albrecht Dittrich, was a young East German chemist when he was recruited by the KGB and assigned the code name DIETER. Rigorously trained in tradecraft, he was sent to the United States with little more than a pocketful of cash and an authentic-appearing birth certificate identifying him as Jack Barsky. The name was appropriated from the birth records of a child who had died young and would have been approximately his age. Barsky spent most of the next decade building an American identity that included employment and educational credentials as well as a personal paper trail. As a Soviet *illegal*, he serviced dead drops, spotted talent for possible recruitment, and received ciphered instructions from shortwave broadcasts from clandestine transmitters known as "number stations" on a portable Sony radio.

The FBI arranged a traffic violation stop on the Portland–Columbia Toll Bridge connecting Pennsylvania and New Jersey as a pretext for questioning Jack Barsky about his past as a Soviet *illegal* in the United States. Barsky cooperated fully and eventually became a US citizen.

Unknown to his KGB handlers in Moscow, their spy created more than just a credible cover to protect him from American counterintelligence. As an information technology employee at the Metropolitan Life Insurance Company in New York City, Barsky worked to achieve the American dream. He married, fathered a child, purchased a home, and acclimated to a lifestyle that would have been unimaginable to most in the USSR or Eastern Europe. He had no intention of returning to the austere life he had left behind the Iron Curtain.

Jack Barsky

In 1988 Barsky received orders to return to Moscow. Unwilling to abandon his family or the life he built for himself, Barsky responded that he had contracted HIV/AIDS, and its treatment was available only in America. If allowed to stay, he promised he would not defect or reveal secrets. Initially, his insubordination elicited threats, but they eventually stopped. As the Soviet Union teetered on the edge of collapse, Barsky was left alone, seemingly forgotten by the Kremlin.

His life of anonymity lasted until 1992 when KGB archivist and defector Vasili Mitrokhin provided a treasure trove of detailed notes on intelligence operations against the West. From clues in Mitrokhin's material, the FBI was able to establish Barsky's identity and intelligence role. The suspected spy was placed under surveillance in 1994, his home was bugged, and the FBI purchased the house next door to monitor his activities. After three years of investigation, the FBI concluded Barsky was no longer an active spy and, with the ruse of the traffic stop, brought him in for questioning.

Barsky cooperated with US authorities and was granted American citizenship in 2014. A year later, he publicly broke his silence with an interview on *60 Minutes* and in 2017 released an autobiography, *Deep Undercover: My Secret Life and Tangled Allegiances as a KGB Spy in America*.

129. FROM JUNKIE TO JIHADIST

MAP I ➤ **Khyber Pass Pub:** 56 South Second Street

When 166 persons were killed in Mumbai, India, in November 2008, it was the world's deadliest terrorist act since the 9/11 attack on the United States. The man responsible for advance operational targeting was David Headley, a Philadelphia resident for nearly three decades.

Headley, born Daood Gilani, was the son of Philadelphian Serrill Headley and a Pakistani journalist she met in Washington, DC, in the late 1950s. They settled in Lahore, Pakistan, but after the marriage failed, Serrill returned alone to Philadelphia in the 1970s and opened the Khyber Pass Pub, 56 South Second Street in the Old City area. The bar, featuring Afghan tents, the hide of a Bengal tiger, and exotic beers, became a Philadelphia hotspot. In 1977 Serrill traveled to Pakistan and returned with her son, Daood, who had been attending Pakistan's Cadet College Hasan Abdal. Daood rented an apartment first on New Street and then at 221 North Clarion Street and immersed himself in the nightlife environment of women, drugs, and booze.

The Khyber Pass Pub, owned by his American-born mother, introduced Daood Gilani to the partying lifestyle.

After the bar was sold in 1988, Daood increasingly expressed contempt for "infidels," even as he engaged in drug smuggling with contacts in Pakistan. After arrests and jail time, he was recruited as an informant by the US Drug Enforcement Administration. In 2001 Daood entered the jihadist training camps of Pakistan's Lashkar-e-Taiba (Army of the Righteous). For four years he trained as a fedayee, a dedicated jihadist warrior willing to sacrifice himself for Allah.

In 2005 Daood was pulled from training because of his unique "Western" looks. With one blue eye and one brown eye, he appeared neither Muslim nor Pakistani. To further mask his Pakistani heritage and radical beliefs, Daood assumed his mother's name, becoming David Coleman Headley and often identifying himself as an American Jew when traveling. Thereafter, Headley made multiple trips to surveil and case Mumbai as part of the operational planning for the attack. By the spring of 2008, he had completed his work.

Daood Galini operated a video rental store on a prime corner in Philadelphia's center city.

Headley remained undetected until 2009 when he was spotted meeting a radical Muslim cleric in the United Kingdom following a reconnaissance trip to Denmark. Authorities determined he was part of an operation called Project Mickey Mouse to kill Kurt Westergaard, the cartoonist famous for his depiction of the prophet Muhammad wearing a bomb-shaped turban. Alerted to his activities, the FBI arrested Headley in 2009 at Chicago's O'Hare Airport as he was boarding a flight to Philadelphia. He eventually pleaded guilty and received a 35-year sentence for his crimes and a promise he would never be extradited to India or Denmark.

David Headley passes through India's immigration at Mumbai in July 2008 to conduct the final reconnaissance of targets that would be attacked that fall.

130. JIHAD JANE

MAP 11 ➤ **Colleen LaRose residence:** 429 Main Street, Pennsburg, Pennsylvania

Colleen LaRose moved to 429 Main Street, Pennsburg, from Texas in 2004 and, after personal loses and an attempted suicide, converted to Islam. On October 16, 2009, after the FBI received a tip from British authorities, she was arrested at the Philadelphia International Airport, 8800 Essington Avenue, aboard a flight from London. She was charged with attempting to recruit Islamic terrorists to wage violent jihad and plotting to murder Swedish artist Lars Vilks, who had sketched the prophet Muhammad as a dog.

LaRose first came to the attention of the FBI after she posted on the internet solicitations for financial support to wage jihad against the West. She used the screen names Jihad Jane and Fatima Rose while posting on Islamic internet forums and social media sites such as Facebook and YouTube to befriend and rally like-minded Muslims. LaRose was considered a useful asset because her appearance and US citizenship allowed her to blend into middle America.

LaRose pleaded guilty in 2011 to conspiracy to commit murder and to providing material support to terrorists. Although facing a maximum penalty of life in prison, she received a 10-year prison sentence in 2014 but was released in 2018. U.S. Attorney Michael Levy commented, "[LaRose] demonstrates yet another very real danger lurking on the Internet . . . that

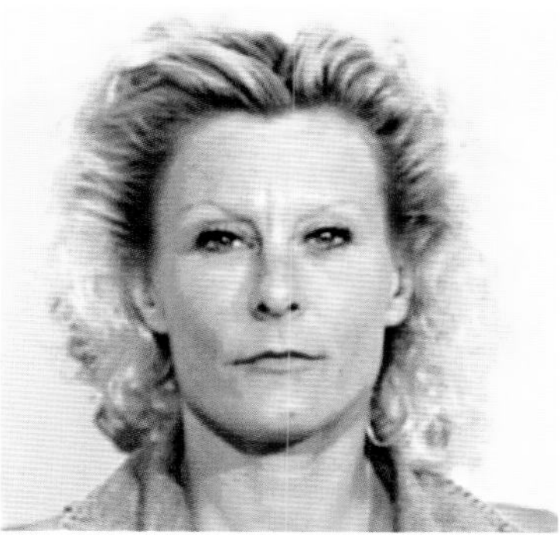

Colleen LaRose, also known as Jihad Jane and Fatima Rose

terrorists are looking for Americans to join them in their cause, and it shatters any lingering thought that we can spot a terrorist based on appearance."

131. TRACKING SPIES AND TERRORISTS

MAP I ➤ **FBI field office:** 600 Arch Street

Philadelphia's FBI field office opened in 1908 with its headquarters in the US Post Office Building on Ninth and Market Streets. In subsequent years, the office occupied multiple locations, including 735 South 12th Street as well as the Liberty Title and Trust Building at Broad and Arch Streets. Today its facility is at 600 Arch Street.

During its earliest years, the FBI focused on German attempts to sabotage explosives manufactured at the Frankford Arsenal and to disrupt shipping during World War I. Following the war, the Philadelphia field office battled the ongoing threat of anarchist terrorism, which was highlighted by the 1919 coordinated bombing attacks on American cities, and eventually led investigators to Philadelphia as the focus of the case.

In the interwar years, the field office sought to stem the growing threat of organized crime and Prohibition-era bootlegging through local gangsters like Max "Boo Boo" Hoff and Michael "Mickey" Duffy. In 1924 FBI special agent Lenore Houston was assigned to the Quaker City field office. Although not the first female agent in the bureau, she was the first and only one hired by the young director J. Edgar Hoover.

Philadelphia's FBI field office was one of the bureau's earliest locations and has successfully investigated espionage, sabotage, and terrorism cases in addition to traditional criminal activity.

World War II again saw Philadelphia become a target of sabotage and espionage. Foreign spies such as Spanish seamen Pablo Meso Legarreta and Emilio Ipes Cazaux Hernandes were arrested in the port city for smuggling messages to German agents in Spain.

Philadelphia's prominence as an espionage hub continued following World War II and into the Cold War. As the Cold War intensified, the Philadelphia field office played significant roles in the investigations of Soviet atomic spies Klaus Fuchs and Julius Rosenberg. Leads from that case also led to the arrest of Harry Gold, a chemist living in Philadelphia, and the identification of David Greenglass, a courier and the brother of Ethel Rosenberg.

Beginning in 1978, the FBI field office participated in what became a highly publicized corruption sting operation known as ABSCAM that ended with the convictions of three Philadelphia city council members, a US senator, six congressmen, and the mayor of Camden, New Jersey. Evidence in the scandal, which involved bribes associated with real estate dealings, included filmed meetings at the Barclay Hotel (today condominiums), 237 South 18th Street.

In May 2007 the Philadelphia Joint Terrorism Task Force disrupted a potentially disastrous terrorism plot by six men planning to attack soldiers at the US Army base at Fort Dix, New Jersey. More recently, in October 2009, the FBI arrested and gained the confession of former Philadelphia resident David Coleman Headley, a key figure in the November 2008 attack in Mumbai, India.

APPENDIX: SPY SITES MAPS

Readers should note that the locations depicted on the maps are approximate and may not represent the precise address of a site. If visiting or looking for a specific site, please refer to the text for the complete address.

To the best of the authors' information, as of press time the addresses cited in the book are accurate. The physical appearance of many sites may have changed since the location was last used for spy activity. Ownership, redevelopment, and business changes have and will continue to occur. Particularly for private residences, we urge readers to respect the privacy of occupants and owners.

MAP 1

PHILADELPHIA

➤ Old City, Chinatown, and Society Hill

south of I-676, north of Lombard Street, west of Delaware River, east of Seventh Street

1. **Independence Hall [2]**
   520 Chestnut Street
2. **Carpenters' Hall [3]**
   320 Chestnut Street
3. **Robert Morris statue [5]**
   Independence National Historical Park, bounded by Second and Sixth and Chestnut and Race Streets
5. **Benjamin Franklin's residence [8]**
   314–321 Market Street (steel frame structure marks the spot where the three-story brick house once stood)
6. **Walnut Street Prison [11]**
   Walnut and South Sixth Streets
9. **Liberty Bell Center [15]**
   526 Market Street
10. **Slate Roof House [17]**
    Corner of South Second Street and Sansom Walk (now the site of Welcome Park)
11. **City Tavern [18]**
    138 South Second Street
12. **The New Market [18]**
    South Second Street between Lombard and Pine Streets
16. **Margaret Shippen residence [23]**
    218–220 South Fourth Street
17. **Joseph Stansbury shop [25]**
    North Second Street (between Church and Filbert Streets, area redeveloped)
20. **Thomas McKean residence [28]**
    312 Chestnut Street (area redeveloped)
23. **Delaware River Piers [31]**
    Independence Seaport Museum
32. **Slate Roof House [43]**
    South Second Street and Sansom Walk
33. **British major John André residence (during occupation) [44]**
    Franklin Court, 314–321 Market Street
34. **Don Juan de Miralles residence [46]**
    242 South Third Street

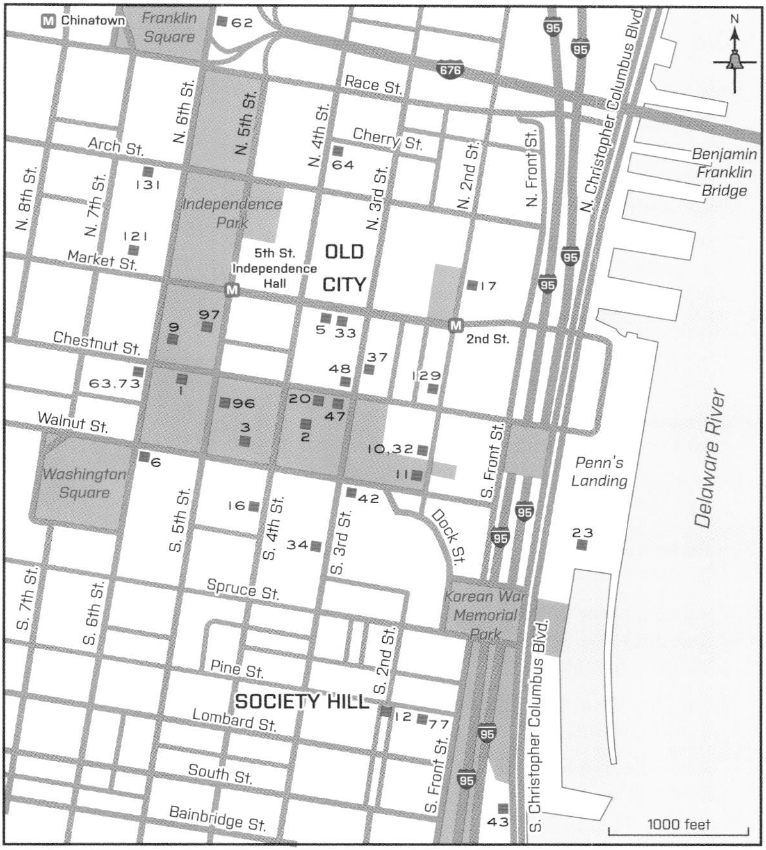
Chinatown
Franklin Square
62
Race St.
676
95
N. Christopher Columbus Blvd.
N
N. 6th St.
N. 5th St.
N. 4th St.
Cherry St.
Arch St.
64
N. 3rd St.
N. 2nd St.
N. Front St.
Benjamin Franklin Bridge
N. 8th St.
N. 7th St.
131
Independence Park
121
Market St.
5th St. Independence Hall
OLD CITY
17
97
9
5
33
2nd St.
Chestnut St.
37
48
63,73
1
129
20
96
47
Walnut St.
3
2
Delaware River
6
10,32
Penn's Landing
Washington Square
11
S. Front St.
16
42
S. 5th St.
S. 4th St.
S. 3rd St.
Dock St.
23
34
Spruce St.
Korean War Memorial Park
S. 7th St.
S. 6th St.
Pine St.
S. 2nd St.
SOCIETY HILL
12
77
Lombard St.
S. Christopher Columbus Blvd.
South St.
S. Front St.
Bainbridge St.
43
1000 feet

MAP 1: continued

PHILADELPHIA

➤ Old City, Chinatown, and Society Hill

south of I-676, north of Lombard Street, west of Delaware River, east of Seventh Street

37. **Pinkerton's National Detective Agency office [54]**
45 South Third Street

42. **Maj. Gen. George B. McClellan birthplace [62]**
248 Walnut Street (near the corner of redeveloped Walnut and South Seventh Streets)

43. **Union Navy Yard [63]**
Federal Street, Southwark neighborhood from Front Street to the Delaware River

47. ***Philadelphia Inquirer* [69]**
304 Chestnut Street

48. ***Philadelphia's Daily News* [70]**
74 South Third Street

62. **Technical School to Aid Soviet Russia [95]**
259 North Sixth Street (demolished, area redeveloped)

63. ***Public Ledger* [96]**
Chestnut and South Sixth Streets, southwest corner (building demolished)

64. **Old Zion Church [100]**
South Fourth and Cherry Streets (razed in 1972)

73. ***Public Ledger* [110]**
South Sixth and Chestnut Streets, southwest corner (building demolished)

77. **Charles W. Thayer residence [120]**
116 Pine Street

96. **American Philosophical Society [154]**
105 South Fifth Street

97. **Law Firm of Biddle, Paul, and Jayne [155]**
505 Chestnut Street

121. **Robert Lipka trial site [189]**
US Courthouse, 601 Market Street

129. **Khyber Pass Pub [199]**
56 South Second Street

131. **FBI Field Office [202]**
600 Arch Street

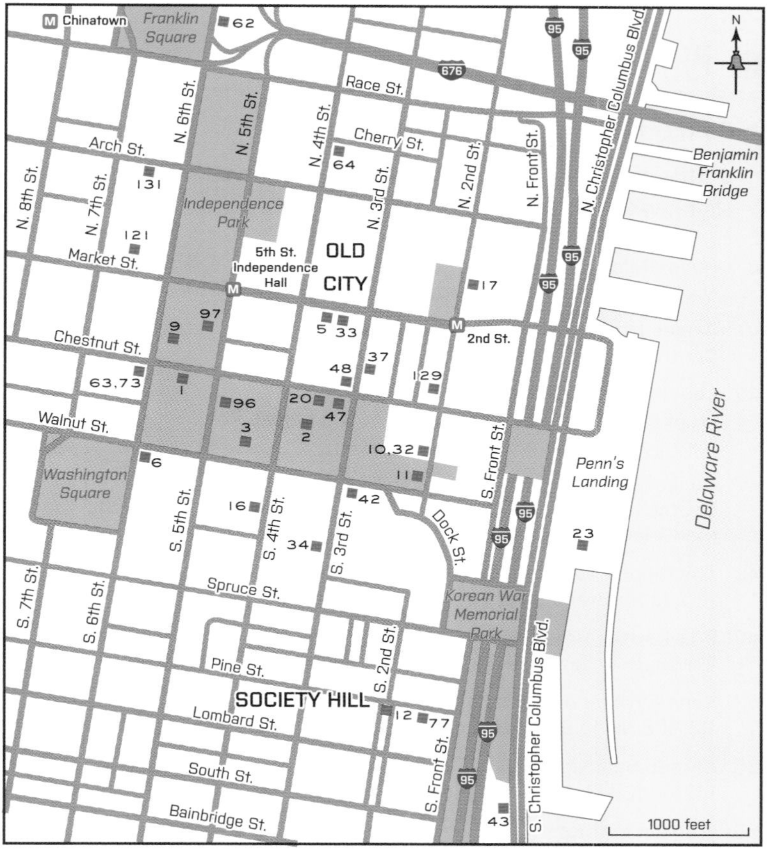
Chinatown
Franklin Square
62
Race St.
Cherry St.
Arch St.
N. 8th St.
N. 7th St.
N. 6th St.
N. 5th St.
N. 4th St.
N. 3rd St.
N. 2nd St.
N. Front St.
N. Christopher Columbus Blvd
Benjamin Franklin Bridge
64
131
121
Independence Park
Market St.
5th St. Independence Hall
OLD CITY
17
2nd St.
97
9
5
33
Chestnut St.
37
48
129
63,73
1
96
20
47
3
2
Walnut St.
10,32
11
6
42
Washington Square
S. 5th St.
S. 4th St.
S. 3rd St.
16
34
Dock St.
S. Front St.
Penn's Landing
Delaware River
23
S. 7th St.
S. 6th St.
Spruce St.
Korean War Memorial Park
S. Christopher Columbus Blvd.
Pine St.
S. 2nd St.
SOCIETY HILL
Lombard St.
12
77
South St.
Bainbridge St.
43
1000 feet

MAP 2

PHILADELPHIA

➤ Center City

south of I-676, north of Lombard Street, west of Schuylkill River, west of Seventh Street

8. **Haym Salomon burial site [13]**
Mikveh Israel Cemetery, South Eighth and Spruce Streets

18. **James Molesworth execution site [26]**
Centre Square at Market and 15th Streets

29. **London Coffee House [39]**
Front and Market Streets (demolished), Thomas Paine Plaza, 1401 John F. Kennedy Boulevard

40. **Quaker School for Negroes [59]**
Southeast corner of Locust and South Hutchinson Streets (site redeveloped)

45. **The Union League [66]**
140 South Broad Street

49. **Ritz-Carlton Hotel [76]**
211 South Broad Street (now site of Daniel J. Terra Building)

52. **Pennsylvania Academy of the Fine Arts [80]**
118–128 North Broad Street

55. **Arcade Building [85]**
1428–1434 Market Street (demolished)

58. **Franklin Institute [88]**
222 North 20th Street

60. **Bellevue-Stratford Hotel [91]**
200 South Broad Street

78. **Ben Franklin Hotel (now the Franklin Residences) [121]**
834 Chestnut Street

84. **War Library and Museum of the Military Order of the Loyal Legion of the United States [132]**
1805 Pine Street

92. **Hyatt at the Bellevue [146]**
200 South Broad Street

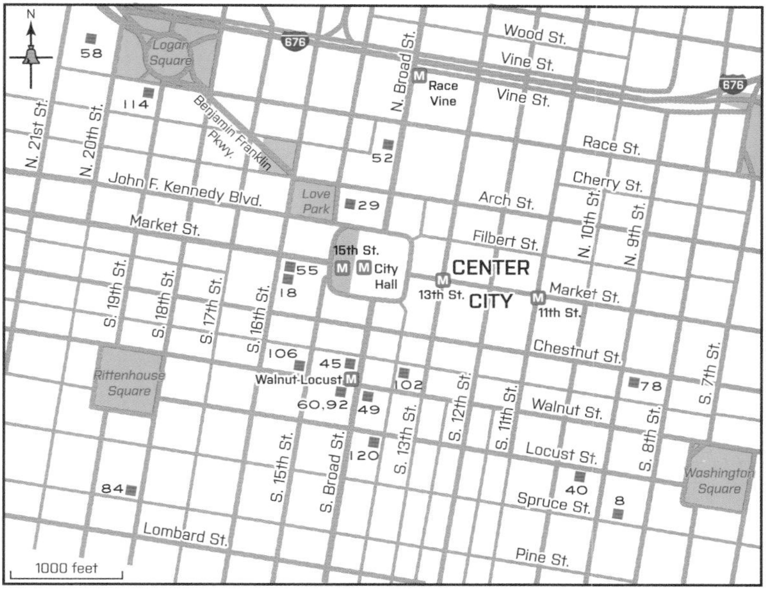

102. **Bankers' Security Building [161]**
1313–1317 Walnut Street

106. **Louis Kahn office [166]**
1501 Walnut Street

114. **Academy of Natural Sciences (today the Academy of Natural Sciences of Drexel University) [180]**
1900 Benjamin Franklin Parkway

120. **Sylvania Hotel [188]**
1324 Locust Street

MAP 3

PHILADELPHIA

➤ South Philadelphia including Navy Yard and Passyunk Square

south of Washington Avenue, to Navy Yard, west and north of the Delaware River, east of South 25th Street

44. **Moyamensing Prison (demolished in 1960s) [64]**
South Tenth and Reed Streets

81. **I. F. Stone birthplace [125]**
636 South Wharton Street

99. **Philadelphia Naval Shipyard [157]**
4701 Intrepid Avenue

111. **Building 638 [176]**
Philadelphia Naval Shipyard, approximate location

122. **Basin Street Bridge [190]**
Philadelphia Naval Shipyard

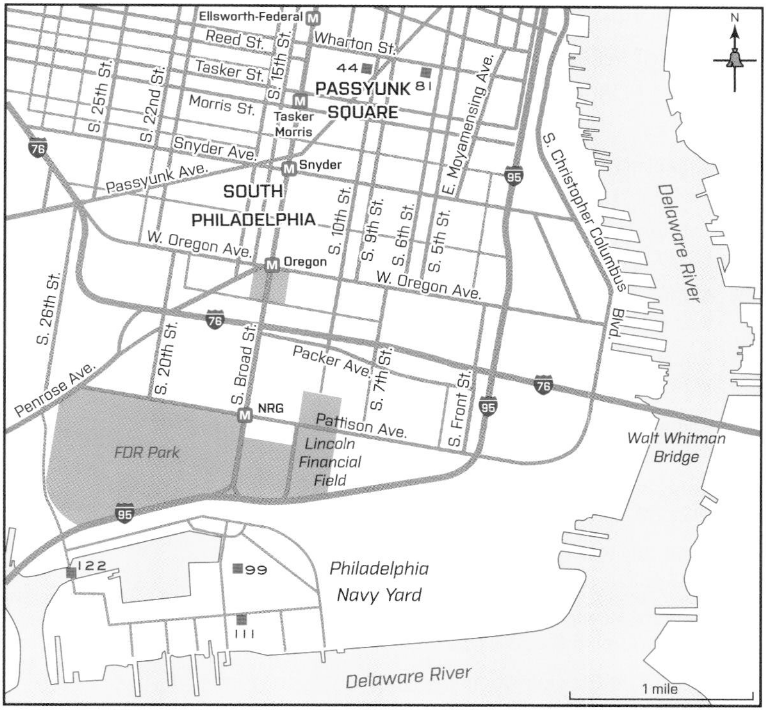
Ellsworth-Federal
Reed St.
Wharton St.
Tasker St.
44
81
PASSYUNK
SQUARE
S. 25th St.
S. 22nd St.
S. 15th St.
Morris St.
Tasker
Morris
Snyder Ave.
Snyder
Passyunk Ave.
E. Moyamensing Ave.
S. Christopher Columbus Blvd.
Delaware River
SOUTH
PHILADELPHIA
S. 10th St.
S. 9th St.
S. 6th St.
S. 5th St.
W. Oregon Ave.
Oregon
W. Oregon Ave.
S. 26th St.
S. 20th St.
S. Broad St.
Packer Ave.
S. 7th St.
S. Front St.
Penrose Ave.
NRG
Pattison Ave.
FDR Park
Lincoln
Financial
Field
Walt Whitman
Bridge
122
99
Philadelphia
Navy Yard
111
Delaware River
1 mile
N
76
95

MAP 4

PHILADELPHIA

➤ North Philadelphia including Franklintown, Fairmount, Norris Square, Poplar, and Yorktown

north of I-676, east of North 25th Street, west of I-95, south of West Dauphin Street

36. **Edgar Allan Poe residence [53]**
532 North Seventh Street

39. **Lafayette C. Baker residence [57]**
1737 Coates Street (later renamed Fairmount Avenue)

56. **Arthur Brock Jr. Headquarters [86]**
533 North Eleventh Street (site redeveloped)

59. **Moose Hall of the Loyal Order of Moose Lodge 54 [90]**
1314 North Broad Street

71. ***Philadelphia Record* [108]**
317–319 North Broad Street

79. **Charles W. Berg Laboratories [123]**
1827–1829 North Fifth Street

93. **John Jay McCloy residence [148]**
2136 North 19th Street

98. **Packard Motor Car Company Building [156]**
317–321 North Broad Street

108. **ITE Circuit Breaker Company [169]**
North 19th and Hamilton Streets (site redeveloped)

112. **Whittaker Chambers birthplace [177]**
2232 West Diamond Street (vacant lot)

W. York St.
W. Dauphin St.
N. Broad St.
W. Cumberland St.
W. York St.
W. Dauphin St.
93
112
N. 21st St.
W. Diamond St.
Susquehanna-Dauphin
W. Norris St.
NORTH PHILADELPHIA
W. Diamond St.
N. American St.
N. Hancock St.
York-Dauphin
N. Front St.
N. 22nd St.
W. Berks St.
W. Montgomery Ave.
Temple University
N. 25th St.
W. Berks St.
N. 2nd St.
Frankford Ave.
N. 19th St.
Cecil B. Moore Ave.
79
Cecil B. Moore
Berks
Ridge Ave.
N. 17th St.
N. 16th St.
N. 12th St.
N. 11th St.
N. 10th St.
Germantown Ave.
Master St.
N. 7th St.
N. 6th St.
N. 5th St.
N. 4th St.
Girard College
59
Girard
W. Girard Ave.
FISHTOWN
N. Broad St.
Girard
39
Fairmount Ave.
Fairmount
95
SPRING GARDEN
Poplar St.
Fairmount Ave.
Spring Garden St.
N. 21st St.
108
56
36
Spring Garden
Spring Garden St.
N. Delaware Ave.
Callowhill St.
Spring Garden
676
95
71, 98
Delaware River
Callowhill St.
Race Vine
676
1/2 mile
N

MAP 5

PHILADELPHIA

➤ Allegheny West, Brewerytown, Fairmount Park

north of I-676, both sides of Schuylkill River, east of Parkside Avenue North, south of I-76, west of North 29th Street

15. **Benedict Arnold residence [22]**
3800 Mount Pleasant Drive

19. **Joseph Reed burial site [27]**
Laurel Hill Cemetery, 3822 Ridge Avenue

25. **Rebecca Shoemaker home [35]**
Laurel Hill, 7201 North Randolph Drive

26. **Rinker's Rock [35]**
Fairmount Park, 4231 North Concourse Drive

41. **Belmont Mansion [61]**
2000 Belmont Mansion Drive

80. **Yellow Cab Company [124]**
1206 North 31st Street

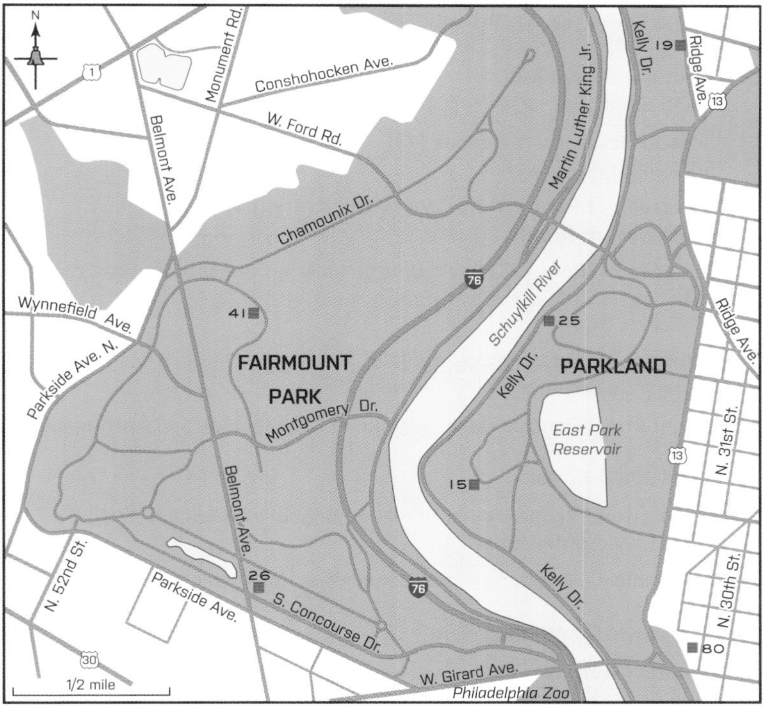
N
Conshohocken Ave.
Monument Rd.
W. Ford Rd.
Belmont Ave.
Chamounix Dr.
Martin Luther King Jr.
Kelly Dr.
19
Ridge Ave.
Wynnefield Ave.
41
Parkside Ave. N.
FAIRMOUNT
PARK
Montgomery Dr.
Schuylkill River
25
Kelly Dr.
PARKLAND
Ridge Ave.
East Park
Reservoir
15
N. 31st St.
Belmont Ave.
N. 52nd St.
26
Parkside Ave.
S. Concourse Dr.
Kelly Dr.
N. 30th St.
80
W. Girard Ave.
Philadelphia Zoo
1/2 mile

MAP 6

PHILADELPHIA

➤ West Philadelphia, University City, and Kingsessing

west of Schuylkill River, south of Haverford Avenue, east of 57th Street, north of Kingsessing Avenue

38. **West train depot [56]**
North 32nd and Market Streets

51. **Joseph McGarrity residence [79]**
5412 Springfield Avenue

54. **University of Pennsylvania, Van Pelt Library [83]**
3420 Walnut Street

61. **Our Lady of Victory Catholic Church (now St. Joseph Baptist Church) [93]**
5412 Vine Street

76. **William C. Bullitt Jr. grave site [118]**
Woodlands Cemetery, 4000 Woodland Avenue

107. **University of Pennsylvania Museum of Archaeology and Anthropology [167]**
3260 South Street

109. **University of Pennsylvania Perelman School of Medicine [170]**
3400 Civic Center Boulevard

110. **The Municipal Auditorium and Convention Hall (demolished in 2007) [174]**
3400 Civic Center Boulevard

115. **General Electric Re-entry Systems Building [181]**
3198 Chestnut Street

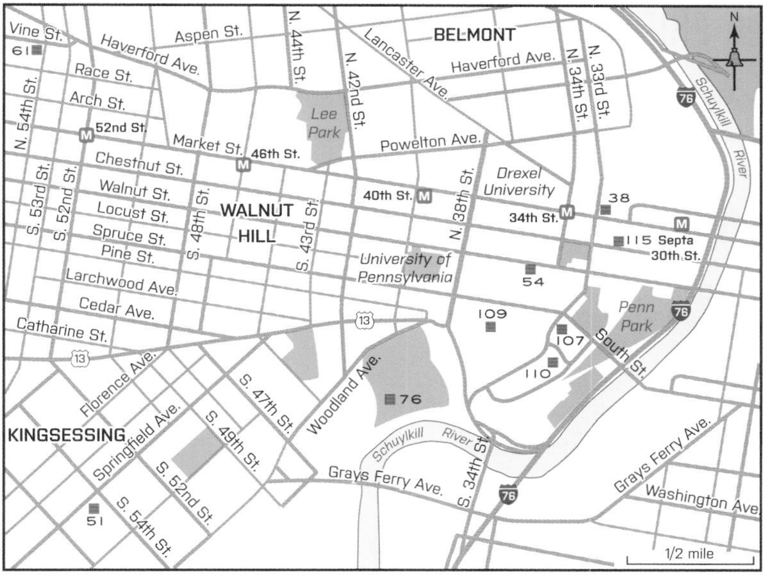
Vine St.
61
Haverford Ave.
Aspen St.
N. 44th St.
Lancaster Ave.
BELMONT
Haverford Ave.
N. 34th St.
N. 33rd St.
N
Race St.
N. 54th St.
Arch St.
N. 42nd St.
Lee Park
Schuylkill
52nd St.
Market St.
46th St.
Powelton Ave.
River
Chestnut St.
S. 53rd St.
S. 52nd St.
Walnut St.
S. 48th St.
S. 43rd St.
40th St.
N. 38th St.
Drexel University
38
Locust St.
WALNUT HILL
34th St.
Spruce St.
115 Septa 30th St.
Pine St.
University of Pennsylvania
54
Larchwood Ave.
Cedar Ave.
109
Penn Park
Catharine St.
13
107
South St.
110
Florence Ave.
S. 47th St.
Woodland Ave.
76
KINGSESSING
Springfield Ave.
S. 49th St.
Schuylkill River
S. 52nd St.
Grays Ferry Ave.
S. 34th St.
76
Grays Ferry Ave.
Washington Ave.
51
S. 54th St.
1/2 mile

MAP 7

PHILADELPHIA AND BALA CYNWYD

➤ Bala Cynwyd and Northwest Philadelphia including Roxborough-Manayunk and Germantown

south of Chew Avenue, east of Bala Avenue North, west of Wister Street, north of US Route 1

31. **Christopher Ludwick grave site [41]**
Saint Michael's Lutheran Church, 6671 Germantown Avenue, Philadelphia

53. **Vernon Park [83]**
5818 Germantown Avenue, Philadelphia

119. **Robert Ames childhood residence [187]**
4624 Pechin Street, Philadelphia

124. **Chuck Barris hometown [192]**
Bala Cynwyd

127. **West Laurel Hill Cemetery [196]**
225 Belmont Avenue, Bala Cynwyd

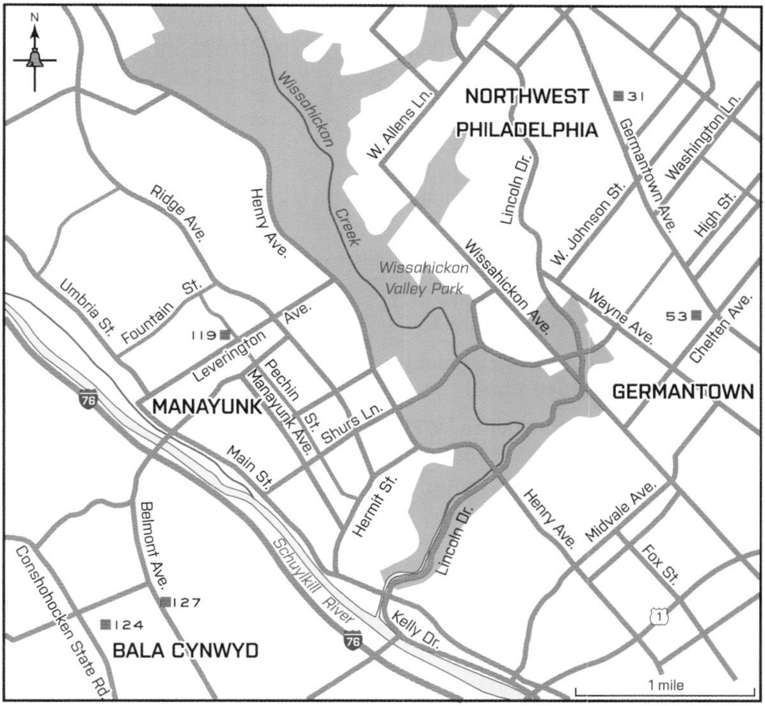
N
NORTHWEST
PHILADELPHIA
GERMANTOWN
MANAYUNK
BALA CYNWYD
Wissahickon Creek
Wissahickon Valley Park
W. Allens Ln.
Lincoln Dr.
Germantown Ave.
Washington Ln.
W. Johnson St.
High St.
Wissahickon Ave.
Wayne Ave.
Chelten Ave.
Ridge Ave.
Henry Ave.
Umbria St.
Fountain St.
Leverington Ave.
Pechin St.
Manayunk Ave.
Shurs Ln.
Main St.
Hermit St.
Midvale Ave.
Fox St.
Belmont Ave.
Conshohocken State Rd.
Schuylkill River
Kelly Dr.
76
1
31
53
119
124
127
1 mile

MAP 8

PHILADELPHIA

➤ North and Northeast Philadelphia, including Glenwood, Kensington, Port Richmond, Frankford, Bridesburg, and Oxford Circle

south of 66th Avenue, east of Ogontz Avenue, west of Delaware River, north of West Dauphin Street, including the Port of Philadelphia

4. **Rising Sun Tavern [6]**
Corner of Germantown Avenue and Old York Road (site redeveloped)

24. **Elias Boudinot residence [34]**
Rosehill and East Cambria Streets (site redeveloped)

28. **Allan McLane headquarters [37]**
Jolly Post, 4606 Frankford Avenue (site redeveloped)

65. **Khaki Shirts of America headquarters [101]**
4430 North Broad Street

66. **Gerhard Kunze residence [102]**
6501 North Smedley Street

69. **Carl Krepper residence [106]**
1906 East Allegheny Avenue

74. **Port of Philadelphia [112]**
Port of Philadelphia

82. **Harry Gold residence [126]**
6823 Kindred Street

91. **Frankford Arsenal [145]**
Tacony and Bridge Streets

103. **Port of Philadelphia [162]**
Port of Philadelphia

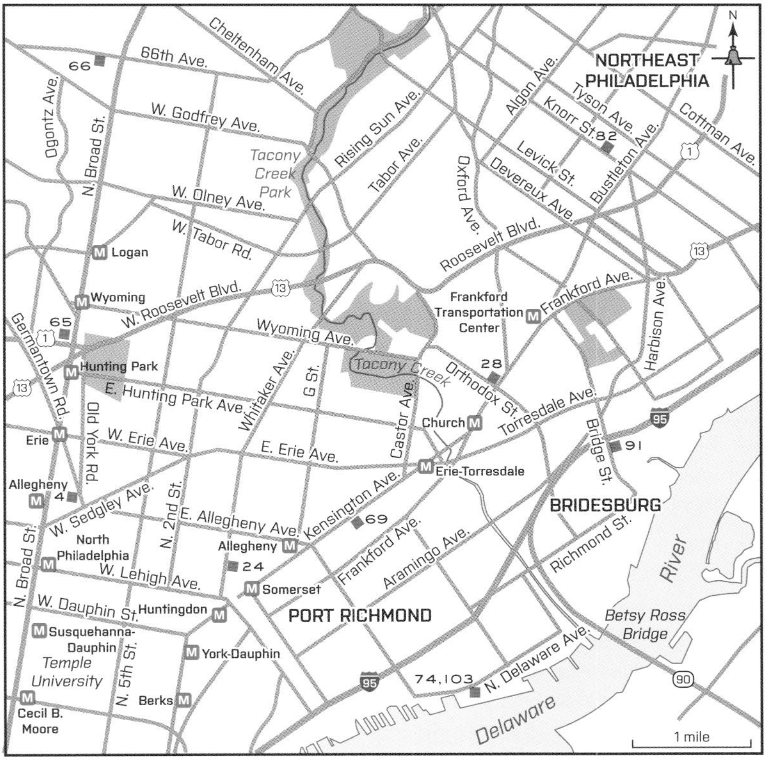
NORTHEAST
PHILADELPHIA
N
66th Ave.
Cheltenham Ave.
66
Ogontz Ave.
N. Broad St.
W. Godfrey Ave.
Tacony
Creek
Park
Rising Sun Ave.
Tabor Ave.
Algon Ave.
Tyson Ave.
Knorr St.
82
Levick St.
Bustleton Ave.
Cottman Ave.
Oxford Ave.
Devereux Ave.
W. Olney Ave.
W. Tabor Rd.
Roosevelt Blvd.
Logan
Wyoming
W. Roosevelt Blvd.
Frankford
Transportation
Center
Frankford Ave.
Harbison Ave.
Germantown Rd.
65
Wyoming Ave.
Hunting Park
E. Hunting Park Ave.
Whitaker Ave.
G St.
Tacony Creek
28
Orthodox St.
Torresdale Ave.
Old York Rd.
Castor Ave.
Church
Bridge St.
Erie
W. Erie Ave.
E. Erie Ave.
Erie-Torresdale
91
Allegheny
4
W. Sedgley Ave.
N. 2nd St.
Kensington Ave.
69
BRIDESBURG
E. Allegheny Ave.
North
Philadelphia
Allegheny
Frankford Ave.
Aramingo Ave.
Richmond St.
River
W. Lehigh Ave.
24
Somerset
N. Broad St.
W. Dauphin St.
Huntingdon
PORT RICHMOND
Betsy Ross
Bridge
Susquehanna-
Dauphin
York-Dauphin
Temple
University
N. 5th St.
74,103
N. Delaware Ave.
Cecil B.
Moore
Berks
Delaware
1 mile
1
13
95
90

MAP 9

MAIN LINE SUBURBS OF PHILADELPHIA

➤ Ardmore, Bryn Mawr, Haverford, Merion Township, Villanova, and Wayne

outside City of Philadelphia, west of city, north of Connestoga Road and Route 30, east of North Valley Road, west of Penn Valley, Pennsburg at far north

75. **Eugène Jules Houdry residence [113]**
Righters Mill and Mill Creek Roads, Ardmore
83. **Henry Collins childhood home [131]**
151 North Merion Avenue, Bryn Mawr
94. **William P. Davis III residence [150]**
111 Ringwood Road, Bryn Mawr
95. **Conyers Read home [152]**
Wistar Road, Villanova
100. **George H. Earle III residence [158]**
Gray's Lane, Haverford
105. **Brooke Dolan II residence [164]**
417 Fishers Road, Bryn Mawr
116. **Catherwood Foundation [183]**
807 Lancaster Avenue, Bryn Mawr
118. **Richard Helms birthplace [185]**
Cambria Court, St Davids (Wayne)
126. **Samuel Cummings residence [194]**
639 Hazelwood Avenue, Ardmore

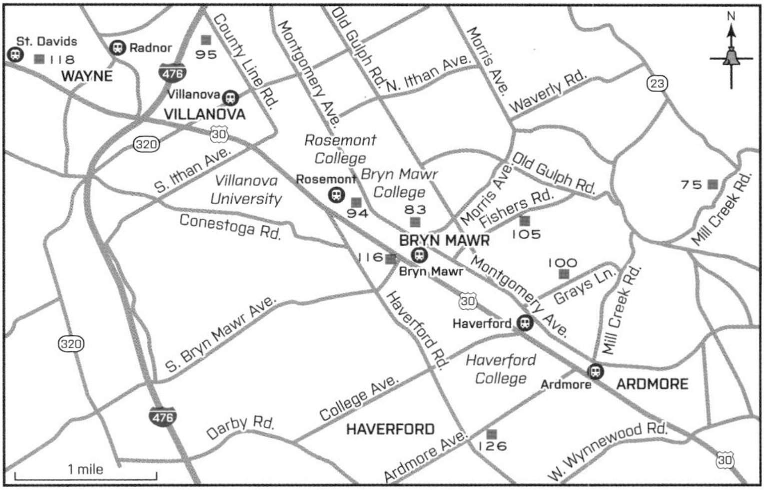
St. Davids
118
Radnor
95
WAYNE
476
Villanova
VILLANOVA
County Line Rd.
Montgomery Ave.
Old Gulph Rd.
N. Ithan Ave.
Morris Ave.
Waverly Rd.
23
N
30
320
S. Ithan Ave.
Rosemont College
Villanova University
Rosemont
Bryn Mawr College
94
83
Old Gulph Rd.
Morris Ave.
Fishers Rd.
105
75
Mill Creek Rd.
Conestoga Rd.
BRYN MAWR
116
Bryn Mawr
Montgomery Ave.
100
Grays Ln.
S. Bryn Mawr Ave.
Haverford Rd.
Haverford
Mill Creek Rd.
320
Haverford College
Ardmore
ARDMORE
College Ave.
Darby Rd.
HAVERFORD
Ardmore Ave.
126
W. Wynnewood Rd.
1 mile

MAP 10

DELAWARE COUNTY, PENNSYLVANIA

➤ Newtown Square, Swarthmore, Chester

north of Delaware River, east of Providence Road, west of Route 30, Goshen Road and south

13. **John Clark operational headquarters [19]**
    4111 Goshen Road, Newtown Square
50. **Unidentified Victims Memorial [78]**
    Chester Rural Cemetery, 412 West 15th Street, Chester
87. **Swarthmore College [137]**
    500 College Avenue, Swarthmore
90. **Swarthmore College [143]**
    500 College Avenue, Swarthmore
117. **Sun Shipbuilding and Drydock Company (today the site of Harrah's Philadelphia Casino and Racetrack) [184]**
    777 Harrah's Boulevard, Chester

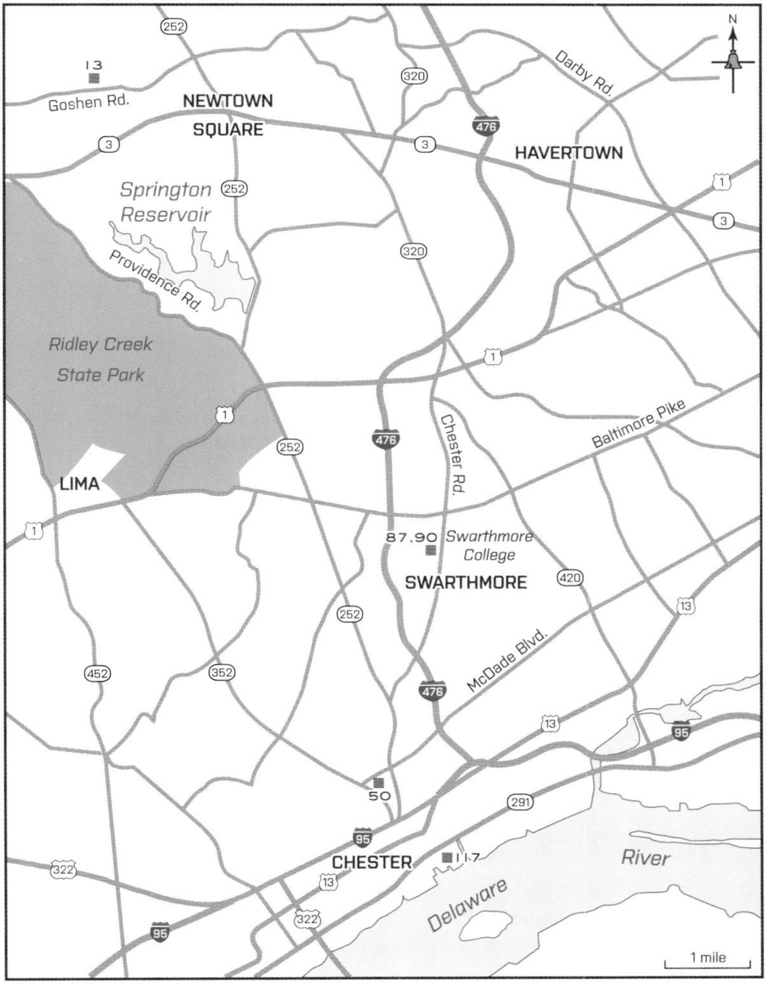
13
Goshen Rd.
NEWTOWN
SQUARE
HAVERTOWN
Darby Rd.
Springton
Reservoir
Providence Rd.
Ridley Creek
State Park
LIMA
Chester Rd.
Baltimore Pike
87,90
Swarthmore
College
SWARTHMORE
McDade Blvd.
50
CHESTER
117
River
Delaware
1 mile
N

MAP 11:

MONTGOMERY COUNTY AND BUCKS COUNTY, PENNSYLVANIA

➤ Bensalem, Doylestown, Morrisville, New Hope, Pennsburg, Quakertown, and Sellersville

north of I-276 except for Bensalem, east of I-476, south of I-78, west of Delaware River

7. **Parade Grounds at Valley Forge National Historic Park [11]**
King of Prussia

14. **Washington's army headquarters [20]**
Valley Forge National Historic Park, King of Prussia

21. **James Galloway residence [29]**
Trevose Manor (also known as Gen. James Wilkinson House and Joseph Growden House), 5408 Old Trevose Road, Bensalem

22. **Doan grave site [30]**
Plumstead Friends Meeting House and Cemetery, 4914-A Pt. Pleasant Pike, Doylestown

35. **Summerseat [47]**
Clymer and North Morris Avenues, Morrisville

46. **Thaddeus S. C. Lowe House [67]**
823 West Main Street, Norristown

67. **Deutschhorst Country Club [103]**
Sellersville (site redeveloped)

68. **Philadelphia Salt Manufacturing Company's Cryolite Plant (now Waterside neighborhood development) [104]**
2375 State Road, Bensalem

70. **William Colepaugh residence [107]**
245 Holstein Road, King of Prussia

86. **Schulberg residence [136]**
US-202 and Lower York Road, New Hope

88. **Springhouse Farm [139]**
2184 Springhouse Lane, Quakertown

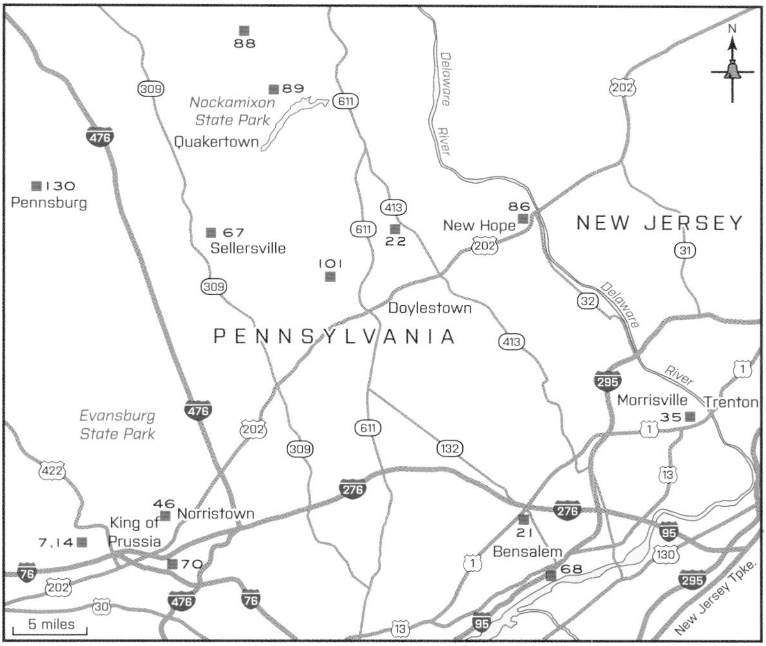

89. **Hede Massing residence [142]**
1767 Country Lane, Quakertown

101. **Katyn Massacre Memorial site [160]**
The National Shrine of Our Lady of Czestochowa Cemetery, 654 Ferry Road, Doylestown

130. **Colleen LaRose residence [201]**
429 Main Street, Pennsburg

MAP 12

PENNSYLVANIA

➤ Lancaster, York, Bellefonte, Mt. Bethel, and Perry County

27. **Thomas Mifflin burial site [36]**
Holy Trinity Lutheran Churchyard, 31 South Duke Street, Lancaster

57. **Anna Wagner Keichline birthplace [87]**
Bellefonte

104. **David Ogilvy home [163]**
420 West King Street, Lancaster

113. **Defector's grave site [178]**
Greenmount Cemetery and Cremation Garden, 721 Carlisle Avenue, York

125. **Big Spring State Forest Picnic Area [193]**
Blain

128. **Portland-Columbia Toll Bridge [198]**
Portland-Columbia Toll Bridge connecting Portland, Pennsylvania, and Columbia, New Jersey

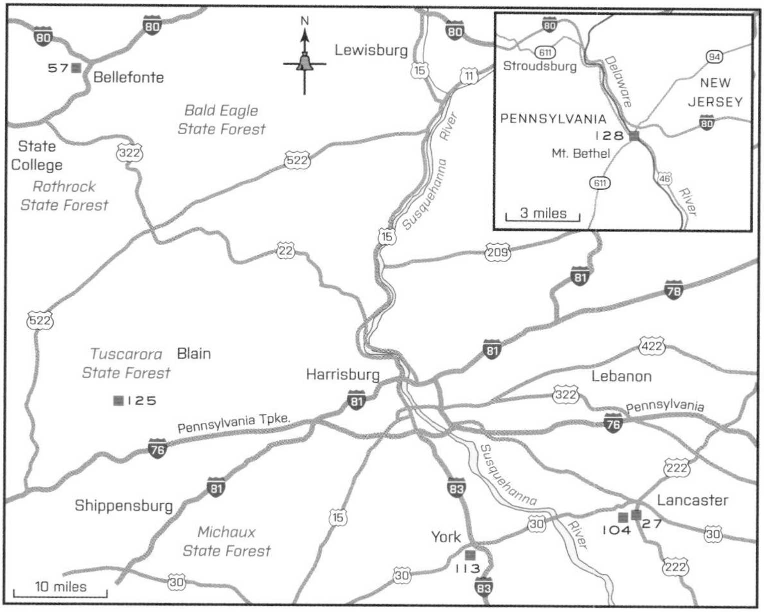

Lewisburg
57
Bellefonte
Bald Eagle
State Forest
State
College
Rothrock
State Forest
Tuscarora
State Forest
Blain
125
Harrisburg
Pennsylvania Tpke.
Shippensburg
Michaux
State Forest
York
113
Lebanon
Pennsylvania
Lancaster
104
27
Susquehanna River
10 miles
Stroudsburg
Delaware River
NEW
JERSEY
PENNSYLVANIA
128
Mt. Bethel
3 miles

MAP 13

NEW JERSEY

➤ Gloucester City, Bordentown, and Loveladies Harbor

30. **Patience Wright residence [40]**
    100 Farnsworth Avenue, Bordentown, New Jersey
72. **Immigration Detention Center [108]**
    101 South King Street, Gloucester City, New Jersey
85. **Loveladies Harbor [134]**
    Long Beach Island, New Jersey

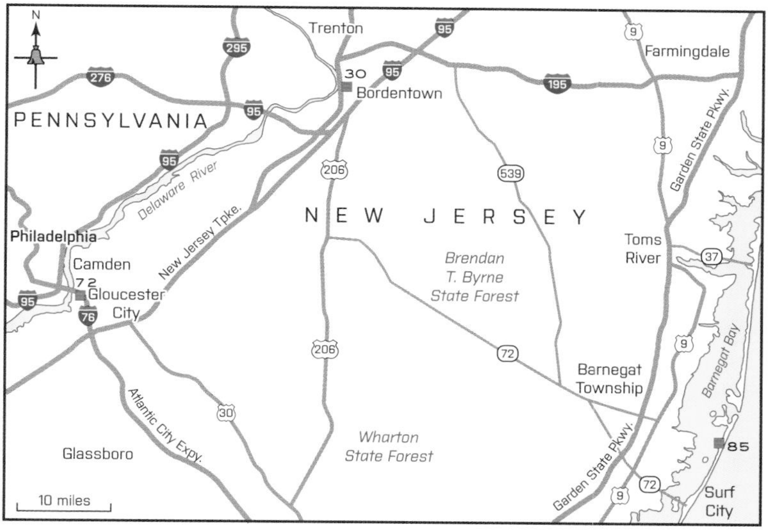
N
Trenton
295
276
95
30
Bordentown
195
Farmingdale
9
PENNSYLVANIA
Garden State Pkwy.
206
539
Delaware River
New Jersey Tpke.
NEW JERSEY
Philadelphia
Camden
72
Gloucester City
76
Toms River
37
Brendan T. Byrne State Forest
206
72
Barnegat Township
Barnegat Bay
Atlantic City Expy.
30
Wharton State Forest
85
Glassboro
Garden State Pkwy.
72
Surf City
10 miles

SELECTED BIBLIOGRAPHY

Allen, Susan Heuck. *Classical Spies: American Archaeologists with the OSS in World War II Greece.* Ann Arbor: University of Michigan Press, 2011.

Andrew, Christopher. *Defend the Realm: The Authorized History of MI5*. New York: Vintage, 2010.

———. *For the President's Eyes Only: Secret Intelligence and the American Presidency from Washington to Bush*. New York: Harper Perennial, 1996.

Andrew, Christopher, and Vasili Mitrokhin. *The Mitrokhin Archive: The KGB in Europe and the West.* New York: Alan Lane/Penguin Press, 1999.

———. *The Sword and The Shield: The Mitrokhin Archive and the Secret History of the KGB*. New York: Basic Books, 1999.

Bakeless, John. *Turncoats, Traitors and Heroes*. New York: Da Capo Press, 1998.

Baker, Lafayette C. *History of the United States Secret Service*. Philadelphia: L. C. Baker, 1867.

Baker, Robert. *Rezident: The Espionage Odyssey of Soviet General Vasily Zarubin.* Bloomington, IN: iUniverse, 2015.

Barris, Chuck. *Confessions of a Dangerous Mind: An Unauthorized Autobiography.* New York: St. Martin's Press, 1982.

Barsky, Jack. *Deep Under Cover: My Secret Life & Tangled Allegiances as a KGB Spy in America*. With Cindy Coloma. Carol Stream, IL: Tyndale Momentum, 2017.

Barzun, Jacques. "Findings: Meditations on the Literature of Spying." *American Scholar*. December 1, 2007. https://theamericanscholar.org/meditations-on-the-literature-of-spying/#.XnPnkC2ZOf5.

Blum, Howard. *Dark Invasion: 1915: Germany's Secret War and the Hunt for the First Terrorist Cell in America*. New York: HarperCollins, 2014.

Bond, James. *Birds of the West Indies*. Philadelphia: Academy of Natural Sciences of Philadelphia, 1936.

Brands, H. W. *The Frist American: The Life and Times of Benjamin Franklin*. New York: Anchor Books, 2002.

Breindel, Eric, and Herbert Romerstein. *The Venona Secrets: The Definitive Exposé of Soviet Espionage in America*. Washington, DC: Regnery, 2014.

Brown, Anthony Cave. *The Last Hero: Wild Bill Donovan*. New York: Times Books, 1983.

Bullitt, William C., Jr. *It's Not Done*. New York: Harcourt, Brace, 1926.

Chambers, Whittaker. *Witness*. New York: Random House, 1952.

Christie, Greg. *Knight: Yorkshireman, Storyteller, Spy*. Folkestone, Kent: Ouen Press, 2018.

Conant, Jennet. *A Covert Affair: Julia Child and Paul Child in the OSS*. New York: Simon & Schuster, 2011.

———. *The Irregulars: Roald Dahl and the British Spy Ring in Wartime Washington*. New York: Simon & Schuster, 2009.

Cook, Andrew. *Ace of Spies: The True Story of Sidney Reilly*. Gloucestershire: Tempus, 2004.

Coulson, Thomas. *Mata Hari: Courtesan and Spy*. New York: Harper & Brothers, 1930.

Creel, George. *How We Advertised America: The First Telling of the Amazing Story of the Committee on Public Information That Carried the Gospel of Americanism to Every Corner of the Globe*. New York: Harper & Brothers, 1920.

Daigler, Kenneth A. *Spies, Patriots, and Traitors: American Intelligence in the Revolutionary War*. Washington, DC: Georgetown University Press, 2014.

Donovan, James. *Strangers on a Bridge: The Case of Colonel Abel and Francis Gary Powers*. New York: Atheneum, 1964.

Dring, Thomas. *Recollections of the Jersey Prison Ship, from the Original Manuscripts of Capt. Thomas Dring, One of the Prisoners*. Edited by Henry B. Dawson. Morrisania, NY: 1865.

Dulles, Allen. *The Craft of Intelligence*. New York: Harper & Row, 1963.

Earley, Pete. *Comrade J: The Untold Secrets of Russia's Master Spy in America after the End of the Cold War*. New York: Berkley, 2009.

Farago, Ladislas. *The Game of the Foxes*. New York: David McKay, 1971.

Ford, Corey. *Donovan of the OSS*. Boston: Little, Brown, 1970.

Freud, Sigmund, and William C. Bullitt. *Thomas Woodrow Wilson, Twenty-Eighth President of the United States: A Psychological* Study. New York: Houghton Mifflin, 1966.

Gazur, Edward. *Alexander Orlov: The FBI's KGB General*. New York: Carroll & Graf, 2003.

Gehman, Geoff. *Down but Not Quite Out in Hollow-weird: A Documentary in Letters of Eric Knight*. Scarecrow Press, 1998.

Gimpel, Erich. *Spion für Deutschland* [A spy for Germany]. Munich: Süddeutscher Verlag, 1956.

Goodwin, Doris Kearns. *No Ordinary Time: Franklin and Eleanor Roosevelt: The Home Front in World War II*. New York: Simon & Schuster, 1994.

Graydon, Alexander. *Memoirs of a Life, Chiefly Passed in Pennsylvania, within the Last Sixty Years*. Harrisburg: John Wyeth, 1811.

Grose, Peter. *Gentleman Spy: The Life of Allen Dulles*. New York: Houghton Mifflin, 1994.

Hall, Roger. *All My Pretty Ones*. New York: W. W. Norton, 1959.

———. *19*. New York: W. W. Norton, 1969.

———. *You're Stepping on My Cloak and Dagger*. New York: W. W. Norton, 1957.

Halles, Richard [Eric Knight]. *You Play the Black and the Red Comes Up*. New York: R. M. McBride, 1938.

Haynes, John Earl, and Harvey Klehr. *Early Cold War Spies: The Espionage Trials That Shaped American Politics*. Cambridge: Cambridge University Press, 2006.

Haynes, John Earl, Harvey Klehr, and Alexander Vassiliev. *Spies: The Rise and Fall of the KGB in America*. New Haven CT, Yale University Press, 2010.

Horan, James D. *The Pinkertons: The Detective Dynasty That Made History*. Prineville, OR: Bonanza Books, 1967.

Isaacson, Walter. *Einstein: His Life and Universe*. New York: Simon & Schuster, 2007.

Isaacson, Walter, and Evan Thomas. *The Wise Men: Six Friends and the World They Made: Acheson, Bohlen, Harriman, Kennan, Lovett, McCloy*. New York: Simon & Schuster, 1986.

Kahn, David. *The Codebreakers: The Comprehensive History of Secret Communication from Ancient Times to the Internet*. New York: Scribner, 1996.

Kalugin, Oleg. *The First Directorate: My 32 Years in Intelligence and Espionage against the West*. New York: St. Martin's Press, 1994. Reprint: *Spymaster: My Thirty-Two Years in Intelligence and Espionage against the West*. New York: Basic Books, 2009.

Knight, Eric. *Lassie Come-Home*. Illustrated by Marguerite Kimse. Chicago: John C. Winston, 1940.

———. *A Short Guide to Britain*. Washington, DC: War and Navy Departments, 1942.

———. *Songs on Your Bugles*. New York: Harper & Brothers, 1937.

———. *This Above All*. New York: Harper & Brothers, 1941.

Loftis, Larry. *Into the Lion's Mouth: The True Story of Dusko Popov: World War II Spy, Patriot, and the Real-Life Inspiration for James Bond*. New York: Berkley Caliber, 2016.

Lota, Vladimir. *GRU I atomnaia bomba* [GRU and the atomic bomb]. Moscow: OLMA-Press, 2002.

Lycett, Andrew. *Ian Fleming: The Man behind James Bond*. Nashville: Turner Publishing, 1995.

Macrakis, Kristie. *Prisoners, Lovers, and Spies: The Story of Invisible Ink from Herodotus to al-Qaeda*. New Haven, CT: Yale University Press, 2014.

Marble, Alice. *Courting Danger*. With Dale Leatherman. New York: St. Martin's, 1991.

Massing, Hede. *This Deception*. New York: Duell, Sloan and Pearce, 1951.

McCullough, David. *Truman*. New York: Simon & Schuster, 1982.

Molzahn, Rev. Kurt E. B. *Prisoner of War*. Philadelphia: Muhlenberg Press, 1962.

Moody, James. *Lieut. James Moody's Narrative of His Exertions and Sufferings in the Cause of Government, since the Year 1776*. London: 1873.

Morgan, Ted. *A Covert Life: Jay Lovestone: Communist, Anti-Communist, and Spymaster*. New York: Random House, 1999.

Morros, Boris. *My Ten Years as a Counterspy: As Told to Charles Samuels*. New York: Viking Press, 1959.

Nash, Robert Jay. *Spies: A Narrative Encyclopedia of Dirty Deeds and Double Dealing from Biblical Times to Today*. Lanham, MD: M. Evans, 1997.

Ogilvy, David. *Blood, Brains & Beer: The Autobiography of David Ogilvy*. New York: Atheneum, 1978.

Orlov, Alexander. *Handbook of Intelligence and Guerrilla Warfare*. Ann Arbor: University of Michigan Press, 1963.

———. *The Secret History of Stalin's Crimes*. New York: Random House, 1953.

Paine, Thomas. *Common Sense*. Philadelphia: William and Thomas Bradford, 1776.

Papen, Franz von. *Franz von Papen Memoirs*. Translated by Brian Connell. New York: E. P. Dutton, 1953.

Pennell, Joseph. *Joseph Pennell's Pictures of War Work in America*. New York: J. B. Lippincott, 1918.

Persico, Joseph. *Roosevelt's Secret War: FDR and World War II Espionage*. New York: Random House, 2001.

Pinkerton, Allan, ed. *The Spy of the Rebellion: Being a True History of the Spy System of the United States Army during the Late Rebellion*. New York: G. W. Dillingham, 1883.

Polmar, Norman, and Thomas B. Allen. *Spy Book: The Encyclopedia of Espionage*. New York: Random House, 1997.

Read, Conyers. *Mr. Secretary Walsingham and the Policy of Queen Elizabeth*. 3 vols. Oxford: Clarendon Press, 1925.

Reed, John. *Ten Days That Shook the World*. New York: Boni and Liveright, 1919.

von Rintelen, Franz. *The Dark Invader: Wartime Reminiscences of a German Naval Intelligence Officer*. London: Frank Cass, 1933.

Salten, Felix. *Bambi, a Life in the Woods*. Translated by Whittaker Chambers. New York: Simon & Schuster, 1928. Originally published as *Bambi: Eine lebensgeschichte aus dem walde* (Berlin: Ullstein verlag, 1923).

Schulberg, Seymour. *The Harder They Fall*. New York: Random House, 1947.

———. *What Makes Sammy Run?* New York: Random House, 1941.

Shea, John Gilmary. *A Child's History of the United States*. 2 vols. New York: McMenamy, Hess, 1872.

Sheean, Vincent. *Personal History*. Garden City, NY: Garden City Publishing, 1937.

Shirer, William. *Berlin Diary: The Journal of a Foreign Correspondent, 1934–1941*. New York: Alfred A. Knopf, 1941.

Spivak, John L. *A Man in His Time*. New York: Horizon Press, 1967.

Stashower, Daniel. *The Hour of Peril: The Secret Plot to Murder Lincoln before the Civil War*. New York: St. Martin's Press, 2013.

Stephenson, William Samuel, ed. *British Security Coordination: The Secret History of British Intelligence in the Americas, 1940–1945*. New York: Fromm International, 1999.

Stevenson, William. *A Man Called Intrepid: The Incredible WWII Narrative of the Hero Whose Spy Network and Secret Diplomacy Changed the Course of History*. Boston: Harcourt, 1976.

———. *Spymistress: The True Story of the Greatest Female Secret Agent of World War II*. New York: Arcade Publishing, 2007.

Sulick, Michael J. *Spying in America: Espionage from the Revolutionary War to the Dawn of the Cold War*. Washington, DC: Georgetown University Press, 2014.

Thayer, Charles W. *Bears in the Caviar*. Philadelphia: Lippincott, 1951.

———. *Hands across the Caviar*. Philadelphia: Lippincott, 1953.

———. *Unquiet Germans*. New York: Harper, 1957.

Tucker, Spencer C. *American Revolution: The Definitive Encyclopedia and Document Collection*. Vol. 5, *Documents*. Santa Barbara: SBC-CLIO, 2018.

Viereck, George Sylvester. *Spreading Germs of Hate*. New York: Horace Liveright, 1930.

Waller, Douglas. *Lincoln's Spies: Their Secret War to Save a Nation*. New York: Simon & Schuster, 2019.

Washington, George. *The Papers of George Washington*. Revolutionary War series. Vol. 7, *21 October 1776–5 January 1777*. Edited by Philander D. Chase. Charlottesville: University Press of Virginia, 1997.

Weiner, Tim. *Legacy of Ashes: The History of the CIA*. New York: Doubleday, 2007.

Weinstein, Allen, and Alexander Vassiliev. *The Haunted Wood: Soviet Espionage in America—the Stalin Era*. New York: Modern Library Paperbacks, 2000.

West, Rebecca. "Extraordinary Exile." *New Yorker*, September 7, 1946. https://www.newyorker.com/magazine/1946/09/07/extraordinary-exile.

Yardley, Herbert O. *The American Black Chamber*. Indianapolis: Bobbs-Merrill, 1931.

ILLUSTRATION CREDITS

All images and photographs are property of the authors except as noted below (with page numbers):

Academy of Natural Sciences Archives, Collection 64, Drexel University: Dolan on horseback (165).

American Russian Institute: *The Face of Soviet Art* book cover (131).

Annals of Philadelphia: Walnut Street Jail (11); Slate Roof House (17); London Coffee House (39).

Beyond My Ken, Wikipedia: Public Ledger Building (111); American Philosophical Society (154).

Bibliothèque Nationale de France, Wikipedia: Basil Zaharoff (196).

Blue Ribbon Books: *Mata Hari* book cover (89).

Bobak Ha'Eri, Wikipedia: Franklin Institute (88).

Bruce Linder, findagrave.com: Mendelsohn grave (83).

Central Intelligence Agency: Richard Helms (186); CIA seal (185).

Charles J. Mendelsohn Cryptology Collection, Kislak Center for Special Collections, Rare Books and Manuscripts, University of Pennsylvania: *Polygraphiae* (Mendelsohn) book cover (84).

Clint, Wikimedia Commons: Big Spring State Park (193).

Corinna Sicoutris: Christ Church (25).

David Mink: George Mink (124).

David Shankbone, Wikimedia Commons: Budd Schulberg (136).

Dillon Collection, The Athenaeum of Philadelphia: Fox Theater (127); Randolph Theater (188).

Donald Palochko, Moose International: Moose Lodge (90).

E.T. Simantiras Design, LLC: Emerald Street (106).

Federal Bureau of Investigation: Molzahn mug shot (100); Carl Krepper (106); William Colepaugh (107); Harry Gold (126); Murphy/Guryev passport (192); Murphy/Guryev birth certificate (191); FBI seal (203).

Franklin Institute, *The Institute News* (May 1950): Thomas Coulson (88).

Free Library of Philadelphia: Ritz-Carlton Hotel (76).

Glazer Theater Collection, The Athenaeum of Philadelphia: Earle Theatre (127).

Government of India: Headley entering Mumbai (201).

Henry R. Schlesinger: Independence Hall (3); Carpenters' Hall (3); Robert Morris statue (5); Robert Morris grave (5); Friends Meeting House (7); Valley Forge Parade Grounds (11); Salomon grave site (14); Zion Reformed Church (15); City Tavern (18); New Market (19); Humphrey home (19); William Lewis Farm House (19); Little Stone House (21); Shippen House (24); Joseph Reed grave stone (27); Plumstead Friends Meeting House (31); Laurel Hill (35); Rinker's Rock (36); Quaker School at Locust and Hutchinson (59); Belmont Mansion (61); McClellan statue (62); Union League (67); Eddystone marker (79); Pastorius Statue (83); Our Lady of Victory (94); Jajieky 1919 bombing site (94); Kunze house (102); Berg Labs (123); I. F. Stone residence (125); Kindred Street Gold residence (126); Gold grave site (128); Frankford Arsenal (145); Navy Yard Philadelphia (161); Penn Museum (167); Building 638 (176); Chambers birth site (177); Basin Street Bridge (191); Khyber Pass Pub (200); Daood video store (200); Philadelphia FBI building (202).

Historical Society of Bensalem Township, Pennsylvania: Salt Company (105).

Historical Society of Pennsylvania: Rising Sun Tavern (7).

Independence National Historical Park: Franklin Court ghost structure (9); Johann de Kalb (17).

Irvin R. Glazer Theater Collection, The Athenaeum of Philadelphia: Stanton Theater (188).

Jack Barsky: Jack Barsky (199).

Jag9889, Wikipedia: Portland-Columbia Bridge (198).

Jerry Freilich, Wikimedia Commons: James Bond (180).

Joan Ruggles, Louis I. Kahn Collection, University of Pennsylvania and Pennsylvania Historical and Museum Commission: Louis Kahn (166).

John Spivak Special Collections Research Center, Syracuse University: John Spivak (141).

Kenneth C. Zirkel, Wikipedia: Benjamin Franklin Hotel (122).

Kzitelman, Wikipedia: I. F. Stone (126).

Library Company of Philadelphia: Jolly Post Hotel (37); Broad and Prime railroad station (56), Philadelphia Navy Yard 1864 (63).

Library of Congress: Lydia Darragh (7); Franklin return to Philadelphia 1785 (8); Washington at Valley Forge (11); Mt. Pleasant (23); Joseph Reed (27); Lt. Moody (28); Elias Boudinot (34); Rivington (43); John Andre capture (44);

Summerseat House (48); Allan Pinkerton (54); Lafayette Baker (58); Joe Hooker on horseback (64); Ben Franklin Chief of Detectives (65); Moyamensing Prison (65); John Reed (91); Bellevue Stratford (92); William J. Flynn (94); A. Mitchell Palmer (95); Constance Drexel (111); William Bullitt (118); Oleg Troyanovsky (138); Allen Dulles (147); William J. Donovan (147); Francis Biddle (155); Nazi saboteur trial (155); George Earle (158); Martha Dodd and Alfred Stern (175); Whittaker Chambers (178); Philadelphia Courthouse (190).

Library of Congress, Brady-Handy Collection: Thaddeus S. C. Lowe (68).

Library of Congress, Historic American Building Survey: Arcade Building (85).

Lutheran Archives Center at Philadelphia: Molzhan Church (101).

Nancy J. Perkins: Anna Wagner Keichline (87).

National Archives and Records Administration: Haym Salomon sketch (14); Benedict Arnold engraving (22); McLane at Frankford (38); Hilken (76); de Ram camera (86); Gloucester City Immigration Detention Center (109); Charles Thayer (121); Nathan Silvermaster (134); John J. McCloy (149).

National Archives, UK: Klaus Fuchs (176).

National Park Service: Edgar Allan Poe House (53).

National Portrait Gallery, Smithsonian Institution: Patience Wright (40).

National Portrait Gallery, Smithsonian Institution, Gift of the Collection of George Buchanan Coale: Thomas McKean portrait (28).

National Reconnaissance Office: Corona camera (182).

New York Public Library, Miriam and Ira D. Wallach Division of Art, Prints and Photographs: Joseph Galloway (29).

New York Public Library Picture Collection, The Branch Libraries, Astor, Lenox and Tilden Foundation: *Battle of the Kegs* engraving (31).

Ogilvy: David Olgivy (163).

Olympia-Film G.m.b.H., Wikimedia Commons: Leni Riefenstahl (136).

Pennsylvania Academy of the Fine Arts: Christ Church sketch (25).

Pennsylvania Academy of the Fine Arts, Gift of John Frederick Lewis: Thomas Mifflin portrait (36).

Penn Museum: Rodney Young (167); Carleton Coon (168).

Russ Dodge, findagrave.com: Hopkinson tombstone (31).

Ryan Gleason, findagrave.com: Mifflin grave marker (36).

Science History Institute: Eugene Houdry (113).

Sergi Kovaleski: Fred Kovaleski (197).

Smallbones, Wikipedia: Railroad Freight Building (182).

Smallbones, Wikipedia: Packard Motor Building (157).

Steven Spielberg Film and Video Archive at the US Holocaust Memorial Museum, Courtesy of the National Archives and Records Administration: Fritz Kuhn (103).

Temple University, *Evening Bulletin*: Berg Explosion (123).

***The Communist* 18, no. 9 (1939), Wikimedia Commons:** Earl Browder (143).

Tom Green County Sheriff's Office, TX: Jihad Jane mug shot (201).

Ugen64, Wikipedia: Swarthmore College (137).

University of Pennsylvania Archives and Records Center: Harry Gold Hospital (128); Conyers Read (153).

US Army, Wikipedia: Christian Lambertsen (170).

US Department of Justice: Jell-O Box (130).

US Department of State: Brooke Dolan OSS (164).

US Navy: USS Eldridge (158).

US Navy, Wikipedia: Yacht Victor (159).

Wikimedia Commons: Benjamin Church (13); *Philadelphia Inquirer* building (69); Sidney Reilly (78); Pennsylvania Academy of the Fine Arts (81); Bund flag (102); Philadelphia German Bund Headquarters (102); George Dasch (105); Ernest Burger (105); Richard Quirin (105); Henrich Heinck (105); France Forever poster (114); Alexander Orlov (133); Alexander Vassiliev (145); OSS poster (151); Archibald Hill (154); Port Security poster (157); Philadelphia Shipyard 1955 (157); Lavrentiy Beria (160); Director of Naval Intelligence (162); Glomar Explorer (184); Chuck Barris (193).

Wikipedia: William Franklin portrait (10); Paul Revere stamp (18); Trevose Manor (29); *History of the Doans* book cover (30); Pinkerton logo (54); John Scobell shooting (61); Balloon barge (68); General Meade (70); Sanderson (70); Joseph McGarrity (79); Philadelphia Branch, Military Intelligence Division, US Army (85); War Department insignia (87); APL badge (93); Luigi Galleani (94); Yakovlev stamp (130); George Koval (176); Robert Lipka (189); NCIS badge (191).

Yale University Art Gallery: Peggy Shippen (23).

York County Heritage Trust: Southwark Theatre (46).

Zeete, Wikipedia: John Honeyman House (21).

INDEX

Page numbers in italics refer to photos and illustrations.

H

Y

Z

ABOUT THE AUTHORS

H. KEITH MELTON is the owner of the world's largest private collection of espionage artifacts, an intelligence historian, and the author of several intelligence-related books, including *Ultimate Spy: Inside the Secret World of Espionage*. He is also the coauthor of *Spycraft: The Secret History of the CIA's Spytechs from Communism to al-Qaeda*; *The Official CIA Manual of Trickery and Deception*; *Spy Sites of New York City*; and *Spy Sites of Washington, DC.*

ROBERT WALLACE is a retired senior intelligence officer. He is a coauthor of intelligence-related books with H. Keith Melton, including *Spycraft: The Secret History of the CIA's Spytechs from Communism to al-Qaeda; The Official CIA Manual of Trickery and Deception*; *Spy Sites of New York City*; and *Spy Sites of Washington, DC*. He is also the coauthor, with Paul A. Newman and Jack Bick, of *Nine from the Ninth*, a collection of essays about the Vietnam War.

HENRY R. SCHLESINGER is a New York–based writer who has collaborated previously with the authors on several books, including *Spycraft: The Secret History of the CIA's Spytechs from Communism to al-Qaeda*; *Spy Sites of New York City*; and *Spy Sites of Washington, DC*.